Nibley's New Year Rite

Isaiah's Promised Protection

By

Joy Bischoff

Poetry by

Sharon Price Anderson

ISBN-13: 978-0692377369

ISBN-10: 0692377360

Published and distributed by Raqia Publishing

For more information regarding this and other books, please visit www.RaqiaPublishing.com

Cover design and diagrams by Rebecca J. Greenwood

Illustrations by Terrie Soberg

Dedication

This book is dedicated to the late Ina Castleberry, Joy's mother who taught the Gospel to her seven children in a way that gave them all very strong testimonies. Although they were not allowed by their father to attend the LDS church in their youth, they all became strong members because of her example of faith.

Behold, I sent you out to testify and warn the people, and it becometh every man who hath been warned to warn his neighbor.

Doctrine and Covenants 88:81

And the eyes of them that see shall not be dim, and the ears of them that hear shall hearken.

Isaiah 32:3

Nibley's New Year Rite

Table of Contents

Nibley's New Year Rite

Foreword

You are about to embark on an exciting journey of discovery, one where you will encounter new information and make connections between many concepts with which Latter-day Saints are already familiar. In *Nibley's New Year Rite* you will be exposed to the ideas of the ancient Hebrews and Egyptians, the writings Hugh Nibley, the teachings of the prophets, the wonders of astronomy, and a variety of other subjects. You will be invited to ponder all these in light of the restored Gospel and to consider why these things are significant and how you can apply them today.

There are a few underlying principles that are worth introducing or reviewing as you begin your journey.

Is it the end or the beginning? We are familiar with the concept that each ending also serves as a beginning. This is true on many levels. We leave the presence of Heavenly Father and are born into mortality. An old year ends and a new one begins. At baptism, we are buried in a symbolic grave and arise to a new spiritual life. Learning by degrees and completing one course of study, we graduate to another level of learning and call the ceremony which marks our accomplishment a commencement.

As Latter-day Saints we understand the plan of salvation which explains how we progress from our premortal existence into mortality and then on into immortality. We especially relate to the words of the poet William Wordsworth. "Our birth is but a sleep and a forgetting. The soul that rises with us, our life's star, has had elsewhere its setting and cometh from afar. Not in entire forgetfulness and not utter nakedness, but trailing clouds of glory do we come from God who is our home." These lines resonate with truth and we rejoice in our understanding of the great plan of salvation, but Wordsworth might also have accurately said, "our birth is but a <u>death</u> and a forgetting," for in many ways birth and death are synonymous.

A Period of Transition. Although there may be a particular moment when the change from one realm to another takes place, often there is a period of transition. This can be a time when the ending and the beginning overlap. For example, a baby who has received nourishment and oxygen from her mother, passes through the birth canal and enters the world to take her first breath. We sleep during the hours of darkness and then arise to a new day. When a snake swallows its tail, as depicted by the symbolic ouroboros, there is a space where both the beginning and the end of the serpent occupy the same part of the circle.

The specific instant when one period ends and a new one begins may be variously noted. The transition from one day to the next, for example, may be marked by the setting of the sun, the stroke of midnight, or the dawn of a new day. Either Saturday or Sunday can be used to mark the first day of a new week.

Not only can the period of transition be a time of darkness, but it can be a time of intensifying opposition and testing when further progress hangs in the balance. This is a critical interval when further advances might be slowed or prevented all together. Consider how potentially dangerous the birth of a baby can be and how many in Israel were afraid to make the transition into the Promised Land causing a forty year delay. As the earth passes from its telestial existence into the terrestrial condition of the seventh thousand year period known as the millennium, there will be great temporal, moral, and spiritual upheavals. This is the time when Satan viciously persecutes the Bride (the Church) in an effort to prevent the coming marriage. If he could, he would lock her in a dungeon, never to see the light of day. During this period many will question whether or not the earth will even survive.

"Turning the Age". This is a time when we need to remain focused on the prophesied outcome: Christ will come to rule and reign. The Earth *will* be celestialized and the meek and righteous *will* inherit it. We need to overcome doubt with faith, faith in God's promises and in the efficacy of the Atonement. It is also important to understand that we have an important role to play. We are preparing for the Second Coming of the Lord. We are helping "turn the age" but this does not mean we are part of the popular New Age movement. It means that by learning, loving, and serving, by spreading the Gospel and living it teachings, we are actively engaged as the Earth transitions to the millennial condition which has been anticipated and prophesied throughout the ages, even from the beginning of time.

Ascending. Atheists and agnostics have a pessimistic view of the mindlessness of starting and finishing the same thing over and over again, but as Latter-day Saints we understand that we do not spin aimlessly and unendingly in the same place for ever. Instead, there is a law of eternal progression which moves us and all creation to progressively higher realms. We may sleep, but when we awake we enter another and hopefully higher state of existence. We may experience death, but at the same time we are born into another dimension where we can continue to progress. Cycles repeat, but as they do we are ascending and spiraling ever upward.

Various Alignments. Interestingly, the beginnings and endings of various cycles of existence can occur simultaneously. Picture the various ways of measuring time as circles of progressively larger sizes, with the smaller ones each encircled by the next larger. Mark a point (or a small arc) on each circle which can represent where the circle starts. Then imagine that every so often, as the circles spin, all of those points line up. For example, the stroke of midnight between December 30, 2011 and January 1, 2012, marked the beginning of a new minute, hour, day, week, month AND year. The marks on the circles all lined up.

These simultaneous alignments occur not only in time but in space. Consider how earth, moon, sun and even certain stars and constellations are aligned at significant times. Joy will address several significant astronomical events that will occur during 2012 and will suggest what they can symbolize.

The Importance of Symbolism. The scriptures teach us much about symbolism. "And behold, all things have their likeness, and all things are created and made to bear record of me, both things which are temporal, and things which are spiritual; things which are in the heavens above, and things which are on the earth, and things which are in the earth, and things which are under the earth, both above and beneath: all things bear record of me" (Moses 6:63). Nature can teach us spiritual truths. Tokens, metaphors and parables are examples of how one thing can effectively represent another. Of course, one of the fascinating things about symbols is that they are not subject to just one interpretation. They can be understood on many different levels; they can represent different things to different people, and more than one person can have it right!

Each of us looks at symbols from a unique perspective which colors our interpretation. For many years, Joy has researched ancient writings, civilizations and religions, along with the standard works. She studied scientific principles and considered how all creation operates according to the laws of science. Joy has been fascinated to learn that not only were many of the myths and teachings of the ancients related to the principles of the Gospel but that they were based on scientific principles as well. In this volume, Joy shares a small portion of what she has learned. She will show that, as we progress, there are many patterns that can symbolize the ascension process and that each such connection can reaffirm that all things really do testify of Christ and the eternal truths of His Gospel.

The Three Pillars of the Gospel. The law of eternal progression applies as we advance from one round or realm of existence to the next. Understanding that some parts of the process are repetitive and reoccur as we spiral upward can give us a new appreciation for three great principles that have been called the Three Pillars of the Gospel. When we speak of the Creation, the Fall, and the Atonement, we usually have in mind the creation of the Earth where we now dwell, the Fall that took place when Adam and Eve partook of the forbidden fruit, and the Atonement which was brought about by the infinite and eternal sacrifice of our Savior Jesus Christ.

While each pillar does represent one of these events, the three pillars also signify principles that extend beyond our present sphere. On each level, as we progress from exaltation to exaltation, there will be the creation of a new world, one which falls short of the glory of the next realm of existence towards which we are moving. An atoning sacrifice will be necessary as we continue to progress. We will still need the infinite and eternal Atonement, the mercy and grace of One greater than ourselves to fit us for that next realm of glory. .

What You Can Do as You Read. This book offers much to inquiring minds, but it also asks something of the reader. Skimming the surface of doctrine will stifle our progression. We must drink deeply. So as you read, be prayerful and ponder these concepts, measuring them against scripture. Not only will these ideas stand up to scrutiny, they will open up scripture in a way that will astound you.

Usually acquiring understanding requires effort, focus, and persistence. You are invited to be patient as you consider the ideas presented here. In our pursuit of truth, we should keep our hearts and minds centered on the Savior and rely on the Scriptures and the counsel of the prophets. These become our standard, much like the star Robert Frost's poem "Choose Something Like a Star" which ends with these lines:

> And steadfast as Keats' Eremite,
> Not even stooping from its sphere,
> It asks a little of us here.
> It asks of us a certain height,
> So when at times the mob is swayed
> To carry praise or blame too far,
> We may choose something like a star
> To stay our minds on and be staid.

Keep in mind that new concepts can be hard to process. Often our first impulse is to reject an unfamiliar idea. We might wonder, "If it is true, why haven't we heard this before?" Or we might discount something because the Prophet didn't say it. But neither the scriptures nor the prophets assert that they have included or taught everything that is true. The Lord doesn't indiscriminately parade all truth before the masses of mankind. Some things are too sacred for that and gaining understanding is usually a step-by-step process where we gain knowledge, apply it, and then acquire further understanding.

Sometimes new ideas are discounted because they oppose popular or private interpretations of the scriptures. We often have traditional or preconceived notions about what the scriptures really say, but if we discard our prejudices, we might discover that what seemed new and strange does not contradict the scriptures after all. So, if something you read doesn't seem to gel, try setting it aside and letting it simmer for a while as you move on. Then you can come back later and check it out again.

During the Winding Up Scenes. These are perilous times when we need the extra strength and protection that comes from working together in our families, wards, and stakes. By joining with others as we move forward in love and unity we can prepare for the marriage supper of the Lamb. The Bridegroom is Jesus Christ, the Church is the Bride, and we have an important role to play. The concepts discussed in *Nibley's New Year Rite* will help us to fulfill that role.

Sharon Price Anderson.

Acknowledgements

Special thanks to all who helped edit or gave feedback for this book: Marissa Bischoff, Sharon Price Anderson, Terrie Soberg, Roy Bischoff II, and Bryon Bischoff.

Preface

Dear Reader:

The second edition of our book comes with a new title and an answer to the question; why should Latter-day Saints concern themselves with a study of the meaning behind the Maya 2012 calendar ending, especially since that time is in the past?

There are four good answers to this question:

First, the Mayas believed that the winter solstice of 2012 was a door. A door to what? That is a question that should interest all who want to understand the temple. Also the answer will open up a new understanding to latter-day prophecy and our role in what is to come.

In Chapter One, we discuss the elliptical crossing of the galactic plan by the "new sun". One of the ways the Mayas describe this event is the crossing of a river. What is on the other side should not be ignored any more than Ancient Israel could have ignored what was waiting for them in the Promised Land after crossing the Jordan River. In fact, the parallels prove rather striking.

Our second reason this subject is so pertinent is that Hugh Nibley taught that every temple endowment is as if it were happening at the dawn of time on the first day of the new year. We believe our book brings forth strong evidence that the winter solstice of 2012 was part of the endowment process for the earth. We will provide evidence that it was the first step for the earth to symbolically move into the endowment room that will begin the process of her moving from a telestial back to a terrestrial condition. As those of us who have attended the temple know, this takes more than a moment in time. We understand that the earth will be a terrestrial sphere after the Second Coming but we attempt to show that the process happens spiritually before it becomes physically apparent. In studying how this spiritual ascension works for the earth, we can learn a great deal that can be applied to our own spiritual progression.

The third reason behind our book is to expound on the role we have to play as the symbolic Bride of the Bridegroom. The principles found in the ancient New Year Rite which Nibley made his greatest area of study, hold crucial keys that can help us more effectively fulfill that role. Additionally, found within the book of Isaiah, Nephi's commentary on that book and also the Ascension of Isaiah, is the same basic message as the ancient New Year Rite. Since the Savior told us that "great are the words of Isaiah" (Third Nephi, 23:1) a new look at that message is astonishing in light of Nibley's work.

Lastly, but perhaps the most personally crucial information that we can come away with is that this information can help us more effectively stand in holy places and in fact draw spiritual protection over our loved ones. This material becomes even more important as we are past the Maya 2012 date.

Feedback from those who have read our book may help our readers. First, those who had intensely studied Dr. Nibley's writings were the most comfortable with this book. Many others were confused and even distressed because symbolism was not a comfortable mode of study for them. A few people told us that when they read the book a second time, the symbolism came alive and they gained much more and became excited about these concepts. When we had a book signing in BYU, one student told us that he had been reading our book and that he had learned to pray intently each time before picking it up again. In that manner he was able to gain much more from its pages.

Dr. Nibley was a humble man who wisely refrained from sharing the fact that his wonderful collection of information actually had a focused purpose. We have no hesitation to declare that according to our research, almost everything Nibley wrote pointed to the temple. Some of his stories may seem like a random collection of myth and history but he was unveiling deep information that can help us become endowed with power and knowledge. One of Dr. Nibley's son's bought a copy of our book and told the owner of the bookstore that his father often talked about 2012 and its significance. Nibley understood cycles and their symbolism like no one else due to his lifetime of study into the ancient New Year Rite.

December 21, 2012 was only the beginning of a very interesting era. Come with us to learn why.

Nibley's New Year Rite

Chapter One: The Crossroads

Besides some fellow-scholars who were offended by the fact that Hugh Nibley broke the cardinal rule of academia, most readers were not offended by his books. His writings were filled with fascinating translations from many manuscripts that have been unearthed the last two centuries as well as many offerings from ancient texts. The fun anecdotes held our interest and subtle hints suggested that there were eternal truths hidden within his books. People find it both fascinating to try and mine for nuggets and frustrating to fail to fully grasp subtle hints.

The rule Nibley broke was that he refused to pretend that he did not know the gospel was true. I know from my classes that we are to always maintain complete objectivity in scholarly writing, never suggesting that the material we are studying supports the truth of the gospel. Nibley would not play those games. Thank goodness. In this age of specialization, many are deeply studying the elephant's tail or ears, etc. but hardly anyone is piecing together the whole puzzle picture.

A professor once told the students in a class I was taking that Nibley was the only scholar who was allowed to get away with such things. The last day of that class, however, that professor invited us to join a group of academics that were going through all of Nibley's work to show how off-base he was. A few times that professor tossed out what he considered to be very strange concepts that Nibley had written of. Hoping that I would see the absurdity of the quotes, that professor became frustrated when I would calmly explain the symbolism behind Nibley's work and exclaim over how breath-taking such teachings were.

We are now breaking an even more serious cardinal rule with this book. Not only are we agreeing with Nibley, that the gospel is true, we are actually making the claim that Hugh Nibley did not just share a jumble of collected anecdotes. He actually was humbly and subtly teaching us how the temple works; and thus, how to become like our Heavenly Father. Although most readers did not become upset with him, we will admit here in our second edition of this book that some readers have become upset with us. Many have become frustrated trying to piece together a pattern we insist Nibley uncovered. It seems prideful of us to assert that the ancient New Year Rite and even the

1

temple teachings themselves are filled with eternal truths. We apologize for this but with a scholarly movement to debunk Nibley's crucial work and with a ban on similar work, we refuse to play the game. This is not a book to be offered to scholars who may take offence. It is for the member who desires to seek an understanding of the things Nibley strove to share.

It is difficult to understand why some people become irritated or resentful when they suspect they may not already have a complete understanding of the gospel and that there is more to learn. Indeed, since the temple holds the framework of how we can learn to become gods and create worlds, it would seem that we should all see we have a long way to go. How boring it would be to think there was not more to understand. Perhaps some are uncomfortable with trying to untangle symbolism. If so, this is an issue to overcome because the meat of the gospel is woven together with symbolism. So please, dear reader, have an open mind and be excited by the fact that there is a whole beautiful world of truths out there to explore.

Dr. Hugh Nibley made a serious mistake. He thought we were all smarter than we are. It takes work to untangle the amazing insights to the temple and the scriptures that he shared. It is time we do that.

Many years ago, friends and family would ask me to explain the writings of Hugh Nibley. After two decades of research including many readings of Nibley's works, we were excited to offer this book to help simplify his deep research. Imagine our surprise and disappointment when we learned that what we had believed had answered that goal, had fallen short of the mark. The feedback we received made it clear that for most people, it took two readings before they grasped what we were sharing.

My children were always telling me that I had spent so much time in the world of my research that it was like I had learned a different language and I had no idea that it was foreign to most people. In light of this feedback, we have made some edits and have added a new beginning to help our readers start with a better idea of where we are going. That means we will be spoiling some of the fun of discovery and not springing as many interesting surprises on our reader as our plot unfolds but it has to be better to supply a touchstone in the hopes that the reader will not have to struggle so much. However, please remember that some of the topics have to be treated with a light hand because of the sacredness of the subject. We each must connect some of the dots ourselves in order to preserve sacred ground and also for personal growth.

We will skip some sources for this introduction in an attempt to freely give our personal view of the subject without getting bogged down. Later sources should cement these ideas as the book progresses.

The story behind 2012 is an important piece of the pattern and truly does help us understand the temple to a greater degree, unveiling our part in helping to prepare for the Second Coming. It also holds the keys of protection that we desire for our families. Just because that event has come and gone does not take away from the powerful significance behind that date. To grasp the true meaning behind cycles, especially the major ending and beginning that came with the 2012 event, opens our eyes to a pattern that is invaluable for personal progression as well as that of the earth herself.

One may ask, "Why didn't anyone notice this earth shaking event if it was so important?"

The kingdom of heaven is likened to a mustard seed in Mathew, chapter thirteen; we learn that a tiny seed can grow very large. No one knows it is there except those involved in the planting or anyone peeking over her shoulder.

And just what kingdom would that be? The kingdom of the Second David. Chapter Two will give evidence that connects the latter-day establishment of the throne of David with the Maya prophecies about the establishment of the throne of Quetzalcoatl on December 21, 2012. This happened quietly and the seed remains in the ground, hidden from the eyes of most of the world.

The Mayas taught that the establishment of the throne of Queztlcoatl would prepare the way for the resurrection to increase dramatically and also the future political kingdom of the great white God.

The Lord often works by proxies, authorized representatives here in mortality who work in His name. The ancient prophets and most of the kings were believed to be an earthly representation of the Son of Heaven. This concept is thoroughly explored here.

Joseph Smith is head of this last dispensation but in addition to his role, as we show later, Christ will personally reign in the role of David, the king. If the political throne was established in 2012 but the Lord won't personally reign on the earth until the Millennium, then what does the seed of the new political kingdom mean? Is there another proxy for that event?

Yes, there is. Joseph Smith ran for president but his life was taken well before the election. The Lord works by common consent so Joseph not gaining the vote of the nation wouldn't fulfill that role. No, that was to be accomplished when the Mayas said it would be, at the end of 2012. How that happened is found in Chapter Two.

A few more concepts we will explore regarding the purpose of the New Year Rite are as follows:

The establishment of kingship and the interactive role of that king and his kingdom, often likened to his bride.

We will also discuss Nibley's assertion that each endowment is as if it is the beginning moment of the new year. This is one way cycles will begin to make sense to us. Sanctification happens step by step. It is as if we die and are reborn to a higher spiritual level with the ending/beginning of each cycle if we have qualified ourselves. If we follow the Savior's example and keep our covenants with Him, we can also be established as a king or queen in a smaller sphere. He has promised us that we can become joins heirs with Him, sharing His thrones as we move from exaltation to exaltation. Nibley wrote about the brightness and enlightenment of the temple endowment in *Abraham in Egypt*. He goes on to write: "In the temple of my father Amon-Re, I was endowed with the authority of a god."[1] How important is proper authority and its connection to light.

We will establish that winter solstice 2012 was the day that the Second David's throne was quietly brought forth. The physical Millennium will begin with the Second Coming in glory of the Lord but first a re-creation begins spiritually, with light – the rising of the new sun, a new cycle of life. From there the blue print is brought forth, the plan is put in motion but first it is a quiet, spiritual establishment of the throne of Christ with Zion assisting the king.

It is our opinion, after years of research, that 2012 was the first step for earth to move from a telestial condition to a terrestrial one with the symbolic rising of a new sun as it rises above the galactic plan. Each New Year represents another ending and beginning of a spiral as the spiritually prepared initiate move up the rungs of Jacob's ladder striving for higher and higher levels of sanctification. Eventually the initiate is qualified for exaltation and even then there are more rungs as we strive to move from exaltation to exaltation. Much progression can take place in this life and it should. For those who are laboring under such adverse conditions that they cannot progress properly, this will all be made up for in the next life. This life may not be fair but the eternities certainly will be.

---

[1] Nibley, Abraham in Egypt, p. 532

Nibley wrote on a variety of topics but most of his work illustrated various aspects of the temple. The New Year Rite opens breathtaking vistas of temple understanding. Why should we worry about some obscure rite in this busy world? Can't we just wait until the next life to worry about understanding the temple? Yes, but if we pass up genuine opportunities for spiritual progression then we may be limiting ourselves to a lesser exaltation. Worse, we may not be keeping premortal covenants to help do our part in preparing for the Second Coming and we may even be unknowingly passing up exaltation altogether.

It is not enough anymore to just keep to the shallow end of the pool. With greater knowledge comes a greater endowment of power and we are now in a day when people are needed who have made the effort to become temples, lively stones in a spiritual house (Peter 2:5). This is what the sanctified Bride of Christ must do to assist more effectively in helping to bring to pass the peculiar work of the latter-days. The Bridegroom cannot do it alone contrary to the belief of many members. It is the interaction between the Bridegroom and the Bride, as we will see from Isaiah's writings, which bring about a joining of heaven and earth.

As more and more temples are built and more homes, and individuals become temples, eventually we will reach the point when they, like points of light through a cloth, will pull down the curtain of heaven and the Son will be revealed (D&C 88:95). It is the unity of Zion that will join with the King of kings to make this happen.

The symbol of the Bridegroom is only one of many types and shadows that can illustrate the interaction between the Lord and His Church that brings about a joining of heaven and earth with its accompanying spiritual protection. In the ancient New Year Rite we find the new King being established on his throne then preparing himself for the symbolic sacred marriage to his kingdom. There is always a battle for the bride from another claimant either in reality or in a staged production, until the king is victorious and saves his bride. We will take a closer look at the New Year Rite later as well as the role of the Bride.

How fascinating it is to ponder the reason countless Egyptians worked for decades to build a pyramid for their ruler. That question has perplexed the world for generations. Modern cultural thinking is very different than the deeply-rooted ideas of the past. The Egyptians understood very well the interdependence between king and kingdom. Nibley believed this was the reason that land enjoyed so much stability compared to other early cultures. The people knew they weren't just doing all this for their pharaoh. Just as they painstakingly set block by massive block, we must also strive with all our strength to hew our stony hearts into vessels of light and take our place as lively stones in the house of God, the temple. We are organized around the earthly representative of the King of Kings. This mortal representative is our prophet.

From what we are now witnessing, it appears that a major divider between the righteous and rebellious members is the decision to fully center around that prophet. Early Israel had to learn that hard truth in the days of Moses. Modern Israel is now dividing along those same lines. Some will humbly allow their heart to be broken and hewn and place their stone around the prophet; others will take their stone home and try to build their own spiritual structure.

We will later explore in greater detail valuable clues regarding this hewn stone in the symbolism found in the *Sefer Yetzirah*, an ancient book that Jewish scholars and Hugh Nibley maintain was written by the hand of Abraham. This book explains that we, as initiates striving to return to God, are tried and tested, becoming like a hewn stone that is placed in the rock fortress of God. That manuscript beautifully explains how we become lively stones in the temple of God. Now is the time for Zion to come together, as if one temple, as the Bride of Christ, to fulfill her mighty work in assisting to bring to pass the Second Coming of the Lord Jesus Christ.

As the Bride surrounds the Bridegroom as He sits enthroned at the center place (the altar/throne), the energy of faith is produced. The unity of hope is focused on the center and this together opens the portals of heaven. These windows of heaven allow the blessings of charity, the endowment of light and power to descend and be distilled upon those prepared (*D&C* 121:45). What this process means will take the whole of this book to even begin to explain.

Isaiah's Promised Protection

If the Lord encouraged us to search Isaiah, a good place to begin may be within the verses He shared at the time of His visit to the Americas. In Third Nephi, chapter 22, the pattern is outlined beautifully but symbolically.

As families surrounded King Benjamin in their tents and as the tents of the 12 tribes surrounded Moses, so we spiritually place our tents around the king. As the Bride, we encircle the Bridegroom or His priesthood representative in what Nibley often referred to as the ancient Round Dance. In Third Nephi, chapter 22, we read: "Enlarge the place of thy tent, and let them stretch forth the curtains of thy habitations; spare not, lengthen thy cords and strengthen thy stakes;" (3 Nephi 22:2). Zion ascends the hill of the Lord and stretches out her tents around the center place of Zion. We focus on God and upon His representative in the center place, the prophet.

Even though Israel often proved unfaithful, in the last days the Savior, as our symbolic husband, calls us as His Bride to return to Him. Continuing with Isaiah's words as shared by the Savior in 3 Nephi 22:

5 For thy maker, thy husband, the Lord of Hosts is his name; and thy Redeemer, the Holy One of Israel—the God of the whole earth shall he be called.

6 For the Lord hath called thee as a woman forsaken and grieved in spirit, and a wife of youth, when thou wast refused, saith thy God.

7 For a small moment have I forsaken thee, but with great mercies will I gather thee.

8 In a little wrath I hid my face from thee for a moment, but with everlasting kindness will I have mercy on thee, saith the Lord thy Redeemer. (3 Nephi 22:5–8)

The Old Testament is filled with stories and comments about Israel whoring after other gods and being an unfaithful wife or bride. Through her actions, we read above that she became as a woman forsaken. But now, in the latter-days, her symbolic husband forgives her and gathers her to Himself.

Another type for the Bride is a sacred city, the city of light on the hill. A unified people of Zion both spiritually and physically fulfills this role. At this time we are gathering spiritually to Zion, the sacred city of the Lord. At a later time we will in fact physically fulfill the following description when the temples at the New Jerusalem are built:

11 O thou afflicted, tossed with tempest, and not comforted! Behold, I will lay thy stones with fair colors, and lay thy foundations with sapphires.

12 And I will make thy windows of agates, and thy gates of carbuncles, and all thy borders of pleasant stones.

13 And all thy children shall be taught of the Lord; and great shall be the peace of thy children.

14 In righteousness shalt thou be established; thou shalt be far from oppression for thou shalt not fear, and from terror for it shall not come near thee. (3 Ne. 22:11-14)

The Book of Revelation tells of this future city and compares her to a bride: 2 And I John saw the holy city, new Jerusalem, coming down from God out of heaven, prepared as a bride adorned for her husband. (Rev. 21:2)

Verses 17 through 21 of Revelation chapter 21 go on to describe the city, especially the precious stones. This ties in perfectly with Isaiah's words as quoted by the Savior in Third Nephi. Even before the physical New Jerusalem is built, the spiritual city on the hill, His Bride, will be in danger as His enemies seek to destroy His bride but Isaiah's Promised Protection is sure as we continue reading in 3 Nephi 22 we learn that the Bridegroom will protect us:

15 Behold, they shall surely gather together against thee, not by me; whosoever shall gather together against thee shall fall for thy sake.

16 Behold, I have created the smith that bloweth the coals in the fire, and that bringeth forth an instrument for his work; and I have created the waster to destroy.

17 No weapon that is formed against thee shall prosper; and every tongue that shall revile against thee in judgment thou shalt condemn. This is the heritage of the servants of the Lord, and their righteousness is of me, saith the Lord.(3 Nephi 22:11–17)

Throughout this book we will look deeper into how the Lord will protect Zion as He makes His arm bare in the battle between the true Bridegroom and the usurper who desires the Bride. In fact, we will learn that we have a part to play in bringing about that protection. The Doctrine and Covenants holds a lot more information about this protection and how it ties into the temple:

22 And we ask thee, Holy Father, that thy servants may go forth from this house armed with thy power, and that thy name may be upon them, and thy glory be round about them, and thine angels have charge over them;

23 And from this place they may bear exceedingly great and glorious tidings, in truth, unto the ends of the earth, that they may know that this is thy work, and that thou hast put forth thy hand, to fulfil that which thou hast spoken by the mouths of the prophets, concerning the last days.

24 We ask thee, Holy Father, to establish the people that shall worship, and honorably hold a name and standing in this thy house, to all generations and for eternity;

25 That no weapon formed against them shall prosper; that he who diggeth a pit for them shall fall into the same himself;

26 That no combination of wickedness shall have power to rise up and prevail over thy people upon whom thy name shall be put in this house;

27 And if any people shall rise against this people, that thine anger be kindled against them;

28 And if they shall smite this people thou wilt smite them; thou wilt fight for thy people as thou didst in the day of battle, that they may be delivered from the hands of all their enemies. (D&C 109:22–28)

No weapon formed against Zion will ultimately succeed against the majority of the Church because of the protection of the Bridegroom in the defense of His Bride: 51 But if they will not, make bare thine arm, O Lord, and redeem that which thou didst appoint a Zion unto thy people. (D&C 109:51)

Nephi continues to quote Isaiah and here it gets really interesting:

4 When the Lord shall have washed away the filth of the daughters of Zion, and shall have purged the blood of Jerusalem from the midst thereof by the spirit of judgment and by the spirit of burning.

5 And the Lord will create upon every dwelling-place of mount Zion, and upon her assemblies, a cloud and smoke by day and the shining of a flaming fire by night; for upon all the glory of Zion shall be a defence.

6 And there shall be a tabernacle for a shadow in the daytime from the heat, and for a place of refuge, and a covert from storm and from rain. (2 Ne. 14:4–6)

So according to Isaiah, the same power that protected Ancient Israel in the wilderness will protect modern Israel. How does that happen? We hope to reveal the answer to that question and clarify what we do to fulfill our part of that interaction between the Bridegroom and the Bride that joins heaven and earth and opens the way for the cloud by day and the pillar of fire by night. In no other way can the Church survive the end times and we absolutely must fulfill our part.

The story is told of Isis, the famous Egyptian goddess, who one day traveled to Byblos and began quietly taking the Queen's young son through the purifying process of sanctification. One night she was discovered holding the boy in the fire as she was purifying him. She had almost completed the process with only his heel left but the Queen was furious and stopped her. Isis was saddened and informed the Queen that now her boy would not be immortal. Truly we must be completely refined as gold so that we will be able to withstand the eternal burnings where God dwells.

That Second Coming is preceded by the opening of the seventh seal with a number of events still needing to be fulfilled. The role of David is a key. John wrote in the Book of Revelation:

5 And one of the elders saith unto me, Weep not: behold, the Lion of the tribe of Juda, the Root of David, hath prevailed to open the book, and to loose the seven seals thereof. (Rev. 5:5)

At the end of the New Testament, these important words are found:

16 I Jesus have sent mine angel to testify unto you these things in the churches. I am the root and the offspring of David, *and* the bright and morning star. (Rev. 22:16)

We will show that the latter-day throne of David is called both the sunthrone and the lion throne and will show how the Maya teachings of 2012 are intimately involved in describing how that throne opens the seventh seal. We will also explain the role of the bright and morning star and tie it directly into the importance of cycles like 2012.

Be prepared to see three main positions that this latter-day kingdom of kings and high priests need to fulfill in order to do our part in helping to bring to pass the Second Coming of the Lord.

1. When we gain membership in the kingdom we become spiritual sons of God.

2. When we keep our temple covenants and gain a certain level of sanctification, we become part of the symbolic Bride of Christ with specific duties to perform that fall with the priesthood umbrella and involves both men and women even females do not exercise the priesthood outside the temple.

3. If qualified, we can be gathered into the throne of God that he promises to share with the righteous. This is the King position. Now is the time when Christ must have a nation of kings and priests to assist

Him. A king without a queen is no king at all so women will be shown to be intimately involved in this process. It will take a perfect balance of male and female righteousness to do our part.

Our Journey

Studying the Gospel has been a passion of mine since I was kicked out of a prominent protestant church when I was five years old. With an anti-Mormon father who would not allow my family to attend the LDS Church, we were forced to grow up attending other denominations. This experience brought quite an education as we were constantly being confronted with anti-Mormon attacks. Through the years, I learned to keep my doctrinal differences quiet and simply enjoy fellowship with other Christians. This did not mean, however, that they would leave me alone.

For a time, Thursday night youth meetings at our town's largest church were for the express purpose of studying anti-Mormonism. This happened as a result of a discussion I had with their youth minister. I was thirteen when I joined their youth group and the first night, the youth minister, having been told I was Mormon, decided to straighten me out. I asked the man not to discuss Mormonism and just continue with his lesson but he persisted. After hours of intense debate late into the night, I went home discouraged, guessing what was coming. That weekend, the church board and the two ministers met and decided to ask me not to return and informed me that they considered me an anti-Christ. So began the meetings to protect their youth from my beliefs. Fridays at school, I was challenged by skewed facts they presented which kept me on my toes studying.

Often I would also find tracts or books hidden in my dresser drawers by my father. Although I do not recommend most people waste time wallowing in the lies and twisted views expounded in this kind of literature, it did nothing but strengthen my testimony and perception as I studied the Gospel and uncovered the misconceptions. This taught me to discern truth and error.

Studying the Gospel and researching religions became a life-long habit. Near the end of my mission I had an experience that led me to make the decision to mostly study just the scriptures until I felt impressed to move on. This helped me to be better grounded in the fundamentals and to postpone the study of other subjects that interested me so much such as ancient rabbinical works, apocrypha, writings on prophecy, origins of world mythologies and similar subjects. I did not realize that the impression to move on would take almost ten years. How grateful I am for this guidance because those esoteric subject I have been studying for the last two decades have needed to be measured against the scriptures for accuracy.

When I learned that Dr. Hugh Nibley had already done most of the hard work on what interested me most, I became a student of his writings in addition to my own research. If I were to summarize his focus, I would say that he studied how we can use the temple teachings to learn to become like Heavenly Father and to prepare ourselves to become creators. Many people I have talked to did not seem to realize that Nibley was very focused in the things he shared. What may seem like a fun collection of ancient stories all point like arrows directly to the temple.

During 2003, Roy and I began to discuss the furor surrounding the Maya 2012 calendar. During our studies we kept coming across references to cycles, especially 2012. At first we were irritated, but then the subject began to intrigue us. The patterns we found first in Egyptology and then in many other ancient mythologies and also in rabbinical writings, began to become clearer, starting to tie in with what we knew of the Maya teachings. At length, we decided to read John Major Jenkin's book, *Maya Cosmogenesis 2012* and many articles on 2012. What emerged was a decided connection between Nibley's New Year Teachings and the Maya beliefs. For a couple of years we toyed with the idea of writing about 2012 and did in fact describe some of the connections in our religious website. Nibley slipped many references to cycles into his writings and it soon became clear that he was well aware of the important patterns found in them that held hidden gospel clues.

It took time to decide to write on this subject because we assumed LDS scholars would do so. At length, finding little evidence of forthcoming books or articles on 2012 written from an LDS viewpoint, we decided to move ahead. Eventually a little attention was given the subject by a few members of the Church but the bigger picture of its meaning was not to be found. We believe that because 2012 was taken over by New Age and extreme groups, scholars were reluctant to seriously look into the subject. Indeed, it would probably be harmful to their careers had they done so. For this reason, I am happy I was not able to pursue the PhD I desired, for I would have been stifled in the direction my studies have taken, and concerns for my academic career would have limited what I could write.

In 2006, I began extensive study of cycles and was shocked to come to understand that the full meaning of their significance belonged to the restored Church. We began putting together files and accumulated over 5,000 pages of notes and quotations. The outline for the book was over 1,000 pages and still far from complete. Everywhere we turned, confirmation of the pattern found surrounding 2012 was seen. Along with the subjects already mentioned, we spent years studying astronomy, physics (especially quantum mechanics), chemistry, sacred geometry, sacred architecture and many other subjects that reaffirmed our understanding of the pattern we had identified. Egyptology is all about this pattern. Most of all, the scriptures, especially Isaiah, opened up to us in an amazing way. The one thing we did not want to do was simply parrot Nibley's writings, so we stayed away from his books for a few years and concentrated on our own research.

When our friends and relatives would ask about our book, I tried to explain what we were doing but from the reaction we received, I knew we had to do a much better job of refining and explaining our premise. The problem was that the pattern was the Three Pillars of the Gospel and held within those pillars is the totality of the Gospel…a very broad subject.

Again and again we tried to narrow down the subject and get to the core of what we wanted to share without going into too much of the science and mythologies. Our files grew larger and we wrote different versions of several chapters. We felt we were drowning in information with no idea how to shape it. Then, an amazing thing happened that scared us into action; I read the newly released post-mortem book that Brother Nibley had been unable to finish before his death, *One Eternal Round*. I read the book twice in a week and was stunned at what I found. He had not brought so much to the table in previous books but now it was clear that his message was the same as ours. He was writing about the very same thing but in a different way. Of course, his scholarship far surpasses ours and we do not compare ourselves to him but the core message was the same.

We also received a powerful message from his introduction. He had written many versions of chapters in *One Eternal Round* and had dozens of boxes of research he was trying to wade through. When I was at BYU from 1996 to 2000 I remember hearing every year that Nibley would finish the book he was working on the next year. Finally and thankfully, Michael D. Rhodes was able to do a noble work finishing Nibley's book. Roy and I knew we could easily fall into the same situation, never finishing our book because of the enormous amount of supporting evidence and all-inclusive scope of the subject. If we did not have a deadline of 2012, I feared we might never finish our work. So we began again.

And still the months passed without significant progress. Mostly, we kept trying different ways to simplify and explain the concepts. After a great deal of prayer, we finally felt that we should go ahead and include Nibley's books in our sources. In fact, we now feel that we are only a second witness to help explain many of the concepts contained in Dr. Nibley's writings. These are very sacred since they are temple oriented but by focusing on 2012, we can illustrate the patterns he taught without trespassing on ground that is too sacred.

December 21st 2012 marked the end of a 5,125 year cycle of the Maya Calendar. We never believed this date would bring the end of the world. With this revised edition, it is now after the fact so we are taking out some of the information about 2012 and what some groups of people believed that date signified. Our focus instead remains on how this cycle helps unfold deeper understandings of the temple and also gives clues to latter-day unfolding of prophecy and the pattern that prophecy will follow.

Millions of well-meaning people believed 2012 was a New Age of new spiritual dawning which would have only positive results. Sadly, human progression needs the law of opposition to succeed. As good grows, so does evil and there will come a decided showdown between those forces as we move further into the new cycle.

Many people feel justified in believing anyone is a fool who believed there was any significance to the ending of the Maya Long Count Calendar.[2] With books and movies like the Hollywood blockbuster *2012*, it became embarrassing for many to even speak of that past event. Like Y2K it became a joke. Just because mortals do not recognize and acknowledge a significant spiritual event does not mean the significance is missing; it can simply mean they are in ignorance of that even. Many LDS people were uncomfortable with showing any interest in 2012 because they feared being labeled a New Age adherent. Fear of labels is a terrible reason to pursue a path of ignorance.

So what do we know about 2012? A significant astronomical event occurred on December 21st. Most people believe this date to be the lone significant even in 2012 but by the end of this book, we will have revealed other days with powerful symbolisms and tie into the major cycle of the 2012 event. Several ancient cultures were able to predict astronomical events with amazing precision. Both Enoch and

---

[2] The Maya Long Count Calendar is a cycle of 5125 years, which ends 12/21/2012

Abraham were said to have been very knowledgeable in astronomy. The wise men who found the Christ child were guided by their knowledge of astronomy. The prophet Alma from *The Book of Mormon* declared: "all things denote there is a God; yea, even the earth, and all things that are upon the face of it, yea, and its motion, yea, and also all the planets which move in their regular form do witness that there is a Supreme Creator." (Alma 30:44)

Astronomers have described what happened on the winter solstice of 2012. At the time of the winter solstice our sun crossed the central plane of the Milky Way galaxy, causing the zodiac constellations to appear to recede backwards in the night sky. This event was symbolic of the birth of a new day. Astronomical events take on spiritual meaning when they are connected with significant religious events. It was not a coincidence that the wise men correctly connected the appearance of a new star with the birth of Jesus Christ.

In the book *Maya Cosmogenesis 2012*, the author, John Major Jenkins, asserts that the main theme of 2012 dealt with the accession rites of the king.[3] What king is this? Jenkins maintains that the king is Venus-Quetzalcoatl.[4] Many Latter-day Saints believe Quetzalcoatl is Jesus Christ who visited the Americas after His resurrection. In fact, on my mission we used to share a filmstrip with investigators about Christ's visit to the Americas and the legends that grew into myths about Quetzalcoatl, the great white God. The Maya believe that "Venus-Quetzalcoatl is born and/or reborn upon passing through the rich, fertile waters of the Milky Way. This birth must occur along the ecliptic[5] and the dark-rift in the Milky Way"[6]

But how could Christ be born on winter solstice of 2012 if He had already been born, then had died and been resurrected 2000 years ago? The answer is simple for Latter-day Saints who understand eternal progression. Our progression from exaltation to exaltation can be thought of as a series of rebirths, with each birth symbolized by another step as we ascend Jacob's ladder. The rebirths of the ascension process apply spiritually and temporally to us as individuals but also to the

---

[3] Jenkins, John Major, *Maya Cosmogenesis 2012: the True Meaning of the Maya Calendar end Date*, Bear and Company, Rochester VT 1998, xli
[4] Venus, the evening and morning star, was thought by the Maya to be Quetzalcoatl's star and by ancient Christians to be Christ's star.
[5] This actually refers to an ecliptic plane. Imagine a plane (flat or two dimensional geometrical object which extends forever in four directions) which is based on the orbit of a particular astronomical body. Astronomical intersections and positions are often based on ecliptic planes.
[6] http://alignment2012.com/waters.htm

Church and to the earth itself. Christ, as the King of Kings, has a very important role to play as we move through the seventh thousand year period. His return was foreshadowed by a series of astronomical events which correspond to prophesied events of the last days. One of our goals in writing this book is to help the LDS people understand the significance and symbolism of these events and how it helps open up temple teachings. Learning about the Ancient New Year Rite, which was Dr. Hugh Nibley's prime focus of study, will put 2012 into perspective and help us learn how to use that knowledge as a blueprint for understanding prophecy and for protecting our families.

Astronomers have identified a phenomenon which occurs approximately every 26,000[7] years. It is called the "Precession of the Equinoxes," also known as the "Great Year." This precession is caused by the slow wobbling of the earth's axis. "That wobble causes the position of the equinox to precess[8] backwards against the background of stars."[9]

When the winter solstice sun passed through the "birth canal"[10] of the Milky Way in 2012, it ushered in the beginning of a new great cycle of time, a resetting of the great celestial star-clock of precession. Many cultures around the world believed this event would announce an unprecedented shift in both civilization and human consciousness.

The winter solstice, on December 21st, has always been celebrated as an important time for cultures to ritually help encourage the sun to be put in motion for a new year. The end of the Great Year cycle is considered the winter solstice of the 26,000 period. The Navajos believe that metaphorically, the winter solstice sun represents the beginning of the return journey to the life-giving warmth of summer.

---

[7] Although there is some disagreement among astronomers most would say the actual period is 25,800 years.

[8] Precess is movement in the axis of rotation of a spinning object. When a top is spun clockwise the point in contact will describe a counterclockwise circle and the top will wobble changing the axis of its rotation. Spinning astronomical bodies such as the earth do the same thing. Precess, as used here describes the wobble, which changes our view of the stars from the earth's surface.

[9] Jenkins, *Maya Cosmogenesis*, 42

[10] There is a wide dark area in the Milky Way that is referred to as the dark rift or bulge and is believed by ancient cultures to represent a womb. When we speak of the sun passing through this "birth canal" it is the ecliptic plane that we reference since the sun is quite far away from what we call the Milky Way.

16

This new great cycle seems very different from all the previous histories as we are now entering the winding up scenes before the Millennium. Could this be the beginning of the return journey of earth to Kolob?[11] Some Native American cultures believe we now live in a time when the Earth's energy is lower than it has been in the past; in fact they maintain that its energy is at its lowest point.[12] At the beginning of the new age (i.e. after winter solstice 2012), they believe the embers of a new life will stir and will burst forth born anew.[13] They maintain that life will die and be resurrected, noting that this is a Christian concept. In fact, they connect this renewal with the many world religions which teach that the winter solstice is a period of holiness to be celebrated by ceremonies and festivals and ties in directly to the Ancient New Year Rites.

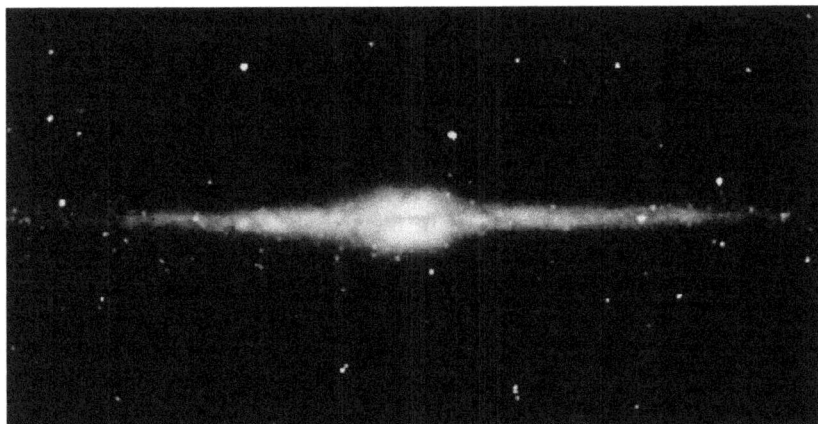

http://www.kui.name/NEWS/astroimg/view_81.html
This is an image of the Milky Way galaxy.

The more we have learned of the concepts behind 2012, the greater our surprise has grown that LDS scholars were not writing about this subject. After all, the sacred Maya writings were from the area and time of the people of *The Book of Mormon*. The Maya Long Count Calendar dates back to 37 B.C.[14] This is pertinent for Latter-day

---

[11] See Andrew Skinner, "The Book of Abraham: A Most Remarkable Book," Ensign March 1997 p. 16 quoting Brigham Young.
[12] Astronomers have data that show that Earth's magnetic field is at a low point at this time.
[13] This is understood to be a whole new creation but we look at it as everything progressing to a new spiritual level.
[14] Jenkins, *Maya Cosmogenesis,* xxxiv.

Saints because we know that the Jaredite plates had been translated by that time and that the teachings of the Meso-American peoples contained a wealth of information that was sacred and profound. We believe the Olmecs were the Jaredites. Their teachings fall right in line with those of the Maya and ancient Egyptians. According to Jenkins, the Olmec civilization dated from around 2,000 B.C.[15] and most scholars say Olmecs faded by 400 B.C.[16] which agrees with the general timetable in which the Jaredite king, Coriantumr, lived with the Mulekites as described in *The Book of Mormon*.

Jenkins says that most of the monuments to the Long Count Calendar are dated after 41 AD. This is significant for Mormons, for we know that this was a period of great righteousness when all the people on the face of the land, both Nephite and Lamanite, were converted to the true Church following the visitation of Jesus Christ.[17] We, as members of the Church of Jesus Christ of Latter-day Saints, should take a very close look at anything that came from those early members who were very righteous and obviously progressing in gospel understanding.

The Maya believed that their lunar calendar of 260 days, which is the approximate gestational cycle for a baby, was echoed in the larger cycle of almost 26,000 years as the birth cycle for our species. They believed 2012 is the zero point in the process.[18] They taught that "a door into the heart of space and time opens in 2012."[19] Fascinatingly, the earth is 26,000 light years away from the Galactic Center.[20] This is one of the reasons we suggest that the earth, which is now entering the galactic plane, may be beginning her journey back to the center of the galaxy. Knowing that the earth will be taken back to Kolob after the Millennium is a dramatic but true teaching in the Church.[21] Our studies seem to indicate that the center of our galaxy[22] will act as a doorway to return the earth to its position as a footstool for Kolob after the Judgment. The Maya taught that in the center of the galaxy there is a hole in

---

[15] Ibid, 5
[16] Ibid, 221
[17] 4 Ne. 2
[18] Jenkins, *Maya Cosmogenesis,* xlvi.
[19] Ibid, xlvii.
[20] Ibid, 199
[21] See Skinner, The Book of Abraham, quoting Brigham Young Journal of Discourses, 17:143 see also Journal of Discourses 7:163.
[22] We will discuss the recently discovered black hole at the center of our galaxy and its affect on astronomical objects in more detail later in this book.

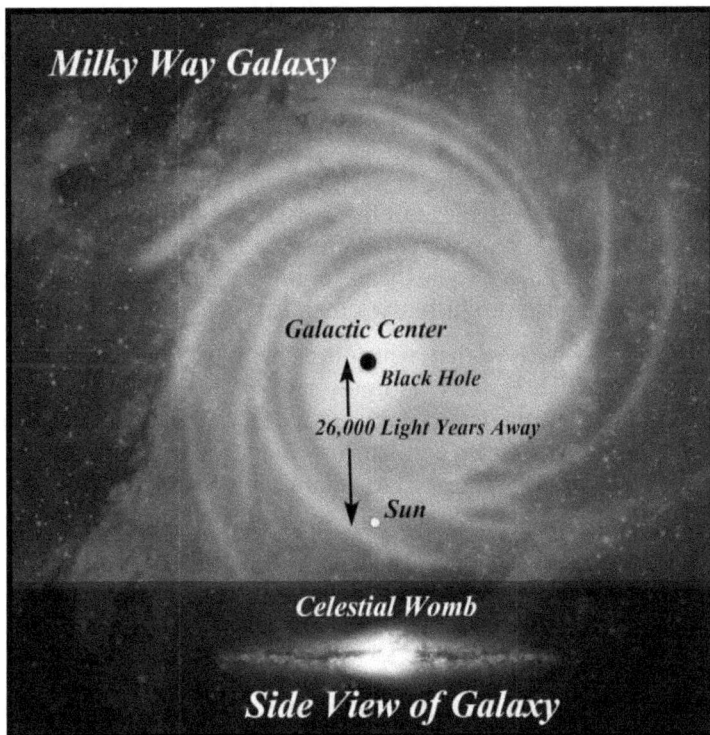

the sky. Jenkins describes it as a wormhole, which is something scientists are just beginning to understand.[23] Many Native American legends describe the sun as being a door to another sun behind it and that there is a spiritual process in gaining access to that sacred place. It is interesting to note that many doors to our temple endowment rooms have a sun carved over the lintel.

The prophet Brigham Young taught: "When Adam and Eve lived in the Garden of Eden, the Earth was closely orbiting Kolob, like God's home planet. But when Adam and Eve fell, so did the Earth and it was hurled across the cosmos and placed in orbit around our sun in this planetary system. After the Millennium, the Earth will return to its rightful place near God, orbiting Kolob."[24]

Now brace for some Egyptian symbolism. Remember, it is simply a type and shadow of real things but not to be taken literally. In Facsimile 2, figure 4,[25] we can see the 'sunship' which we must enter

---

[23] Jenkins, *Maya Cosmogenesis,* 200
[24] Skinner, The Book of Abraham, 16
[25] All references to "facsimiles" are those from the Book of Abraham in the Pearl of Great Price LDS scriptures.

for the return trip to God. This sunship, ship of a thousand or ship of Zion, symbolizes an important eternal concept. Without that ship, we will fall prey to the crocodile shown in Facsimile 1. Many crossroads[26] scenes depict a monster with an open maw ready to snatch up the person who is thrown from the ship for iniquity. How do we get into that ship? Only through becoming one with Christ can we be purified, gathered in and taken safely through the crossroads that lead to a spiritual rebirth. We come to many spiritual crossroads in life and it is at these times that the Adversary stands wait to grasp us in its jaws if we fail to make the crossing successfully. Helaman explains that spiritual rebirth:

29 Yea, we see that whosoever will may lay hold upon the word of God, which is quick and powerful, which shall divide asunder all the cunning and the snares and the wiles of the devil, and lead the man of Christ in a strait and narrow course across that everlasting gulf of misery which is prepared to engulf the wicked—

30And land their souls, yea, their immortal souls, at the right hand of God in the kingdom of heaven, to sit down with Abraham, and Isaac, and with Jacob, and with all our holy fathers, to go no more out. (Hel. 3:29–30)

Some may balk at an idea, like wormholes mentioned above, that smacks of science fiction because they have not kept up with the actual science that has quietly been unfolding in the fullness of times. Neal A. Maxwell spoke about the gains in astronomy in a BYU devotional: "Astonishingly, to those who have eyes to see and ears to hear, it is clear that the Father and the Son are giving away the secrets of the universe! If only you and I can avoid being offended by their generosity."[27] We love this quote but it became more significant to us as we have travelled and given lectures throughout the west. Most of our fellow saints have responded with enthusiasm to the things we have to share but we have also ran into more than a few who are offended that we suggest there is anything more than the most basic primary knowledge of the gospel. They are convinced that we should always stay on a spiritual diet of milk and never move to the meat of the gospel. Line upon line is important but to refuse to move beyond step one and even, as Elder Maxwell said, it be offended by Heavenly Father's generosity in sharing more is simply a travesty.

---

[26] This is a common reference in apocryphal works and refers to a time of trial.

[27] Neal Maxwell, "Meek and Lowly," devotional address given at BYU 21 Oct. 1986

During the New Year Rite of the Ancient Egyptians, the king would ride on a sacred boat up the Nile. This solar boat symbolized the sunboat that would sail here in mortality and also into the heavens, where Nut, the Milky Way goddess represented a river that birthed the boat into the heavens. [28] This reminds us of the sun crossing the galactic plane through the central bulge (womb) of the Milky Way as we come to an end of this 26 thousand year round. The goddess Nut represents the redemptive progression found through the priesthood as we will confirm later. That goddess is one of the representations of the redemptive power of the priesthood in gathering in the sanctified. In the symbolic sunship, she takes those who have taken upon themselves the name of Christ and are one with him, then they are lifted to a higher spiritual state.

In the traditional Navajo view, life is a constant cycle of growth. Death and new life flow in a circular motion and all things must begin and end at the same point. In their traditional culture a person's umbilical cord is buried at birth and when that person passes away he is returned to the Earth in a similar way. The religious teachings of the Navajo offer a guide for daily living that flows with the cycles of the days and seasons. [29] The umbilical cord ties us to our mother. The priesthood, represented as a mother for the rebirthing process, attaches an umbilical cord to us as we gestate, so to speak, in the womb of the sunship. This process eventually returns us to our Heavenly Father, birthing us into His presence in a higher dimension.

Is there a reason for Christians to see any significance in the turning of the age? What could possibly interest members of the LDS Church about this date? Yes, there will be disasters during the period leading up to the Lord's coming in glory. Surely the scriptures are clear on this point. We simply have a far different purpose in mind, a different road to travel than any other that we have found concerning the real story behind 2012. In fact, we hope to show that it is the unprecedented building of temples that smoothed the turning as we passed through 2012 and will in fact hold the earth together in coming years. We believe things will get more difficult eventually if the temples are closed for a period of time and then disasters will increase greatly.

No one can truly grasp what the Maya end date of 2012 means without comprehending the mission of the prophet Joseph Smith. It will

---

[28] Nibley, *An Approach to the Book of Abraham*, 371

[29] Roman Bitsuie, "Holy Wind and Natural Law: Natural Law and Navajo Religion/Way of Life," April 21, 1995
http://www.indians.org/welker/dineway.htm

take the whole of this book to prove these previous points but we believe our assertions will be convincing to any open minded Latter-day Saint. For some readers, the evidence will seem inconclusive because the ideas we will be exploring will seem new and strange but they are neither new nor strange. They are old and they are woven throughout scripture, embedded in time itself.

By the end of this book we hope to establish our thesis, which is: there is a link between the sixth and seventh seals that can be shown in a pattern of time that corresponds to the Three Pillars of the Gospel. The union of effort between the head of the final dispensation, Joseph Smith and Jesus Christ in His kingly role as the Second David, is as a hand clasp across the gulf of the old cycle and the beginning of the new one at winter solstice of 2012.

The Four-Fold Purpose of this Book:

In the magnificent book, ***Temple and Cosmos***, Hugh Nibley explained in the first chapter how the Church in the Americas was able to remain pure for so long after the visit of the Savior. Order is preserved by great mental efforts.[30] When spiritual focus wavers, things begin to decay. First to decay is faith, then knowledge, followed by morality. As a result of such decay, society crumbles and when the cup of wickedness is full, the earth itself becomes affected and chaos ensues. Nibley wrote that temples are the force that works against this degradation.[31] We must not only attend the temples, we must prayerfully work to gain an understanding of what is taught within their walls and even more, we must strive to become temples ourselves to help establish enough stability in the world to gentle the journey through the upheavals we know are coming.

Having a clearer understanding of the plan of salvation helps us grasp the importance of cycles. Alma the Younger perceived that his youngest son broke the commandments because Corianton's understanding of the Gospel was shaky.[32] Instead of railing on him at length for his misdeeds, Alma called him to repentance, then proceeded to clarify doctrinal points for his son. After this, Corianton was as firm

---

[30] Nibley, Hugh, *Temple and Cosmos,* CWHN Vol. 12, Deseret Book, Salt Lake City UT and FARMS Provo UT, 14
[31] Ibid, 6–8
[32] Alma 40:1

and faithful as his two older brothers. Although it is not necessary for members to read this book in order to fulfill their mission in life, anything that helps clarify a principle can help create a stronger focus and mental energy to bring about righteousness. With this book we hope to expound truths that have already been revealed in a way which will assist each of us in seeing the role of the Church in the winding up process and also help us understand what we as individuals can do to more firmly stand in holy places and be not moved.

Although there are many aspects of cycles that we would love to cover, we will attempt to narrow our focus to four main areas, as follows:

1. **To explain the connection between the Gospel principles and 2012.** We will show the pattern of the three pillars of the Gospel (the Creation, the Fall and the Atonement) in terms of space and time and we will discuss the physicality and geometry of the pattern. Einstein's theory of relativity (space/time) is a true eternal principle. Winter Solstice of 2012 is one of the markers or "mileposts" of the pattern in relationship to time. The interrelatedness of space and time is just as relevant in God's science as it is in man's. One of the points we will attempt to show by the 2012 space-time junction, is that the 2012 date is a piece of the puzzle in understanding the resurrection.

2. **To show how obedience to Gospel principles will provide protection during the perilous times we are facing.** We believe that the principles of Zion hold the key to protection for our loved ones and we will attempt to show that we have moved into a time when this protection will be more necessary. We will identify the Gospel steps that clarify how we can increase this protection and discuss a little of the science behind how this all works. The meaning behind the 2012 date will help explain this process.

3. **To provide information that will help us and our loved ones recognize truth and identify New Age counterfeits**. The widely held misconceptions about the 2012 date, make it hard for some people to take the subject seriously. For others, even members of the LDS Church, the New Age teachings are luring many away from truth or polluting and confusing correct teachings. We believe that within the coming years this problem will increase dramatically. Sadly, we know that even some of the very elect will be fooled. Learning the difference between truth and error and explaining how we can help loved ones discern those differences, is one of our major goals in writing this book.

4. To describe the Ancient New Year Rite and show that the Great Year ending in 2012 was a large cycle of the pattern of that ancient rite. We will tie this concept into the temple, often using Hugh Nibley's work. This knowledge illustrates the important role of the Church and its members now and in the coming years. What will be the focus of the Church during this important transitional time? What will be the role of families and individuals in furthering the Lord's purposes? We will attempt to answer these questions and also show where 2012 fits in terms of prophecy and the Second Coming and how Deseret fits into that role.

The Ties that Bind

One evening, as I sat beside my daughter-in-law at a memorial service, the face of a friend haunted me. It was not the righteous young man, my son Roy's friend who was being memorialized; instead, I began thinking about a much older man, a friend who by appointment, came to my home one day to gain a better understanding of Dr. Hugh Nibley's writings. This was a wise and powerful priesthood holder who had held important offices and callings and was very knowledgeable about the Gospel. He had long desired to study Nibley's work and knowing I had a lot of background in this area, he wanted a shortcut to understanding the challenging works of this great scholar. I was very excited because nothing interests me more than the study of the Gospel and related esoteric subjects.

After an hour trying to cram as much information as I could into a willing listener, I noticed my friend was becoming distant and quiet. Searching my memory for more exciting bits of Nibley's golden teachings, I tried to regain his interest. Finally, I grew quiet and sat back, waiting to see if he would share what was weighing on his mind. At length, he leaned forward, clasping his hands between his knees and looked intently into my eyes. "I guess what I really want to know is this," he quietly said. "How is this information going to help me protect my family? Nothing is more important to me than that."

Looking back on that exchange as I sat in the memorial service brought tears to my eyes as I listened to a heartbroken father speak of his only son. I looked at two of my sons sitting on the bench near me, wondering how they were holding up. They had both been roommates with the newly married victim of the crash and my oldest son, Roy had remained close friends with him.

I knew my daughter-in-law, sitting by my side, must be thinking of the recent death of her best friend's brother, a young man who was like a brother to her. He had died along with his mission companion in Romania from a gas leak. A few months before that, two girls from our stake were killed in a car accident while traveling to girls' camp. In our close-knit community in Southern Nevada, we all felt the losses deeply. My children went to school with the ones that died and the others who were injured, one barely pulling through.

My daughter-in-law told me she felt she was growing stronger in her ability to bear the pain of losing people she loved. I was sad it was necessary but glad for this growing strength as I thought upon the prophecies of difficult times that I know must be faced in the coming years.

Believing my son would find some relief in comforting his friend's parents and new wife, I offered to go with him to greet them. He gratefully agreed. They lit up to hear his name and hugged him tightly. Watching my son struggling with his emotions, I thought of the reason why death affected him so deeply. On a Sunday morning when he was eight years old, we awoke to see him standing by our bed holding our seven-month-old son. Gently placing the child into my husband's arms, my son asked his father to fix his brother.

My eldest was now twenty-five, strong and confident, but still bearing the scars of losing his early morning cartoon buddy to SIDS. I mentioned to his friend's father that we had also lost a son. I explained that normally I would not have mentioned it but that our son had what I considered a sacred name. At that point, the mother, who I did not think had been listening, stepped past the men and wrapped me in her arms. "Beloved," she whispered, her voice breaking. I thought of the beautiful headstone on my child's grave engraved with the meaning of his first and middle name, David Jesse, Beloved Gift. We had each lost a David and we mourned as mothers who could never forget.

This book is dedicated to the ties of love, the only thing powerful enough to bring the courage to face the final battles before the Second Coming, a continuation of the age old War in Heaven. We are living in the day that has been prayed for these two thousand years; "thy kingdom come, thy will be done, on earth as it is in heaven." (Matt. 6:10[33]) The protection to make it through what lies ahead will be easier to understand as we discuss the significance of the throne of Da-

---

[33] All citations to the Bible refer to the King James Version unless otherwise noted.

vid, the doorway to establishing that political kingdom of God upon the earth, and its tie to 2012.

The Lord is preparing His armies of Sabaoth and placing some on this side of the veil, some on the other side. In the larger scheme of things, it does not matter which side of the veil we are on as long as we are on His side. The protection of Christ in His Latter-day office of David and how it ties into the New Year rites is the theme of this book and the subject of Chapter Two.

Knowledge Flooding the Earth

In the year 1441, Johannes Gutenberg completed his version of the printing press, revolutionizing the world. Mass communication completely changed society in a way that is often called the democratization of knowledge. A great struggle was waged by heroic men to spread the word of God to the common man. Although a massive attempt was made to keep new knowledge from the general population, because of Gutenberg it was only a matter of time for the people to have access to that new knowledge too because of the printing press.

Similarly, we are living in the fullness of times when knowledge is flooding the earth. Ancient manuscripts are being unearthed and information is being disseminated throughout the world. As with the advent of Gutenberg's printing press, the knowledge beginning to flow forth will not be stopped. Those who try to suppress this knowledge and tell people to leave it alone will find many who will not listen, especially among the youth. What is to be done?

We have been profoundly disturbed while doing research for this book to learn that the sacred truths we are discussing are becoming more and more public. What we painstakingly piece together from scriptures and the writings of Latter-day prophets is being handed out on a platter to any searcher. Yet woven within that readily available information are falsehoods that are leading many astray. One of our main goals in writing is to help Latter-day Saints, who may be confused, see the dangers and pitfalls in pursuing esoteric subjects outside the bounds the Lord has set. In addition, we believe that these kinds of studies should be done in a careful, measured way and pace, line upon line or very serious spiritual consequences can result by becoming obsessive and going beyond the mark.

Many members of the Church say we should leave esoteric knowledge alone. Hugh Nibley did not leave the subject alone because it is the sacred understandings of the temple that we are discussing here and we are to move forward in learning those truths. They lead to exaltation. While attending a regional conference in Tennessee in 1994, we heard Thomas S. Monson ask the congregation if we were studying Nibley. He said that he was and encouraged us to do likewise.

Some members argue that these things should be left until the next life. Hopefully, we can show why this is not the answer for most members and that it is in fact crucial that we move forward in seeking the proper mysteries. And what are those? They are the plain, basics of the Gospel that lead to salvation. Anything that cannot be broken down and placed into the basic principles of Church doctrine, we leave alone. As long as we are patient, prayerful and humble and use the scriptures as our daily touchstone, then we should seek pertinent knowledge.

What is lacking in the understanding of many in the New Age Movement (and throughout history) seems to be one or more of the following: (1) Christ and His Atonement is the center piece and the power and foundation upon which everything rests. (2) Obedience to the commandments, repentance and the concept that sacrifice brings forth the blessings of heaven, are indispensable. (3) That receiving saving ordinances through the true priesthood is the only means of returning to our Heavenly Father's presence.

Without these three things, there is no efficacy in the work of trying to achieve salvation through the ascension process. There are many counterfeits offered by those who are guided by the false priesthood. Using the ascension process without proper authority is one way the idea of the false priesthood is represented. This can be done knowingly or by deceived sincere people. There are also many good people who recognize pieces of truth and desire more but do not know where to look for the power of God on earth.

A few years ago, a woman who attended my Gospel doctrine class told me that she came from a family who were active but blended many New Age beliefs in with the Gospel. They were more 'social' Mormons than true believers. After a discussion on where the New Age ideas had stemmed from, that they lacked the priesthood, the Atonement as the centerpiece and also the necessity of repentance, this woman was able to see the truth. She bravely approached family and friends with her new clearer perception and was able to help dozens of people weed out doctrinal pollutions from their beliefs and turn fully to the Gospel. Because so many New Age groups have gained more information from the 2012 concepts and also because last day prophecies will unfold in a way that ties in with many of those understandings, there will most likely be a tremendous explosion of New Age adherents within the next decade or two.

More and more, as the restoration of all truths comes forth in the last days, we will need to address and correct the misconceptions. That means we should understand what brought about the muddying of truth in the past, resulting in apostasy. It may be that one of the reasons there will be no widespread apostasy in this last dispensation is because the Saints will be able to learn the meat of the Gospel without going beyond the mark and becoming prideful, believing their knowledge alone can save them. It is so easy when grasping the beauty of the pattern, to begin worshipping the process instead of God who empowers that process. This is the religion of Humanism that has taken over much of the modern way of thinking. Humanists spread the gospel of pride, teaching that mankind is the only real god and we have the power to save ourselves.

Let us have the courage to not be afraid of truth as many religious leaders were with the advent of the printing press. Knowledge will not be stopped from flooding the earth and our children are curious and very intelligent. Brother Nibley wrote that "In the time of the gathering of all things together, we gather everything good that ever was - not just people - that nothing be lost, but everything will be restored in this last dispensation."[34] Truth cannot be stopped from spreading abroad but what can be stopped is ignorance and the counterfeit teachings. If we become armored with knowledge, we will much more successfully protect our loved ones in the coming trials.

Protection

Throughout the time we were researching how the Great New Year Cycle tied into the gospel, we were anxious to share these exciting findings with our friends. Much to our surprise, many people showed only mild interest in the subject. What the burning desire on their minds was, "please, just tell me, how do I protect my family from what is coming?" The answer to that question is the beauty of the true story behind 2012. As we begin to comprehend the true significance of this

---

[34] Nibley, *Temple and Cosmos*, 25

period of time comes we experience a dawning of understanding about how we can protect our families. In the following chapters, we will share details on how to find the safety that Nephi spoke of:

O Lord, wilt thou encircle me around in the robe of thy right-eousness! O Lord, wilt thou make a way for mine escape before mine enemies! Wilt thou make my path straight before me! Wilt thou not place a stumbling block in my way—but that thou wouldst clear my way before me, and hedge not up my way, but the ways of mine enemy. (2 Ne. 4:33)

We will discuss this process of the protection provided by the uniting of heaven and earth which creates the doorway that will bring about the beginning of the earth's reinstatement from a fallen telestial condition back to a terrestrial state. That process is illustrated by any number of examples from scripture, science, mythology and indeed everything around us for all things do indeed testify of Christ and the Plan of Salvation. We will lay out our belief that 2012, the New Year of the cycle we have now entered, was the first step in the earth's rising to a terrestrial state. It is important to remember that the spiritual oc-curs before the physical and that this is a process more than an event, so this step   occurred without most people's knowledge.

The whole earth will be living under the protection of Christ during the Millennium and He shall be our light[35] but we can and must stand on holy ground now so that we are kept hidden in the shadow of His hand.[36] In this way, if death or struggles come, we can be sure that Heavenly Father's will is being done and we can still consider our-selves held within the safety of His hand, regardless of which side of the veil we are on.

Providing protection for us and our loved ones is only one of the reasons to overcome the effects of the fall and become a temple of God. It is the uniting of those who have overcome the world that brings about the stirring from below that makes the path straight for the Lord. The righteous have a major part to play in helping to bring about the Second Coming. President Spencer W. Kimball spoke about the part we need to play that can affect the Second Coming:

There are things we must do before the end does come, and perhaps that controls it to some extent…The time of Christ's return is affected by our conduct…In my estimation,

---

[35] Rev. 22:5

[36] 1 Ne. 21:2

the Lord's timetable is directed a good deal by us. We speed up the clock or we slow the hands down and we turn them back by our activities or our procrastinations. [37]

A fullness of understanding is found in the truths that have already been revealed by both ancient and Latter-day prophets; nothing new is needed. We only need to piece together the available information. Many clues are found in the words of Isaiah which we will be exploring. Not only will we investigate the 'what' and 'why', but we will discuss later in this book 'how' we prepare. For readers to have any faith in the answer to that question, they must grasp at least a portion of the pattern.

So, do we feel this book is necessary for people to find understanding or safety? Not in the least. We bring no new truth to the table. We hope instead to bring clarity and structure to what has already been given in light of the Mayan teachings becoming available in the dispensation of the fullness of time and tie this exactly to the ancient temple-inspired New Year Rite. Why does that help? The Nephites understood that focus and concentration on gospel principles helped keep chaos at bay. They followed the laws that prevented breakdown for two hundred years. So what went wrong? According to Nibley it was too strenuous; it required great mental exertion. "They spent their time constantly in meetings and prayer and fasting – in concentrating on things."[38]

The more we understand the temple and how the Atonement works and the more we concentrate on these principles, the greater endowment of Spirit for which we can qualify. Knowledge is power and at this time in history, the unifying power of Zion is crucial. Nibley wrote: "The temple represents that organizing principle in the universe which brings all things together."[39] Breaking this down, Nibley maintained that the Atonement is the principle working against chaos and bringing things into one, which maintains order in the cosmos.[40] The reason we were not concerned with 2012 doomsday speculation was because of the stabilizing force of the temples and those who became temples (as the apostle Paul said in 1 Cor. 3:16), because the power of the temples and those who became temples was a stabilizing force.

---

[37] Kimball, Edward L. ed., *Teachings of Spencer W. Kimball*, Salt Lake City: Deseret, 1982, 141-142.

[38] 4 Ne. 1:12

[39] Nibley, *Temple and Cosmos*, 9

[40] Ibid, 11

On Sunday, Oct. 2, 2005, Gordon B. Hinckley said in General Conference: "someone has said it was not raining when Noah built the ark. But he built it, and the rains came."[41] It is obvious that President Hinckley was well aware of the powerful symbol of standing in holy places and also the companion concept of finding safety on Zion's Hill from the following quote and song from his talk:

The primary preparation is also set forth in the Doctrine and Covenants, wherein it says, "Wherefore, stand ye in holy places, and be not moved, until the day of the Lord come" (D&C 87:8).

We sing the song:

When the earth begins to tremble, Bid our fearful thoughts be still; When thy judgments spread destruction, Keep us safe on Zion's hill. ("Guide Us, O Thou Great Jehovah," HYMNS, no. 83)[42]

Does time have a similar representation for the hill of the Lord, the temple? We believe the answer to that is a resounding yes. The hill or mountain of the Lord's house is represented by Deseret's beehive and learning to discern the signs of the time and the keys of protection will help us know when we need to establish ourselves firmly within the beehive of safety, the hollow of the Lord's hand.

As described earlier, the events associated with 2012 marked the beginning of a new great cycle of time, a resetting of the great celestial star-clock. These events were part of a dramatic transition into a great new year that will eventually move the earth into a physical terrestrial state. When fully accomplished, it will become apparent to all that things have changed as is expressed in the poem by Sharon Anderson found below:[43]

To make it through the perilous times ahead as the earth moves to a more glorious condition, we need the Lord's protection. Learning the pattern behind 2012 helps us identify events as they unfold around us so we do not give in to hopelessness when the mists of darkness swirl. With this tool we can believe in the words of President Hinckley from the above talk: "We can so live that we can call upon the Lord for His protection and guidance. This is a first priority. We cannot expect His help if we are unwilling to keep His commandments."[44] Hope and

---

[41] "If ye are Prepared Ye Shall Not Fear," *Ensign*, Nov 2005, p. 60

[42] Ibid

[43] Sharon has been a dear friend of ours for many years and is an award winning poet that has been published in each of the church English language magazines including seven times in the Ensign. Sharon is also the author of several books.

[44] "If ye are Prepared Ye Shall Not Fear," *Ensign*, Nov 2005, 60

faith in ultimate safety for us and our loved ones makes it easier to keep those commandments which are the requirements for this promised safety on Zion's Hill as we stand firm in holy places.

After the End

*The clock of chaos has run
its course. Time is no more.*

*Gathering remnants
of our past,
rewind the clock
turn the key,
cross the threshold,
pass through the open door.*

*Enter a dimension
green and new as morning,
young as wet down
of a gosling just hatched,
fresh as a song
we have never heard before.*

©Sharon Price Anderson

Chapter Two: David's Throne

The astonishing blessing of living in this day and the over-whelming significance of the role of the Church helped me in a recent Sacrament Meeting. A member, speaking in monotone, was reading a beautiful account from the scriptures. She looked and sounded depressed. Glancing around, I saw boredom in the faces of the congregation and began to feel irritated. That feeling grew during a musical number that was not well done. Later, another musical number started in an uninspiring way until I noticed that one sister was pouring her heart into it. Quickly repenting of my judgmental attitude, I focused on her testimony through music and felt my spirits lift. I began thinking of the concepts we are writing about and felt ashamed. Pondering the importance of a group of people congregating before the sacrament table and then sustaining those who speak of Christ, brought me back to thoughts of the throne/altar of God and the need to join together in focused love.

It is up to us to bring a cup to our meetings to be filled with the Spirit of the Lord. I remembered when my anti-Mormon father finally allowed me to attend our church when I was 18. A friend asked me why I always had tears in my eyes and a huge smile on my face during Sacrament Meeting. I answered that I was overwhelmed with gratitude to finally be able to meet with fellow saints. Everything I heard at that time, even the simplest testimony of a child, touched my spirit.

Meeting together with fellow believers is not enough to bring about Zion. Bringing humility, reverence, attention, charity and even energy and enthusiasm to the meetings is what it will take for us to rise above a fallen earth. Reflecting upon these things, I knew it was my job to worship Heavenly Father. I was not in Sacrament Meeting to be entertained but to figuratively come before the throne and praise God in my heart as John wrote in Revelation: "And a voice came out of the throne, saying, Praise our God, all ye his servants, and ye that fear him, both small and great." (Rev. 19:5)

Later in the meeting, I had to hide a smile when the choir director led us in a hymn, going faster and faster until we were racing through a song that should have been slow and powerful. It is not up to me to set the conditions whereby I will be humble and appreciative, in spite of what others do. We simply must love one another and be patient in our imperfections and differences. There is no other way for Zion to come forth and fulfill her role in assisting Christ in His Davidic role. It is the combination and unity of roles between David, (the Bridegroom) and the Church (the Bride), that will bring about that protection we all so desperately want. To explain how this process works, we must first break down the parts and examine them.

The Creation

"And God said, Let there be light." (Gen. 1:3) This is the first step in a new round of creation just as it was in the original creation. For the universe, Kolob was the first light, the center place. From there, creation symbolically spread out in the four cardinal directions. There are actually preparatory steps before the light of the new day comes forth.

Each new day is a new beginning (or birth), following the pattern of creation as the sun rises from the darkness that represents the womb. The womb symbolizes sacred space, like the temple, where the profane and corruption of the fallen world does not contaminate the individual about to be born. So although things begin in the womb, the birth is thought of as the beginning for the new creation.

Sunday is the first day of the week because it is the beginning of the cycle of the week. Each New Year is considered a new cycle. It comes on the heels of the winter solstice when the sun is at its lowest point on the horizon in symbolic death that brings about the rebirth of the sun or the year renewing itself. The winter solstice is the shortest day of the year when the Earth's axial tilt is farthest away from the sun at its southernmost (lowest) point. The sun seems to hold still for a few days. Then, around Christmas Day, it appears to begin its journey north again. Other cycles of time, of which there are many, also follow the pattern of creation, beginning with the new sun. We have discussed two of those cycles, the Maya Long Count Calendar of 5,125 years, and the almost 26,000 year cycle of the precession of the equinoxes, both ended in 2012.

In a personal sense, one of the types for the pattern of cycles is represented by Venus as the evening star represents our symbolic death and Venus as the morning star represents our symbolic rebirth. There are many steps up the ladder of ascension and even for those who receive a promise of exaltation while still in mortality, they can continue to progress from exaltation to exaltation. The temple helps us move up that ladder as far as we each have the will and determination to continue.

For 2012, the pattern was for the Church as a whole and the earth following the same spiritual steps of progression that individuals do in the temple. The sun rising from the "river" of the Milky Way is considered a new sun and its rising marks a new first day of the re-creation, moving us from the fallen state of the first six thousand years, into the higher state of the seventh thousand year period which begins with the Seventh Seal beginning to slowly open. This is a process and does not happen in a day or a year. The throne coming forth as a new sun, the first light of the new day, is a major step in our journey back to a paradisiacal state. The Mayas believed that the old evening star of Venus became renewed as the new morning star of Venus at winter solstice 2012. They taught that Venus was the star of the Sun Lord, Quetzalcoatl.[45] The Maya Sun Throne is the symbol for this event.[46]

If Jenkins has identified the accession rites of the king as the core concept behind the Maya 2012 beliefs, then we need to begin by laying the foundation of that idea. The new sun of 2012 is believed by the Maya to signify the old day dying, as Venus the Evening Star in its female aspect. Then Venus rises as the new sun, as the Morning Star of a brand new day in its male aspect.

The throne of David is another symbol for that new sun. How does a king accede to his kingdom? The connection between the throne and the altar provides the place for this rebirthing process for the new king. The enthroning ceremony has always been the method of establishing a king as the father of his people. Nibley wrote that the first sun that rose on the day of creation was hailed as Atum (Adam) rising from the sacred mountain, sometimes depicted as a pyramid. Nibley taught that the pyramid was a symbol for the uniting of heaven and earth.[47] This uniting happens on the First Day or New Year's Day.

The whole idea of coming forth into a new spiritual or physical resurrection on this important day is key. The resurrection only takes place at this time when an effectual door is opened between mortality and the spirit world. Just as each endowment is seen as taking place on New Year's Day, so would each resurrection be seen as 'First Day' for the reborn person, as they ritually come forth from the throne of God clothed upon in glory. Whatever light we attain to spiritually in this life, determines the brightness of our resurrection. Of course the Lord takes into account our circumstances in life and all unfair circumstances are made up for through the Atonement.

There was a re-enthroning of the king for the New Year Rite in most ancient cultures. The throne is the center piece of the beginning of

---

[45] Jenkins, *Maya Cosmogenesis,* 50
[46] Ibid, 311
[47] Nibley, *One Eternal Round,* 171–172

the new cycle of time around which all things were organized. Quetzal-coatl (Jesus Christ) inherits the Sun Throne of David as part of the events surrounding the opening of the Seventh Seal. The Mayas were so excited about this future event that it became one of the main focus-es of their religion.

Defining the basic framework of 2012 and David's throne now will allow us to furnish the various pieces of supporting concepts as we go along. Psalms 89 is one of many examples from ancient scripture and lore regarding David's throne: "35 Once have I sworn by my holi-ness that I will not lie unto David. 36 His seed shall endure forever, and his throne as the sun before me." David was comforted by this promise, knowing that even though he failed to retain his throne, the promise was sure that another would use that throne to save Israel. Donald Parry wrote this about the throne of David:

> Although David was a king, he never did obtain the spirit and power of Elijah and the fullness of the Priesthood; and the Priesthood that he received, and the throne and kingdom of David is to be taken from him and given to another by the name of David in the last days, raised up out of his lineage. The throne is symbolized by the star of David, which in Hebrew is called a shield.[48]

The throne, as the bringer forth of a sanctified initiate, was ac-tually established when the keys of the priesthood were restored to Jo-seph Smith. Accompanying the whole process of founding David's throne is the establishment of the political kingdom of God upon the earth through the principles of Zion. The saints were not able to abide the laws of Zion, as the Lord knew would happen and so the political kingdom and the possession of the sacred land that would be the center place for that kingdom had to wait. Elder James E. Talmage said:

> The saints were not permitted to enter into immediate posses-sion of the land, which was promised them as an everlasting inheritance. Even as years elapsed between the time of the Lord's promise to Israel of old that Canaan should be their in-heritance, and the time of their entering into possession there-of—years devoted to the people's toilsome and sorrowful prep-aration for the fulfillment—so in these latter days the divine purpose is held in abeyance, while the people are being sancti-

---

48 http://maxwellinstitute.byu.edu/publications/review/?vol=4&num=1&id=86

fied for the great gift and for the responsibilities associated with it.[49]

Instead, the Church was taken into the wilderness to grow and prepare for the time when she was ready for the higher responsibilities and blessings of Zion. In the meantime, the throne of David was symbolically kept hidden and protected through the sacred space of the temple. In 2012, the throne burst forth to a higher state from the mountain, so to speak but is still enshrouded in clouds of glory, protected and assisted by the priesthood. The throne symbolizes the center place that organizes and orders the new creation spiritually first, until the time comes to physically build the New Jerusalem, the center stake of Zion. Only a sanctified people can take part in building that sacred city. Orson Pratt explained:

> When we go back to Jackson County, we are to go back with power. Do you suppose that God will reveal his power among an unsanctified people, who have no regard nor respect for his laws and institutions, but who are filled with covetousness? No. When God shows forth his power among the Latter-day Saints, it will be because there is a union of feeling in regard to doctrine, and in regard to everything that God has placed in their hands; and not only a union, but a sanctification on their part, that there shall not be a spot or wrinkle as it were, but everything shall be as fair as the sun that shines in the heavens.[50]

---

[49] James E. Talmage, *Articles of Faith,* 353; see also Notes and Commentary on D&C 29:8
[50] In *Journal of Discourses,* 15:361

Types and Shadows

Samuel filled the horn
with holy oil, and
among the sons of Jesse,
sought Israel's future king.
He anointed the shepherd
on whom rested,
from that day forth,
the Spirit of the Lord.

When the father sent his son
with bread and corn
to his embattled brethren,
David arose and went
early in the morning
to the valley of Elah where
Goliath, arrogant as Evil,
determined as Death,
defied the armies
of the living God.

The anointed son
descended willingly
into the valley of death,
and in the name of Israel's God,
crushed the giant's head.

Delivered, the men arose
with a mighty shout;
with dancing and joy
women from all the cities
sang his praise.

From Bethlehem beginnings,
the beloved son
ascended to the seat
of power, justice, judgment –
that glorious throne
from which the King of Kings
will one day rule and reign.

© *Sharon Price Anderson*

Throne Upon Throne

Enoch understood that the initiate can inherit throne upon throne in a spiritual ascension process. He wrote: "And I placed for myself a throne, and took my seat on it, and said to the light: 'Go thou up higher and fix thyself high above the throne, and be a foundation to the highest things.'"[51] After the Lord's resurrection, He was enthroned at the right hand of the Father in His Sonship role as the Great High Priest of the Church. Paul wrote to the Hebrews: "Now of the things which we have spoken *this is* the sum: We have such an high priest, who is set on the right hand of the throne of the Majesty in the heavens;" (Heb. 8:1)

The scriptures explain that the Lord will later be established in His own throne, taking the fallen David's place as eternal king of the political and spiritual kingdom of Israel.[52] The Savior will always retain both roles, just as we are always children to our parents and also can have the role of parents.

Parry also wrote concerning the throne of David: "In short, the Messiah, after his divine investiture and enthronement upon the throne of David, will wear the royal robes of his Father and reign as the new King forever and ever. His Saints will call him *Wonderful Counselor, Mighty God, Everlasting Father,* and *Prince of Peace.* Surely, the "zeal of Jehovah of hosts will do this."[53]""

There is some debate among members within the Church about the identity of the latter-day David even though the scriptures make it clear it is the Lord.[54] Also, Bruce R. McConkie, in Millennial Messiah, was very clear about the identity of the latter-day David:

> How little the world knows of the coming day when Christ, as our tenth Article of Faith says, "will reign personally upon the earth," meaning, as the Prophet tells us, that he will "visit it," from time to time, "when it is necessary to govern it." (*Teachings,* p. 268.) And how little even the saints know of the government that is to be, meaning that their King will reign over Israel, on the throne of David, being himself the **Second David**, and that, as a prelude thereto, the "Gentiles" will "lick up the dust" of the feet of the chosen people. (Isa. 49:23) And yet these are profound truths that are spread forth *in extenso* in the revealed word. To understand the Second Coming, we must

---

[51] The Book of the Secrets of Enoch, XXV:5
[52] Luke 1:32–33
[53] http://maxwellinstitute.byu.edu/publications/books/?bookid=46&chapid=252
[54] See Acts 2:30–35

consider them in their proper relationship to all the events of the latter days.[55]

The Jews clearly mixed up the first coming with the latter-day political kingdom they knew would come. They would not have been surprised when Christ indicated in the words of the Lord's Prayer, that we should pray that His kingdom would come and His will be done on earth as it is in heaven. The establishment of the throne of David on a terrestrial level must happen before the kingdom fully comes forth from obscurity.

The life of David himself is a good type and shadow. The boy was first quietly anointed king without the world at large knowing of it. He continued to work as a shepherd for his father until a later time when the enemy of Israel needed to be overcome. Even then, he waited until Saul, who knew he no longer had a right to the throne, destroyed his own kingdom. Only then did David publicly take up his rightful throne. The latter-day David will also begin His work with only those close to Him knowing that He has come to begin establishing His kingdom on earth. First, He brought forth the Bride (Church), who in the role of Deseret brings forth the throne. Again, this signifies the earth beginning her journey from a fallen state to a higher state.

The scriptures strongly seem to indicate that this earth is not only the Atonement earth but that it will also be the winding up scene for the current universal round of creation of our Father. With the judgment at the end of the Millennium, we will receive a new heaven and a new earth: "And I saw a new heaven and a new earth: for the first heaven and the first earth were passed away;" (Rev. 21:1) Everything begins again with all the qualified moving up to a higher dimension. This explains the teaching of eternal progression, even for God.

The above quote from the Book of Revelation, according to Parley P. Pratt, takes place at the end of the Millennium and entails a change not just for earth but the planetary systems.[56] Earth will become celestialized and taken back to Kolob. But first she must become terrestrial again. This happens with another cycle that began in 2012 with the rebirth of the new heaven and new earth to a higher state. These two different stages of the new heaven and earth are also discussed in a Church Education System Manual.[57]

---

[55] Bruce R. McConkie, *Millenial Messiah* ch. 48

[56] Parley P. Pratt, *Key to the Science of Theology*, 61

[57] http://www.ldsces.org/inst_manuals/dc-in/dc-in-041.htm#43-31

In other words, with 2012, the spiritual creation on a terrestrial level took place then with the advent of the Savior that creation will be clothed upon with terrestrial physicality so the earth will be ready for the righteous to live upon. The earth began as a celestial sphere at the foot of Kolob. She then descended to a terrestrial state and then fell to a telestial state. It would appear that her process back up is by steps, as is ours.

2012 was the doorway for 'Alpha' (beginning) of the Lord's higher state as a Heavenly Father and at the same time was also the start of 'Omega' (ending) of this current round. The overlapping of the two will be demonstrated at length throughout this book. For now, we will take a closer look at David's throne as the centerpiece of 2012 and how it relates to exaltation.

Gaining exaltation means an adding upon of thrones and principalities. This applies to qualified Church members as well as the Lord. Just as Heavenly Father placed His heir, the Savior, at His right hand, we can also share the throne of David as joint heirs with the Son. John the Beloved explained this in Revelation: "To him that overcometh will I grant to sit with me in my throne, even as I also overcame, and am set down with my Father in his throne." (Rev. 3:21) The unity of Zion is the key. We need to become one with each other and the Savior, as He is one with the Father.[58]

Nibley wrote that when the throne is established the Lord will gather in the people to sit with Him. Nibley went on to say that after that happens Satan will wage war and lose. Those who flee the 'Great White Throne'[59] will have no place to go. After his defeat, the holy city descends from heaven.[60] So clearly, the establishment of Christ's Davidic throne comes before the actual Second Coming.

The Lotus and the New Year

According to Nibley, the throne is like a lotus bringing forth the new sun at dawn. The new king is birthed forth as the rising sun.[61] Temple baptismal fonts are usually lotus shaped and held up by twelve oxen which correspond to twelve months of a year and the twelve constellations of the zodiac. The pure lotus encircles the king like a womb, keeping him separated from corruption while in the lower realm. Then

---

[58] John 17:11

[59] See Rev. 20:11

[60] Nibley, *One Eternal Round*, 374

[61] Ibid, 412

rising above the waters of chaos, it opens at the dawn of a new year birthing forth the new king into a higher existence. This idea is portrayed in the image on the next page.

Lotus birth motif[62]

The rising of the new sun from the Galactic Plane through the Milky Way symbolizes the river or gulf that must be crossed in a death of the old life and birth into the new life. We are led across that gulf by the hand of the priesthood as ordinances are administered, to become established on the throne that Christ shares with the sanctified. As noted in chapter one, in Hel. 3:24, the man of Christ is led across the gulf of misery.

The successful crossing of that gulf is a birth that places the initiate into a higher state, a new day, endowed with greater light and power to ensure new growth in the New Year. The ancients believed that the return of the brighter light of the sun after the winter solstice was step one (the rising of the sunthrone) that prepared the way for new growth of spring.

The celebration and traditions of the New Year have been so prevalent throughout history that it is amazing more scholars do not wonder at the significance of the elaborate ceremonies. The similarities between the ceremonies of the ancients should make one wonder if there is something to all of this instead of bundling them all into a pile to discard. The full meaning of the New Year is not something we can cover completely in one book but since it is all about the ascension process, we will often refer back to these rites in order to expand our understanding and make further attempts at enlightenment.

The New Year rites and the Atonement are linked by traditions stretching back to the dawn of history. We will examine this connection and also touch on a few of the traditions of the king who suffers either personally or by proxy, in order to bring forth new life each year. Also

---

[62] *Fed By The Lotus* © Katelyn Mariah
http://medicinewomanart.wordpress.com/2010/02/05/day-27-art-as-meditation

a part of the tradition in most ancient societies was the ritual Sacred Marriage which the ancients believed would ensure an abundant harvest. Finally, the correlation will be made between the ancient rites of the New Year and how to apply it to our day.

In many ancient New Year rituals, a reenactment of the creation, the battle between good and evil and coronation of the king were the usual fare. As will be shown throughout this section, Hugh Nibley taught that what goes on in our temples should be viewed as happening at the New Year, as it symbolizes the beginning of all things.

The creation of earth followed the pattern that began with the creation of the universe, beginning with Kolob. The center spot, like an altar, was where it all began but it did not happen without the participation of the faithful. **Nibley wrote that the function of the New Year was to repeat and continue the creation cycle**. He repeatedly made the point in his writings that the process of creation was associated with the birth of the sun when all things were put into motion. Since our sun was lit by Christ,[63] it is clear that Kolob came first. What we do in the temple is a crucial part of the continuation of the ordering process of the ongoing creation, including our own future creations: "We must all participate in the revival of a new year, and a new age, in bringing things to life again, and make our new oaths and covenants for a new time."[64]

Since time as we know it is only relevant to this earth and because we also understand that space is not a barrier to higher beings, it will be helpful if we can see the integral message in Nibley's book *Temple and Cosmos*. The temple can overcome time and space to bring us symbolically back to the point of all creation, the beginning of time itself. He wrote: "The New Year was the birthday of the human race and its rites dramatized the creation of the world; all who would be found in the 'Book of Life opened at the creation of the World' must necessarily attend."[65]

Repeating the pattern of the creation is certainly instructional but why is it necessary for us to continually do the same thing? Nibley quoted the poet Yeats in explaining that: "Things fall apart; the center cannot hold; mere anarchy is loosed upon the world". Nibley goes on: "Our civilization is collapsing, falling apart, because there is no center, everything is loosened."[66] The Center is the throne.

---

[63] D&C 88:7
[64] Nibley, *Temple and Cosmos*, 156
[65] Ibid, 157-8
[66] Ibid, 140

It all begins with the Atonement: "Adam in the presence of God is the quintessential atonement."[67] Since Adam and Eve experienced spiritual death, which was separation from God, their purpose after being cast out of the garden was to return to God's presence. The Atonement makes that possible. The temple, a symbol for the Body of Christ, is the organizing force for the eternities that makes it possible to return to the Father and become joint-heirs with His Son. The Egyptians believed the temple was the primeval mound from which the sun god emerged to begin cosmogony (the creation of the universe). It is all about sacrifice and the symbolic death and rebirth of the individual and the unity and organization of the eternal community, the Church of the Firstborn. The altar/throne of sacrifice is made efficacious through the Atonement of Jesus Christ. The shedding of His blood and sacrifice of His life created the power that makes the center able to hold all things in place like a sun's gravity holding the planets in a structured rotation. It always comes back to the Atonement and being born of God:

For if you keep my commandments you shall receive of his fullness, and be glorified in me as I am in the Father therefore, I say unto you, you shall receive grace for grace. And now, verily I say unto you, I was in the beginning with the Father, and am the Firstborn; And all those who are begotten through me are partakers of the glory of the same, and are the church of the Firstborn. Ye were also in the beginning with the Father; that which is Spirit, even the Spirit of Truth. (D&C 93:20–23)

The Father glorifies the Son, sharing His throne with Him after Christ was resurrected. Jesus, as the Son, stands in the position of the great high priest. This idea is found throughout the Book of Hebrews. Then in the latter days, through the establishment throne of David, Christ gathers all who are begotten through Him to share His throne with him or her, in preparation for the new heaven wherein we will have our own creation.

Nibley taught that "the goal [of the ancient civilizations was always] to restore the primal community of Gods and men, or as we would say, to achieve atonement."[68] The New Year Rites of most of the major ancient societies were all about enthroning and empowering the king so he could bring about a state of organization and oneness in the community he ruled but before the foundation of a community can be stretched out, a center place has to be established.

---

[67] Ibid, 383

[68] Nibley, *Temple and Cosmos,* 400

In Facsimile 1, the lion couch scene gives the story of the establishment of the center place. Creation is empowered because of the Atonement of Christ and our own future creations will come from the temple covenants and blessings which act in place of our own actualized atonement. Anciently, before the new kings could complete their coronation, they would have to symbolically go through the sacrifice that brings about life. The sacrificial scene of the lion couch of Facsimile 1 creates the sacrifice of the center place. This leads us to Facsimile 2, the endowment or ascension process where all things are ordered around the center of sacrifice (figure 1). This brings us to Facsimile 3 where the lion couch of sacrifice becomes the lion throne of a new creation. The new king is established forever upon the throne and his kingdom is sealed upon him.

Christ came as a meek lamb in His first coming but in the last days He comes as a lion to fight for Israel: "And one of the elders saith unto me, Weep not: behold, the Lion of the tribe of Judah, the Root of David, hath prevailed to open the book, and to lose the seven seals thereof." (Rev. 5:5) One of the symbols of the lion throne of Facsimile 3 would seem to be the Latter-day throne of David. The lion was the symbol of Judah and David's kingdom.[69] In the facsimile, Pharaoh stands behind the throne, sharing it with Abraham. Pharaoh was believed to be a representative of the Son of God, who is the Father of Creation. Pharaoh stands as a father to his people in creating an organized community made ready for eternal life. Pharaoh and ancient kings in general were considered the bridegroom of his kingdom and that kingdom is symbolically his bride whom he saves. As already noted, the scriptures teach that Jesus will share His throne with the sanctified that are gathered in as part of the body of Christ, prepared for exaltation.

We normally think of beginning our creation far in the future but the seeds of that creation are begun here for those who have the opportunity of receiving the ordinances and living up to those promises. For those without that opportunity, the blessings of temple proxies will eventually provide that blessing for everyone whether in mortality or during the Millennium.

Each one of us can follow Christ, as Abraham has shown us and begin a center point, then stretch out a foundation in preparation for an eternal family. That was what the ancient kings were doing, symbolically going through the atonement, assisted by the faith of their people who considered the king as both their father and husband depending on

---

[69] http://www.buzzle.com/articles/what-does-the-lion-of-judah-represent.html

which principle was in focus. Christ is both the Father of the faithful and the husband to the Bride, the sanctified members of the Church. Later the king was given rebirth and then assisted his people to achieve rebirth, to become a feather in his cap, a jewel in his crown, a star on the evergreen tree of life. This was all done through the power of Christ, for without His priesthood, the types and shadows are mere teaching tools.

In Egypt, when the king was brought forth during the New Year's rites, the people would celebrate as the king was re-enthroned and the coronation and sacred marriage would take place. Each year would mark a new beginning and so these things would have to take place for each new round of creation. This ceremony was believed to bring about the renewal of life, the growth of all life in the coming spring.

By now it should be clear that the Great Year, this large cycle, follows the same pattern as the annual New Year Rites so prevalent throughout history, which is why the Mayas were so focused on the 2012 event. The redemption of individuals is very important but the redemption of the whole earth and the coming of the Second David's political kingdom is a bigger story.

The six-pointed Star of David represents many things. We feel that one of its meanings is the gathering in of the six dispensations of the faithful as the 'Bride' that brings forth the 'Bridegroom' from the center place, the throne of David. The Egyptian goddess Isis represented the Bride and wore a tiny throne as her crown. Hers was the power to bring forth and establish the new king just as the Church votes to establish a new prophet who was called of God. Other Egyptian crowns depict a small sun rising from the head, hidden and protected by two large feathers. The symbolism behind the concepts we are discussing is prevalent throughout the world and found in the earliest histories.

For earth to begin her transition from a telestial to terrestrial state in preparation for the Second Coming, 2012 was the opening ceremony for a new endowment of power, the first step in the new creation on a higher level. Nibley explains that the throne of David brings everything from a macrocosm into a microcosm.[70] That seems to mean that the followers of Christ and all truth is drawn into the new throne which then symbolically is raised up and opens the way for the higher level of sanctification. Then, on this higher level, the Lord, is His Da-

---

[70] Nibley, *One Eternal Round*, 626

vidic kingly role, begins to spiritually spread out His kingdom beginning at the throne as the center place. This would be the microcosm spreading out into the macrocosm. The devil will challenge the true Bridegroom, trying to hold onto what he considers to be his dominion until this claim is given up completely at the Second Coming in Glory.

The transition to a higher state starts as a small, quiet seed and will grow until it fills the whole earth. It will be like a new Garden of Eden (an outdoor temple) endowed with light and kept clean from worldliness, hidden within God, encircled within the robes of righteousness. Zion, like a sacred city can also be depicted as the wings of a hen protecting her young. Christ lamented His city of Jerusalem comparing her to chicks that He wanted to gather beneath His wings.

Nibley taught that this protection was also symbolized by the Tree of Life, the Seal of Solomon, and the shield (star) of David.[71]

Picture of Panama National Flower,[72] La Flor del Espiritu Santo.[73]

(This photo has not been altered in any way.)

This amazing flower, known as the Flower of the Holy Spirit, is another example of all things testifying of Christ. The dove as a symbol of the Holy Ghost is very familiar to Christians. Being born of the Holy Ghost as from a lily or lotus is a common ancient motif. The wings or arms being sprinkled red are symbolic of the

---

[71] Nibley, *One Eternal Round*, 625

[72] http://iconsecast.wunderground.com/data/wximagenew/s/SATxKat/32.jpg

[73] Holy Ghost Orchid (Peristeria elata).

blood of the Atonement and reminds us of the blood on the door lintels that protected those within the house during the Passover in Egypt.

Traditionally, the lotus has represented Egypt. These flowers grew in the shallow, swampy waters along the banks of the Nile. Coming forth from those waters, protected by the reeds and lotuses, was a powerful symbol to Egyptians. No wonder the daughter of Pharaoh was so intrigued by a baby, hidden and protected in a basket of reeds (lotus stems) coming forth from the Nile. The Egyptians called the Milky Way the Heavenly Nile, which reminds us again of the December 2012 sun rising from the center of the Milky Way in a new birth.

Many cultures show the lotus as a throne or a birth place that brings forth god, as do the Buddhists as shown in the following picture of Buddha being born from a lotus coming forth from swampy waters.

There are many examples in sacred architecture of the throne of a king being set upon a floor made to look like a river or ocean and making us think of the Milky Way bringing forth the sun (throne). Solomon's throne was built upon pavement made to appear like water.[74] The Greeks believed there was a Sea of Heaven in which the stars floated which bore the throne of Zeus.[75] During the middle ages, many churches, especially in Italy had floors made to look like water, with some bearing the images of the twelve constellations of the zodiac and the sun which equate to the 26,000 Great Year.[76]

The Egyptians believed that the god Osiris sits, attended by Isis and Nephthys, upon "his throne in the midst of the waters, from which rises the lotus, bearing upon its expanded flower the four genii of Amenti."[77] The two goddesses act as midwives and protectors. They also stand as witnesses, declaring the initiate clean after the birth, which reminds us of the feminine role of the priesthood in bringing forth

[74] *Architecture, Mystery and Myth*, 206
[75] *Ibid*, 206
[76] *Ibid* 216
[77] Ibid, 216

new births.[78] Osiris is god of the dead and rises up as Re-Horakty (Adam raised up as the new sun god). The four genii represent spreading the new king's realm in the four cardinal directions throughout the new creation. This would seem to show the pattern of the Facsimiles again. Facsimile 1 is the sacrifice of Osiris. Facsimile 2 is the womb or spiritual progression centered around the sacrifice. The initiates spiral around (circumambulate) the center until they are ready to be birthed into the celestial state (room) through the throne/veil of Facsimile 3.

"The Egyptians depicted Osiris under a pillar-borne canopy, seated on a throne placed on the waters, the water being shown by a parallelogram covered with zigzag lines."[79] Most throne scenes from Egyptian art show wavy lines beneath the seat of the throne which symbolizes the waters that bring forth life from the throne.

Dr. Nibley often wrote of the garments of light that are awaiting the righteous to clothe them with an endowment of power. He wrote that crossing the waters at the new birth is when the initiate receives this sacred garment. These garments are metaphorically stored beneath the throne. Nibley identifies two garments, one is a pre-existent garment.[80] To receive this one we must be purified by water. The other is a priesthood garment worn outside the other that is added later.[81] Christ, or those empowered with His priesthood, bring forth the initiate through the throne/altar/lotus.[82] Nibley wrote that the sun-god filled the canopy with light.[83] He, as the Bridegroom, grooms the Bride, pouring water over her, which clothes her with a garment of light as a royal robe. Nibley then identifies this clothing with a ritual embrace.[84] Being clothed upon with light is a symbol of rebirth.[85] Many symbols illustrate various aspects and purposes for this clothing of light including; a cloud of protection, a canopy of light, a beehive protecting the king and many other types.

In the earth's journey through the constellations of the zodiac, we are now approaching the end of Pisces. Metaphorically, we change forms into the higher birth. Drawn from the salty waters of chaos as the Pisces fish, the initiate is cleansed by pure water from the constellation we are moving into for the Seventh thousand year period, the man

---

[78] Nibley, *Message*, 198
[79] *Architecture, Mystery and Myth*, 216
[80] Nibley, *Message*, 489
[81] Ibid, 490
[82] The white lotus represents the veil.
[83] Nibley, *Message*, 439
[84] Ibid, 498-9
[85] Ibid, 441

Aquarius. He pours the living waters over the initiate to purify him/her from corruption. The initiate is now ready to share the throne with the king.

An important part of the Maya symbolism for 2012 is the panther. Nibley showed that the panther skin is a symbol for the high priest. The pelt resembles the night sky with faint stars covering it. This is reminiscent of the Milky Way as the bride that brings forth the sun.[86] It is the high priest who has the job of anointing and placing the king on the throne. The king is represented by the lion skin, golden like the sun.

Moses

The endowment of light and the staff of authority upon Mt. Sinai, was another type and shadow of the sacred rebirth of the king. Moses, as a representative of God, the head of a new dispensation, was commissioned to go back down into Egypt (the world) to have a showdown with Pharaoh, the usurper of the Bride, Israel. This was no easy task. The plagues purified Israel and helped Moses wrest back the Bride from the usurper.

Moses worked hard to sanctify Israel but they rejected the opportunity to live the higher laws. Instead, they were given the law of carnal commandments "and were led, no longer by the Lord's immediate presence, but by his angels."[87]

Latter-day Israel is fulfilling her role with many members living the higher laws. These sanctified members, acting as the unified stars of the Milky Way or the Nile River, will birth forth the new King, the throne of 2012. This means that they will be led by the Lord's immediate presence. This is the gift that was lost with the fall of Adam and Eve. The restoration of this gift signifies that the receiver is in a terrestrial or celestial condition.

Christ, in His Davidic role, will work to birth forth Israel into a higher spiritual state. He will challenge the usurper for possession of the Bride and the earth. The world, like ancient Egypt, will go through great trials as this contest progresses. It is through these trials that Israel will be purified and strengthened so she will fulfill her part. The sancti-

---

[86] Ibid, 440
[87] http://www.ldsces.org/inst_manuals/dc-in/dc-in-101.htm

fied members will assist Christ, the new David, through His representative the current living prophet. As one, we will work to invite our brethren from the grasp of Pharaoh and bring them out of the world. This was symbolized by Moses and the plagues, until Israel was birthed out of Egypt, across the Red Sea and into a higher state.

It seems there are two camps of Israel symbolized by the story of Moses that equates to the latter-days. The first came through the Red Sea as the waters of baptism and began their wilderness experience. Their progression through that experience is a type and shadow of our progression through receiving the blessings of the temple. It takes time for the initiate to complete this process of sanctification.

The second camp would be those who have ascended the mountain and are ready to be born of the Spirit into the Promised Land or in other words, are ready to have the promises of eternal lives sealed upon them. This birth is announced as with the sound of a trumpet, as symbolized by Moroni's statue, ready to bring forth the initiate as from a womb. This group will be spiritually ordered and organized (whether they know it or not) until they are ready for the great day when they vote to sustain the new David on the throne at the council of Adam-Ondi-Ahman.

So how does this bring us back to the principle topic of protection for us and our loved ones? It is important to understand that throne and altar are interchangeable in most applications. When we focus our faith and unified attention on the throne, with our eye single to the glory of God, we turn the key to unlock a canopy of protection, a pillar of fire and a cloud of protection over Israel. These are the same blessings of protection given to ancient Israel in Sinai when the ark was within the Tabernacle and Israel was being faithful.

The connection between the throne and the canopy of protection is represented by the altar of the temple and the prayer circle. The offering we bring of a broken heart and a contrite spirit, along with the unity of the saints, brings about the energy necessary to raise those offering sacrifice to a higher spiritual state if they are prepared. The words 'throne' and 'canopy' come from the same Hebrew root. In fact, a number of words have the same Hebrew root which ties together the idea of the throne, a covering, protection and the temple: "chair, throne, cover, gather, among others, and here are a few very similar roots: canopy, circle/square, concealment, dome, cap, atonement, encircle, surround, shoulder, carry."[88]

---

[88] The New Bantam-Megiddo, Hebrew Dictionary, 109

Hopefully we can begin to put the pieces together that Nibley painstakingly brought to light. If we will do so, the scriptures, including Isaiah, will open up in a dramatic new way. We will learn how to see those principles in light of the basic doctrines of salvation, for truly it is the basics that hold the real mysteries of salvation. These basics can bring us to a Zion state. The unity found within the principles of Zion is crucial in bringing to pass the Second Coming. Earth must mirror the order of Heaven and the stirring of energy of faith from below, as in a prayer circle. The earth must draw down the power of heaven, removing the curtain that separates heaven and earth.[89] The purity and power of the New Jerusalem will attract and draw down the city of Enoch, symbolizing the completion of unity between heaven and earth and usher in the return of Glory.[90]

The final steps leading up to the Second Coming all begin with the birth or bringing forth of the throne of David from the quiet protection of the church in the wilderness of the Sixth Dispensation, to the higher state of the Seventh Dispensation. Eventually conditions will prevail so that the Savior will begin ushering in His political kingdom. As a quick aside, some anti-Mormons believe we will try to take over governments but that is not the case. As governments crumble, the Church will continue to support Constitutional principles that will hold things together. The Lord will rule from the New Jerusalem eventually and in the meantime, we need not worry about the details of how this will all come about politically.

Now back to the spiritual fulfillment of these things, the Son adds throne upon throne, moving upwards to the position of Father in preparation for His own eternal kingdom, bringing all who will prepare themselves to share His throne and transition with Him. The sacred Book of Creation, the *Sefer Yetzirah*, written by the hand of Abraham, expounds on this subject: "One single name is not uttered in the world, the name which the Father gave to the Son; it is the name above all things: the name of the Father. For the Son would not become Father unless he wore the name of the Father. Those who have this name know it, but they do not speak it. But those who do not have it do not know it."[91]

The Seventh Dispensation is a type and shadow for Jesus. The birth of the dispensation occurs in 2000 (or 2001). The new dispensa-

---

[89] D&C 88:95
[90] Moses 7:62
[91] *Sefer Yetzirah*, Chapter VI

tion is young and needs to grow. At twelve years of age, it steps into a higher state, as a type for when the twelve-year-old Jesus went to the temple complex to teach. This is the age to receive the priesthood. It is time for him to be about his father's business. The young Jesus was seated on the steps of the temple. Interesting in light of the fact that most ancient cultures depicted gods as being either seated on a throne or on the ground. They were rooted in in order to draw from the earth or sea the members of their kingdom. Symbolically, they birthed the worthy into a higher state from this seated position. In Egyptology, a man seated on the ground is their hieroglyphic for 'god'. Thus, Christ seated on the temple steps (the temple being often depicted as a throne or holding a throne) gains significance, especially for us as it was at the age of twelve.

The **Sefer Yetzirah** seems to allude to the idea of the son being established while young but still continuing beneath His father's rule, acting in the role of sonship. Later, when he is older, then he takes possession of his kingdom: "What the father possesses belongs to the son, and the son himself, so long as he is small, is not entrusted with what is his. But when he becomes a man, his father gives him all that he possesses."[92]

The Political Throne of David

The ancient and very common motif was played out once again in the latter days with the usurper illegally taking possession of the throne. The United States is at this time the most powerful nation on earth and the president could now be seen in the ancient position of the cosmocrator, the most powerful man on earth. Now this is probably not strictly accurate but he is a place holder or image of that position. Whether the reader is a democrat or a republican or something altogether different, we are intending to make no political statement here as to specific politics. The gospel net gathers in all political persuasions. Hopefully the reader can refrain from crying sour grapes when we share this next part.

I have been a political student since I was a child. I was very active in promoting my candidate in the last two elections and the last month before the voting took place in 2012, I carefully watched all the polling. I began to learn many things such as the fact that a company in Spain, a very socialistic country, had been retained to count the general vote of most of the states. That company in Spain was bought by

---

[92] *Sefer Yetzirah*, Chapter VI

George Soros a few months before the voting took place. That is one of many disturbing things I learned about the extensive voting fraud that took place. Now I am not trying to say that only liberal candidates engage in voting fraud but there is an important point this leads us too.

About a year before the election, I was asked by some family members and later by some close friends if I believed Mitt Romney would be elected. My response was that I felt certain that he would gain the majority of the popular vote. I went on to explain that according to the pattern of a new cycle and especially the time of the quiet establishment of David's political throne, a proxy for the Lord would definitely be expected. With sadness I told them that I believed that Mitt Romney would either be killed shortly after taking office or he would win but the position would be usurped through voter fraud.

The political position of the new throne demanded the proxy of a righteous high priest. Now whether or not someone likes or hates his politics, all who know him agree he is a very good person in his private life and as a Church leader he was deeply loved and respected. The confirmation of the fraud and Romney's crucial role as proxy will most likely have to wait until the next life but we have no doubt of this fact because the pattern insists at this point that the usurper takes dominion from the rightful leader.

Mitt Romney's staff was stunned with the outcome. Their internal polling showed a very different story than we all saw in the returns. I followed closely and blogged about the last few days with huge crowds in swing states being turned away from Romney's stadium events. The stories were everywhere that only Mitt signs were found in most areas of the swing states and this would be a landslide. Mitt's opponent was holding events in barns, schools and other small venues and cameras were careful not to show the small crowds but video would still get out to a stunned internet audience of mostly empty crowds for President Obama.

After the election the stories began coming in about many districts receiving over 100% of the votes for the incumbent. The other states that were being counted by the company in Spain were all wondering how their polling could have been so very far off. Not much of this was heard by regular people because there is a very terrible stigma that attaches to anyone who claims election fraud. That stigma virtually assures that nothing will be done about this growing problem. I have mostly kept quiet about it since the election and only share this now because it is such a strong part of the pattern that it must be explained.

The message within the true meaning behind 2012 is the establishment of the political throne of David and the gathering of Zion, the Bride of Christ. This Zion unity is crucial and has a role to play that can be learned and understood. The Church on both sides of the veil, gathered in from the six dispensations helps bring forth the Davidic throne of the Seventh Dispensation, as symbolized by the star or shield of David. This protection is also symbolized by the beehive of Deseret. The unity of the bees helps protect the king, the sweet honey keeping him from the corruption of the world. The beehive is like the sacred mound of creation or mountain of the Lord that births the king from a lower to a higher sphere. According to ancient mythology: "Bees represent the bridge between two worlds. . . In the ancient Near East and throughout the Aegean world, bees were seen as a bridge between the natural world and the underworld. Bees were carved on tombs. The Mycenaean tholos tombs even took the form of beehives."[93]

In His turn, Christ in His Davidic and kingly role saves and brings forth the Church (Bride) into a Millennial state. The stirring from below is a covenant people making sacrifices and fulfilling the requirements necessary to bring down the kingdom of Heaven to this earth, which is the stirring from above. Once the sacrifice is given and accepted the blessings of Heaven will be showered upon us. A world dotted with temples is making this happen.

The temples can be seen as the womb of rebirth, a feminine aspect of the Gospel. In all ancient cultures, the concept of a bride or a mother goddess is intrinsic to their mythologies. This worship of a feminine deity, in our opinion, is a worship of the process of salvation found in the Three Pillars of the Gospel.

We should remember that the mother aspect, like mother earth, should not be the focus of our adoration. Earth will become the footstool for the throne, Kolob. It is the Father of our Spirits and His Son, the Father of Creation, that we adore. The throne and the concourse of worshippers gathered around it are a good representation of the altar and prayer circle. Together, these powers work to bring about the canopy of protection symbolized by the cloud by day and pillar of fire by night that protected ancient Israel and will be needed to protect modern Israel as we move into more intense times during the lengthy process of the opening of the Seventh Seal.

The seventh thousand year period is the Sabbath of the world but that Sabbath will both begin and end with tribulation. Understanding more of our role as the Bride of Christ is very helpful as we seek

---

[93] http://en.wikipedia.org/wiki/Bee_(mythology)

protection. The energy and reverence we bring to this Sabbath union will make all the difference, just as our attitude in Sacrament meetings illustrates our unity and devotion as we worship before the throne of God.

From the Waters

When Earth began,
the first mountain rose
from waters of chaos.
Surrounded by oceans,
emerging land
would be planted
with grass and garden.

Flying high above
receding flood, the dove
found an olive branch,
and Noah knew
the Tree still grew.

From the Nile,
Pharaoh's daughter
drew an infant who
would lead God's people
through the sea and beyond
to Canaan's promises.

In latter-days, Saints,
baptism clean,
seek a future paradise,
and this year our sun
passes through the center
of a starry river, the Milky Way,
perpetuating the pattern
of progression.

© Sharon Price Anderson

20 June 2012

Chapter Three: The Bride

While on a boat trip to the *Fernandez Archipelago*, archeologist Jim Turner took refuge from a storm on a wild and deserted Island 400 miles from Chile. The archeologist fell and was injured, forcing him to set up camp. With the light of dawn, after a turbulent night, Turner drew back the tent flap and had his first clear view of Apocalypse Island. There, before the stunned scientist stood a giant carved Mayan monument, more than a thousand miles from where anything Mayan should have been.

Turner, an expert on the Maya, understood that the island, so far from their southern Mexico realm meant there had to be something very important about this unlikely location. Why was there a 100 foot megalith of their sungod on a distant obscure island where no one would see it? The building of the statue was obviously a massive undertaking involving large numbers of workers. Behind the sungod, a huge figure of a crouching panther stood sentinel. What did this mean? What made Apocalypse Island such a sacred spot? This incident in 1995 launched Turner on an extensive study, piecing together clues until on a recent return trip for the History Channel, he confirmed his research on what the monument signified.

As it turns out, Apocalypse Island is the only place in the western hemisphere where one could get a perfect view of a solar eclipse that happened on November 13, 2012. Wait a minute…the special date was supposed to be December 21, 2012, so what is up with this new date?

We kept shaking our heads as we watched the intense arguments that surrounded the Maya Calendars. People polarized into camps regarding which date and even which year was to be the focus. What they seemed to miss was that the turning of an age is a process and not just a single event. Just as the Mayas have three major interlocking calendars, like cogs in a wheel, there are puzzle pieces to the winding up scenes of a cycle, especially this new Great Year that needed to be in place according to the pattern of creation or re-creation.

One of the important pieces of the pattern is the feminine aspect that we have discussed. Bringing forth new life through the birthing process is what women do physically, so when a birth or rebirth is brought about it is customary to speak of the facilitator having a feminine aspect. This concept is illustrated in Facsimile 3 figures 2 and 4 where both Pharaoh and Prince of Pharaoh are dressed as women, even though they are male.

The feminine principle of rebirth is what the November eclipse date is all about. But why should any of this interest us? Quite simply, the role of the Church and the priesthood, including individual members, is the key for bringing about spiritual rebirth and without that, we are in trouble. The reason it is so crucial right now to fully step out of Babylon and learn the principles of Zion is that we have entered the period of time when we will be spewed out of the mouth if we are lukewarm.

These astronomical events can help us piece together our job as part of the Bride of Christ. We can describe this chapter as a large painting. It will be a lot to take in but is necessary to understand later chapters. An overall glimpse should be seen like an impressionist painting, standing back to get a feel for what the artist is trying to show, although our painting is actually a puzzle carefully pieced together. A view from too close can confuse a person and look like nothing more than dabs of paint. First, we will lay out the four major players in this process and then we will take a look at each one.

The first player in the completion and renewal of a cycle is the sun as the old god (cycle) that is ready to die and be reborn. Second, is the Bride who brings forth the new sun through her Pleiades aspect. Third, is the new sun (new cycle), the offspring of the old sun and the Pleiades. The new sun is symbolized by the planet Venus in its Morning Star aspect, and fourth is the moon in its role of Great High Priest who watches over the Bride and the sacred birth/rebirth process.

The Sacred Marriage

In chapter two, we discussed the most important role as illustrated by the sun, throne and lotus flower as symbols of the new king that came forth during the winter solstice of 2012. The priesthood in its feminine aspect as the panther is represented in a temple role of birthing the new king or sun. In the New Year Rite, the people unite with one voice to bring forth and establish the king at the center throne/altar. They are led by the high priest. Once the king is lifted upon his throne and established, he then establishes his kingdom or his bride. This aspect of the pattern was demonstrated in some ancient cultures such as in the Sumerian Akitu New Year Rite, where the king symbolically weds the high priestess after his re-enthronement at the New Year.[94]

---

[94] Encounters In The Gigunu. Bibliotecapleyades.net. Retrieved 05-23-2010.

Again, the sun being birthed from the Milky Way womb in 2012 was like the king at the New Year being reborn and established on his throne. He will then challenge any who would claim his bride. A battle reenactment is a common New Year Rite motif. The rightful king wins the day and saves his bride and then the sacred marriage can take place. When does that marriage happen? Midnight and winter solstice of 2012 is considered the midnight of the Great New Year Cycle. When speaking of a cycle that lasts 26,000 years, we can see that a moment in time that is our own midnight does not signify. Midnight will span a number of years. It is our opinion that this sacred marriage has important significance over a period of years lasting from 2012 until the council at Adam-Ondi-Ahman and beyond, ending with the Lord's coming in glory.

We believe that in 2012 those who were spiritually ready were called to the marriage feast. Members of the Church rarely know when they have become sanctified and qualified as part of the Bride of Christ but that does not take away from the blessings. In addition to this, individuals may fulfill the requirements of being called as part of the Bride during an endowment session where they have come with their lamp filled with oil. That is their midnight; their New Year Rite when the Bridegroom lays claim upon them as part of the Bride.

Ideally marriage happens in the temple so we will now discuss how that marriage saves us and why marriage means "to lift up".

According to Brother Nibley, we must reorient ourselves in the temple. As previously discussed, everything is upside down here on the fallen earth. To reverse the fall, we must be spiritually reborn upward. The temple, as a priesthood womb of rebirth, lifts us up with the assistance of the King/Bridegroom office.

We believe one of the ways we reorient ourselves is by thinking of the veil as the separation between dimensions with one example being this telestial state from the terrestrial state. The Garden of Eden was a terrestrial place and in order to be reintroduced into the presence of God by reversing the effects of the fall, we must be pure and perfect so the Adversary has no claim upon us. Only Christ was perfect, so we must become as Christ, taking upon us His name and standing upon His foundation of priesthood authority in order to be lifted above the fallen condition of this earth. Christ is the door to the sheepcote of safety and He alone has the power to gather us in through His Atonement.

The Savior, as the Bridegroom, embraces His Bride as she is reborn into a place of purity. Encircling her in His robes of righteousness, he lifts her up to the terrestrial place of safety. He was lifted up so that He might lift us up. The sanctified become members of the Church

of the Firstborn, the Bride of Christ, in order that we can lay claim upon the Bridegroom for rescue and be lifted up in the sacred and symbolic midnight marriage that we read of in the parable of the Ten Virgins
(Matt. 25:1–13). If we have pure oil in our lamps, then Christ will light
those lamps and give us salvation so we will not be burned at His coming.

Paul wrote in Ephesians about a rising from the dead that
would appear to be a spiritual preparation for a later physical resurrection. We rise above our fallen self who is spiritually dead through the
priesthood ordinance of baptism and further prepare ourselves spiritually through the ordinances of the temple: "Wherefore he saith, Awake
thou that sleepest, and arise from the dead, and Christ shall give thee
light." (Eph. 5:15) We believe that 2012 marked an important step in
the rebirth process for the earth, a spiritual rebirth in preparation for her
physical rebirth into a terrestrial state at the Second Coming. For those
who miss the moment because they are not spiritually prepared, remember that Nibley insisted that the temple endowment overcomes
time and space to symbolically return the initiate to midnight of New
Year's Day. Each person, as they take upon them the name of Christ
and become sanctified, can become endowed with light and spiritually
rise as the midnight new sun on New Year's Day...even if they do not
realize this gift has been given to them.

Paul goes on in the same chapter to write: "For the husband is
the head of the wife, even as Christ is the head of the church: and he is
the saviour of the body." (Eph. 5:23) Paul says the husband must save
the woman, so how does this work? This does not imply that the woman is in any way inferior to the man. It was the woman, Eve, who did
the courageous act of putting things in motion as women often do. She
took the fruit, bringing about the fall and the conditions to have children. Because of this crucial act, she must be saved from the natural
consequences of that act. As Christ draws the Church to Him, lifting
her up and hiding her beneath His robes of righteousness, so does a
man, who desires to marry a woman properly, stand as a representative
of Christ, as a savior of the body of his Bride to be. Carrying the bride
over the threshold takes on new meaning when we remember the Hebrew word for marriage, "nisuin" which means to lift up. The bridegroom symbolically lifts his bride up, protecting her from the Adversary who has possession of this fallen world. Like wooden Russian
dolls carrying a smaller doll within, the bridegroom hides his wife,
metaphorically within his heart, veiling her from the greedy eyes of the
usurper. The enemy both hates and desires the bride. The evil one
would claim that she is not Christ even if she has taken His name upon

her because she is clearly female. She enters the sacred terrestrial Edenic place through the door of her husband's heart. She then stands by his side as an equal; purified from the corruption of the world she left so that the sealing will last for eternity with no corruption to cause a breaking down as science says things must do over time.

The Atonement works against this scientific principle, the second law of thermodynamics or entropy, which insists that all things break down over time. Again we go back to the first chapter of Nibley's book **Temple and Cosmos** where he delves into that subject, explaining that some scientists realize that there is something working against that natural law. Nibley shows that it is the Atonement, tied to the temple that works against the breaking down of matter. A purification process brings the initiate to a state of incorruption that prepares him/her for an eternal linking that maintains the wholeness and integrity of that sealing.[95] In the same way welders know that metals must be clean when welded in order not to break under pressure and time.

Christ set the standard for equality in the sacred marriage when He said we would be joint heirs with Him. (Rom. 8:17) Although He will always be greater than us, He teaches the Zion oneness that places those worthy by His side in a circle of family unity and not in a pecking order. So should a husband see his wife. In priesthood offices, there is a hierarchy but within the eternal family unit, husband and wife are one body…equal.

The counterfeit to this spiritual ascension process is found all over the world in many expressions. The biggest difference between the correct path and the counterfeit is that the false ascension path is an individual process for those who think to try and save themselves. Only the true and authorized priesthood has the power to bind and seal. Unity is the key to Zion and this is what brings eternal happiness.

Pleiades, the Seven Sisters

Various astronomical and metaphorical examples are used to describe the feminine role of the priesthood; the Milky Way, the Pleiades,[96] Venus in its Evening Star role, the Moon, a cow, the mother goddess, a swan, a beehive and many more. The Pleiades is the 2012 feminine symbol because it explains a very sacred level of redemption and unity that lifts sanctified man into a high kingship that qualifies one to become rooted in with the promise of becoming a future Heavenly Father. As discussed in a previous chapter, we feel that Christ will be-

---

[95] Nibley, *Temple and Cosmos,*
[96] The Pleiades or seven sisters is a bright cluster of stars very near to earth and easily visible to the naked eye.

come established as a Heavenly Father during the Seventh Seal as He also begins the winding up scene for this round of creation in His office of Firstborn Son.

We begin with the old sun that brings itself forth into a new cycle. It is very simply the winding down of the old cycle on a telestial level, ready to die and be reborn into a terrestrial state. The whole world will not yet be in this higher state. It always starts with the center place. The Egyptian idea of the opener of the way, illustrates how a God is needed to pierce through new territory. It would seem that Jesus Christ takes the lead in being the opener of the way.

There are seven dispensation leaders who have organized a sanctified people in their own time. The leader of the seventh dispensation has the job of unifying all seven dispensation leaders through sacred priesthood ordinances. Those seven work together like a sacred prayer circle around the center place to birth forth the new cycle. Many ancient mythologies seem to indicate that the seven sisters of the Pleiades have long represented this specific process, as well as other roles.

Elijah restored the sealing power so that children and fathers can be sealed together in holy temples.

1 Behold, I will reveal unto you the Priesthood, by the hand of Elijah the prophet, before the coming of the great and dreadful day of the Lord.

2 And he shall plant in the hearts of the children the promises made to the fathers, and the hearts of the children shall turn to their fathers.

3 If it were not so, the whole earth would be utterly wasted at his coming. (D&C 2:1–3)

The union of heaven and earth through this sealing is necessary to keep the world from being "wasted at his coming". Why would it be wasted? Because at the Second Coming, nothing that remains in a telestial state will be able to withstand His brightness and will therefore burn. The blessings received through keeping temple covenants bring us back from a fallen or telestial state. As we strive to become born again and redeemed from the fall, we become a temple. Then, gathered in as part of the Bride, we work with the Son of God to begin bringing the earth back from a fallen state. This is a job that takes help from both sides of the veil. The hearts of the fathers in the Spirit World and the children in mortality become welded together, joining heaven and earth. A conduit opens up that enables the distillation of light upon the redeemed. That group will act in concert with Christ to prepare that city on the hill, a terrestrial people, so that all is not burned (wasted) at his coming.

The counterfeit priesthood and also many sincere people, who use sacred teachings to attempt an ascension process to God or to a higher state, lack the priesthood and must repent and follow the narrow path emblazoned by the Lord or fail in their attempt at redemption. The linking of heaven and earth can be accomplished only through the glue of valid sealing ordinances. The sealing of husband and wife, when both have achieved sanctification and justification, is the only thing that can overcome the telestial law of opposites between good and evil. The higher celestial law is between man and wife. This is why the legal forms are adhered to in the Church.

Christ is the Bridegroom who prepared and groomed the Bride in the final years leading up to 2012. All who unify in Zion and live up to their temple covenants will be a part of His legal Bride, thus lifting them above the fallen law and establishing them in the higher law.

Joseph Smith received a revelation to explain that Missouri could not at that time be redeemed. The New Jerusalem that will be built in Missouri will be the city that most represents the principle of the Bride and cannot function on lower laws. Zion itself cannot work properly through telestial laws. *Doctrine and Covenants* 105 reveals that members failed because of disunity and disobedience: "And are not united according to the union required by the law of the Celestial Kingdom; And Zion cannot be built up unless it is by the principles of the law of the Celestial Kingdom; otherwise I cannot receive her unto myself." (D&C 105:4–5)

There is a magnetic connection between man and wife, king and queen, which is the glue that holds the Celestial Kingdom together. On a larger scale, the Lord in His Bridegroom aspect is bound together with the Church in her Bride aspect. During the year 2012, the feminine process was in place that brought forth the new king at the end of the year. The king is the first through the veil of the new creation and then he will reach back to bring His Bride through for the sacred marriage.

Nibley spent a lot of time writing about mothers marrying sons, and other strange practices. The explanation can be broken down to female bringing forth male, then alternately, the male bringing forth the female, as they help each other up Jacob's ladder in the ascension process. That sounds so strange, even startling. Nibley had more than his share of detractors and this author has had professors complain about Nibley's odd remarks. The above explanation is so very simple when broken down from the symbolism. It is nothing more than the feminine role of the priesthood in rebirthing people into a higher spiritual condition. Then, in the role of kingship, as a new Adam, the husband reaches down and lifts his bride to his side in preparation for the sacred marriage. Why does it need be so complicated?

Because of the fall, the evil one lays claim on all who come under the effects of the fall. He requires a death. Through baptism and other ordinances, symbolic deaths are given, fulfilling the law and releasing the candidate from the effects of the fall and from the grasp of the author of sin. Lucifer still tries to claim the Bride since woman took the fruit from his hand but the husband saves the Bride and lifts her to himself. She is, so to speak, encircled within his embrace just as Christ as the Bridegroom encircles the Church within His embrace and takes her for His own. The ends of the law must be fulfilled. No twitching of the nose or magic incantation can undo the effects of the law. Legal steps must be taken and this is done through the offices of priesthood and kingship as sons of Adam.

The Bride is represented by the Pleiades star cluster. Every year, during the middle of November (the exact date depends upon your location) the Pleiades is in the zenith of the sky at midnight. Druids and other ancient religions taught that the midnight hour allows people to move from one state of being to another. This is the moment when the old begins to die and the new moves into the birth canal for delivery. For a woman, this usually takes one or two hours but for cosmic events, the delivery takes longer. In this case, the trip down the birth canal lasted from November 13th, to December 21st, 2012. So when the solar eclipse happened on the 13th, it signaled that the old sun was overcome, killed and then reborn. The eclipse was the beginning of the labor pains that brought forth the new sun five weeks later on the winter solstice.

This sacred event was not for profane eyes so the eclipse that was seen from Apocalypse Island symbolized a veiling. The Aztecs always carefully noted and celebrated the Pleiades zenith crossing in November, as did the Mayas before them. Every 52 years, during this November crossing, the Aztecs had the new fire ceremony to celebrate a new feminine cycle of their lunar calendar. At this time, the solar calendar, the Haab, would correlate with the feminine in order to ensure that life would continue into the next 52 year round. All the fires in the kingdom would be extinguished before the ceremony and then relit with the fire from the temple complex where a sacrifice would take place. This new fire represented a new sun, a promise that life would not end with this transition into a new creation cycle.

All of the cycles have significance but the 2012 date represented a new era of unprecedented importance. It opened the doorway to the flood of resurrections that will take place during the seventh thousand year period, and those who have qualified will be established as new Heavenly Fathers/Mothers for their own kingdoms, becoming as it were, new Adams or Eves. Enoch taught that the Pleiades represents the key to physical protocreation; it represents the galactic beginning of the physical Adamic household.[97]

We will always worship Heavenly Father, the Father of our Spirits and honor Him, even those who follow in His footsteps and have their own kingdoms. Just because Abraham, Isaac and Jacob have been established in their own kingdoms does not mean we worship them. The order of the Godhead, and all the principles of the Gospel that members learn in Primary are still true.

Cycles of time may seem strange to modern man but that is because we are taught to see time as linear. The ancients saw time as circular, like a day, week, years, etc. which always had an ending and a beginning. They were comfortable with calendars having spiritual significance. They also understood that darkness and light, like day and night, took turns in dominance. Of the 52 weeks in a year, half were seen as a time of darkness and death and half as light and life. Cycles can also break down into smaller and smaller pieces until we have a 24 hour cycle that also represents an ending, (like Venus as the evening star) and a beginning, (like Venus as a morning star) with the dawn of a new sun. Half of each of these cycles are considered feminine and were dark like the womb. Half were considered masculine and bright with the presence of the sun. The Chinese ying/yang symbol is one of many traditions that depict this half dark/half light aspect of cycles.

The dot of opposite color within each side may represent a veiling and protecting of its counterpart during its dominant cycle. We have now emerged from a dark cycle where the presence of the moon was so important because mankind was not able to withstand the brightness of the sun, or the Son of God. This meant that a representative of God has to help the people in their darkness. We are still within this process and it takes time to be completed. We still need the help of the moon working with the sun to fulfill this overlapping time period. To the Egyptians, the moon and its representative was called Thoth (remember that the Egyptians had the true form of the

---

[97] The Book of Knowledge: The Keys of Enoch, Key 1-0-6

Gospel but without priesthood authority) and for the Greeks, Hermes. For us, this is the Holy Ghost. It is his job at the end, to gather all as one and then to decrease as the Son of God, coming forth from the waters of baptism, begins to increase and organize His forces. The sun will cross the Milky Way at the end of the Mayan Calendar, which symbolizes the Savior coming forth from the Celestial River (Jordon) like a baptism or birth.

The moon has long been seen as representative of the Holy Ghost. Some have been confused whether this is a man or a woman. We believe the evidence clearly shows that it is a man who stands as high priest over the bride, so he is working with the feminine aspect of the Gospel. The moon can be seen as the bride but the best man at the wedding watches over her for the groom until the time is right to hand her through to the true husband. The Pleiades themselves, the seven sister stars, are more directly representative of the mother aspect of bringing forth new life. Each of the seven dispensations, (symbolized by the seven early Christian Churches of Asia) is organized beneath the head of the dispensation leader. The leader of the seventh, Joseph Smith, gathers them all into one to bring forth the Second David, the King of kings, on December 21, 2012.[98]

The Mayas understood the astronomy that represents the Gospel pattern and knew it would play out perfectly in the last dispensation. The black panther behind the sunlord on Apocalypse Island, represents the bride, the era of night, holding within her sable robe, the stars (kings and high priests) that unify to bring forth the new king. For the Egyptians, the Milky Way goddess, Nut, was shown either as a giant woman or a cow arching over the earth and holding within her body, the stars that represent the sanctified members of the Church who work as one to bring forth new kings who have taken upon them the name of Christ. The Milky Way was often referred to by the Egyptians as the Celestial Nile or waters of Nun that birth the new sun.

The Mayas looked forward to the great event of Quetzalcoatl entering the birth canal of the Pleiades when they would reach their zenith over the temple in Palanque, Mexico on November 13, 2012. Together, those seven dispensations (represented by the seven sisters) unify to create the energy needed, like a great chorus, to bring forth the birth.

---

[98] This is in a spiritual aspect not the physical second coming of Christ, which we do not presume to predict.

The Pleiades or seven sisters.

What makes this great New Fire Ceremony, as the Maya would call it, even more astonishing is what happened about six months earlier. On May 20, 2012, there was a rare solar eclipse. The early Native Americans always marked the time of the November Pleiades crossing so they would know that six months later, the Pleiades would be in the zenith at noon. This was the time for planting crops...sowing seeds. It was also a very sacred time for the Mayas and Aztecs. They believed that the sun and the Pleiades, as they cross that day, would bring forth the birth of crops for that year and ensure continuity. On that day in 2012, the sun, representing God and the Pleiades, representing the Bride, unified and that sacred union was overshadowed by the moon, which represented the great Holy Spirit to the ancients. This reminds us of that sacred event found in the book of Luke:

He shall be great, and shall be called the Son of the Highest: and the Lord God shall give unto him the throne of his father David:

And he shall reign over the house of Jacob for ever; and of his kingdom there shall be no end.

Then said Mary unto the angel, How shall this be, seeing I know not a man?

And the angel answered and said unto her, The Holy Ghost shall come upon thee, and the power of the Highest shall overshadow thee: therefore also that holy thing which shall be born of thee shall be called the Son of God. (Luke 1:32–35)

The above scripture is literal and this 2012 event was in some ways symbolic but still a necessary part of the pattern of redemption for the earth and Zion.

In a History Channel special, Turner speaking of the carved sungod and panther, explained that the Mayas saw the 2012 November eclipse as a return of kings and gods at the end times. We feel that the statues on Apocalypse Island, symbolize the power of Zion (represented by the panther statue) in guarding and bringing forth Christ (statue of Quetzalcoatl). During the first coming of Christ, John the Baptist, acting as the forerunner, gathered a people to make straight the paths for the coming of the Lord. Christ was already born, so how could a man born shortly before Jesus, prepare the way for His coming? The Savior began His three year ministry after coming forth from the waters of baptism, brought forth by John representing the Church, which is the Bride. John had fled into the wilderness after his father was murdered. After he began his ministry, the honest in heart sought after him there. When the time was right, he came forward and handed over his disciples to Christ. Similarly, during winter solstice 2012, the sun rose up out of the Celestial River as it was birthed to a higher state.

In the last days, the Church had to flee into the wilderness after the father of our dispensation was killed. Brigham led them and established the Bride in a place of safety where she could stretch out her tent, a canopy of safety and stability. She grew in stature and strength and is now coming out of the wilderness, bringing spiritual Zion from darkness to light in preparation for the future political and spiritual kingdom of David.

We must remember that the spiritual creation or re-creation happens before the physical reality. So before the actual millennial reign of the Son of God, the spiritual aspects are put into place. The Bride and the Bridegroom jointly open the door for the resurrection. The prophet Amos associated the Pleiades with the resurrection.[99] Turner explained that the Mayas believed that Kings were a conduit between god and man. The sun god of Apocalypse Island was seen as that king, a stairway and a door that joined heaven and earth.

Why were the ancients so impressed with the Pleiades? Enoch's writing tells us that The Pleiades is "the cradle and the throne of our consciousness" emphasizing that "the program of Adamic life was created in connection with this region of space. And that it is this

---

[99] Amos 5:8

region of space that will also signal the return of higher intelligence." The word 'throne' represents the spot where the upper Hierarchies "come together to balance lower creation."[100]

Venus

Our third player (not in importance) is the seed (meaning Christ in his Davidic role) that comes forth as the new sun. Venus is the symbol for this seed in its 'morning star' phase. Facsimile 2, figure 4, is that sunboat where all the worthy who die (literally or figuratively) are gathered into the body of Christ, and with Him, come forth into a new kingship. It is important to note that at times members of the Church work in the feminine role, as symbolized by the prayer circle (evening star phase) and sometimes in the kingship role at the altar (throne) where the king, supported by his council, rebirths himself anew. When one is spiritually prepared, that initiate, as a king in the making, steps up another rung of the ladder in a rebirth until they receive the promise of exaltation and on from there as far as they have the capacity to progress. So for 2012, it actually is not just the Lord Himself who is moving from exaltation to exaltation, but all those who have qualified to follow Him in this upward spiritual ascent.

Just days after the sacred union of the sun and the Pleiades, on May 20th, 2012, there was another rare event. The Venus transit occurred on June 5th. This is when that planet crossed in front of the sun, symbolic of the new seed in gestation for a higher birth at the winter solstice.[101]

According to the *Manuscript of Serna*, a missionary report from central Mexico, the natives "adored and made more sacrifices" to Venus[102] than any other "celestial or terrestrial creatures" apart from the sun. They believed Quetzalcoatl transformed himself into that star. They correlated both the sun and Venus as symbols for royal authority,

---

[100] The Book of Knowledge: The Keys of Enoch, Key 1-0-6

[101] http://siderealview.wordpress.com/2010/12/05/galactic-underworld-venus-rising/

[102] Six pages of the Dresden Codex are devoted to Venus. The left hand sides of pages 46-50 (according to the conventional page numbering) contain a table of dates of the rising and setting of Venus as morning and evening star. On each of these pages, the last station of Venus listed is heliacal rise. On the right hand side of each page, deities and auguries associated with heliacal rise are illustrated.
http://www.bibliotecapleyades.net/ciencia/dresden/dresdencodex04.htm

which ties Venus as the morning star in with the throne, the kingdom of God on earth and the new sun at 2012.[103]

The Maya's story of the Hero Twins, Hunaphu and Xbalanque, had everything to do with the resurrection, and the bringing forth of Venus. They believed Venus would lead the sun and indeed, on December 21, 2012, Venus rose at 5:30 in the morning, leading (taking over the position) of the sun for a new dawn. In fact, Mayan artifacts have been discovered that were inscribed with a solar symbol on one side and a Venus symbol on the opposite side. In passing through the veil of the Pleiades, Venus becomes a new sun. The Maya also marked this passing as a time when "dire events could be expected."[104]

The new sun represents the opening of a new era. Remembering that the sun is a star, this reminds us that Kolob was the first creation in this universal round. According to Anthony E. Larson, "the intended meaning of Kolob is 'Heart Star.' The Latin Venus was Verticordia, 'Turning Heart' or 'True Heart.'" [105] Winter Solstice of 2012 was the midnight of the old round, the heart of the night, the dying of the old. Venus pierces the darkness, bringing a new dawn but only for those who gather with the congregations in the north. There is a seeming dichotomy to the 2012 winter solstice end date. Was it midnight, or was it dawn? This date is the midnight of the 26 thousand year period. How can it also be dawn? The sun crossing the Galactic Plane is the dawn.

Now let us take a metaphorical look at the midnight/dawn conundrum. The term "congregations of the north" comes from Isaiah 14:13. The text is referring to Lucifer who attempted to wrest the throne from God and take control of the council: "For thou hast said in thine heart, I will ascend into heaven, I will exalt my throne above the stars of God: I will sit also upon the mount of the congregation, in the sides of the north:" A footnote to this verse refers to the council in heaven. We learn from Psalms 48:2 that the mount of the congregation is the symbol for the holy city: "Beautiful for situation, the joy of the whole earth, is mount Zion, on the sides of the north, the city of the great king." A footnote to this verse tells of a concept that the dwelling place of Deity was in the north. Ancients often referred to North as up and South as down, in addition to their regular points on the compass.

---

[103] Ibid

[104] http://www.bibliotecapleyades.net/ciencia/dresden/dresdencodex04.htm

[105] http://www.mormonprophecy.com/prophecy,_ancient_history_and_the_ restored_gospel_002.htm

They do double-duty. Remembering that Nibley suggested we need to reorient ourselves when we are in the temple, then we can easily picture ourselves lifted upward to rest in the city of light with the Congregation of the North.

We suggest this describes the process of gathering in, like the seven stars of the big dipper that rotate around the North Star. As we have shown earlier, earth is the mirror image of heaven. So when it is winter solstice here, it is summer in heaven. So for those lifted up by the temple mount to a heavenly state, they will find themselves symbolically in the north. This will be the only place mankind will be able to enjoy light in the coming years, as the rest of the earth remains in growing darkness. We must keep our covenants well so we can be endowed with brighter and brighter light as one of the candles set on the hill. The original council of heaven is reorganized on a higher level of progression. In this spiritual city set on the hill, the congregations of the North, like the City of Enoch, must work to lift others to that place of safety. To reach this metaphorical (for now) city, we need a bridge. A beautiful poem by our friend Sharon helps illustrate:

Bright and Morning Star

I am the root and the offspring
of David, [and] the bright and
morning star.
Let God's children shout for joy
and all lights of the morning sing together.
From Jacob's line a star will shine.
Above all things, he is
first in government, last in time,
before the beginning, beyond the end.
He who bends the bow of heaven
by the scepter of his majesty
condescends to know mortality.
Arrowing life into the shadow of death,
the Dayspring comes radiant as dawn.
Arise. Declare the glory of
the Bright and Morning Star!

© Sharon Price Anderson

The Moon Bridge

The ancient Japanese Shinto religion, the American Navajo and many other cultures, believed in a rainbow bridge that led the righteous from this fallen place up the seven colors to heaven.[106] Seven is the number of completion for reaching a higher level, be they days, dispensations, color frequencies, stars, churches or thousand year periods. We are blessed to live in this exciting time and to be a brick in that Bride

---

[106] http://www.novareinna.com/bridge/quote

72

that bridges the gap between the lower wilderness to the upper garden of peace.

The Rainbow Bridge depicted here is one analogy that explains the ascension process from earth to heaven.

To reiterate the four major players, we have (1) the old cycle that dies, and (2) the Bride who gives birth to (3) the new cycle as symbolized by the sun, and this birth is bridged and protected by (4) the servant high priest. And so now we take a look at the high priest position.

The Egyptian story of Isis in the wilderness is enlightening. With destruction bringing a creation cycle to an end, Isis the bride flees into the wilderness to be watched over by Thoth, the Egyptian representation of the Holy Ghost. At times Isis is a fierce lioness when danger abounds. At times she is Hathor, the cow goddess. She has other aspects to her nature which she invokes according to need. Likewise, Thoth can be portrayed as a baboon, an Ibis bird and the high priest Anubis among others. God gives Thoth the job of protecting the bride and cheering her through her difficult journey. At length, they finish their trek and Isis establishes the next creation cycle, creating a new Garden of Eden, slowly bringing order to a world in chaos.[107] What does this story mean for Latter-day Saints?

When ancient Israel wandered in the wilderness, they were watched over by a great high priest. At times Moses (head of a dispensation) worked in the king position, and his brother Aaron was his high priest. In a larger circle, Moses fulfilled the role of high priest to Jehovah. He watched over the Bride (Israel), protecting and cheering, until they came to the Promised Land. There, he handed the Bride over to the

---

[107] http://books.google.com/books?id=gq1LhcH48GQC&pg=PA858&lpg=PA858&dq

true Bridegroom. This was symbolized by Joshua taking the lead. In Greek, the name Joshua is 'Jesus'. The crossing of the Jordan into the Promised Land, the place where Jesus came forth from the waters of baptism, is the Israelite equivalent to the Milky Way, the waters of Nun bringing forth the new sun. Joshua literally came forth from Nun. This was the name of his father and we do not believe that was a coincidence. The handclasp of unity between Moses and Joshua (the type for Christ) bridged those waters, the priesthood miraculously creating a path for Israel to cross. There are many types and shadows throughout history to show this part of the pattern but we will look at only two more because of space.

Peter, the high priest of the early Christian Church, bridged the gap between dispensations by bringing the priesthood order to Joseph Smith, the new dispensation leader. Jesus and His apostles are the head of the sixth dispensation.[108] The high priest is usually assigned to bridge the gaps between dispensations or smaller cycles. Christ moved on to act in higher offices and gave Peter the job as His representative to be the bridge. John the Beloved referred to the early Church as the Bride who had to flee into the wilderness for protection, just as Isis did.

In the latter days, when Joseph moved upward to fulfill a busy agenda, a man very much like Peter in personality, led the Church again into the wilderness. Although both Peter and Brigham were prophets, they are often thought of as the head of the apostles. Both were reluctant to lay claim to the title of prophet for a few years. Brigham led the Church metaphorically to a higher state in the everlasting hills. There he set up the organization of Deseret and spread out the curtains of Zion to bring stability, strength and protection to the Bride. A temporary center stake of Zion was established until Jackson County will someday actively become the center place. Although Joseph is the head of this dispensation, he gave the care of the physical Church into the hand of his high priest.

The word 'bridge' is the root for the name Bridget. This is the name of the Celtic goddess who is considered the sacred bride. The masculine form of her name is 'Brigham'. The name Bridget means; strong,[109] exalted one,[110] bride,[111] and the goddess of fire,[112] which

---

[108] LDS Bible Dictionary, 657

[109] http://www.babynamescountry.com/meanings/Bridget.html

[110] http://www.thinkbabynames.com/meaning/0/Bridget

[111] http://en.wikipedia.org/wiki/Bridget_(given_name)

brings us back to the Pleiades fire ceremony. Brigham, although the masculine form, also means "the Bridge Settlement."[113]

The city set on a hill, bridges the gap to the other hill on the other side of time (2012). This Zion or Deseret watches over the king, hiding him within the sacred space of the beehive, until the new king is ready to come forth into His Bridegroom role. The beehive represents the temple or the womb of the Bride. This is sacred space only for the initiated. The righteous should spiritually unify at that symbolic place and be a light to encourage others to come and join the city on the hill. This symbolic settlement by the bridge is watched over by the high priest, just as Thoth watched over Isis. We are Isis; we are that city symbolically moving upward in the solar boat: "Ye are the light of the world. A city that is set on an hill cannot be hid." (Matt. 5:14)

Sometimes Zion is a physical place, and sometimes it is a spiritual place. It would seem that that city right now is made up of the people that the Lord is calling up out of the world. Each of the citizens of that city of Zion go through the same process we have been discussing. We enter the temple through the waters of baptism in the basement of the temple. Step by step, we progress as if we were moving upwards in the temple, in a series of deaths and rebirths on each rung of Jacob's ladder until finally ready to be born from the womb of the temple or in other words born from the top of Mt. Zion. That birth is announced by a righteous servant of God who symbolically blows the trumpet.

As Isaiah says, "How beautiful upon the mountain [top of the temple] are the feet of those who publish peace." Moroni, gold as the sun, appears to be standing on a sun, born from the temple (throne) to bring forth the initiate to the promise of exaltation. He is now qualified to stand as a savior on Mt. Zion, to help lift others from that place of preparation to step into the boat of Facsimile 2, figure 4, also known as the ship of a thousand. That is the king position. It is the bride's job to help bring forth the king, and also protect him as the wings of the hawk protect that ship.

Another aspect of the story is the Ark of the Covenant, protected by two female angels. Egyptians would recognize the two as Isis and Nephthys. That ark is a type for the grave and preparing the initiate for

---

[112] http://www.behindthename.com/name/bridget
[113] http://www.babynames.com/name/BRIGHAM

the resurrection. Brigham Young taught that the ordinances of the temple are to prepare the individual for resurrection.[114]

With the turning of the age, the high priest over the Bride in the wilderness turns her over to the Bridegroom. Who is it? The current living prophet is the Bridegroom. Then why do we say that it is Brigham Young? His name seems to indicate that there is a masculine office that watches over the Bride in the wilderness. He is the high priest that led the Bride to safety, set up Deseret to protect the waiting political kingdom and organized the beehive to do the work of preparation to tie together the dispensations and spread the Gospel, preparing the Church for her role. The current prophets are the ones who receive revelation to build new temples that now dot the earth, reclaiming fallen telestial pieces of ground. Now let us tie this in to the basics of the Gospel.

The second chapter of the **Sefer Yetzirah** (written by Abraham) explains that there is an earthly organization represented by water and a heavenly organization represented by fire. These are the baptisms of water and fire, which are mothers bringing the initiate into rebirth. Here are the four sacred elements found throughout all ancient cultures: the initiate is earthly matter cleansed by the water, then refined by the fire, and then finally the initiate is sealed by the Spirit (wind or air) to be born as a new creature. The office of Holy Ghost, through the power of the priesthood, brings forth the initiate born of the Spirit. Nibley explained that the unifying covenant described in the **Sefer Yetzirah**, brings together two aspects representing the male and female.[115] Heaven-fire, water-earth and birth through the Holy Spirit in between them are the unifying covenant.

Still too complicated? Fallen man (made from earth) must be baptized in water, baptized by fire through the laying on of hands and then live the Gospel until he/she is ready to be sealed up to Eternal Life.[116] The Bride (symbolized by earth) is saved from the fall by the heavenly Bridegroom. She is lifted up through partaking of the Tree of Life into the sky to be a part of the Pleiades. Their sacred marriage and union is facilitated and protected by the Holy Spirit as symbolized by the moon.

---

[114] Brigham Young Addresses, 1860-1864, A Chronological Compilation of Known Addresses of the Prophet Brigham Young, Vol. 4 [Salt Lake City: Elden J. Watson, 1980]
[115] *Nibley, One Eternal Round,* 518
[116] See D&C 68:12

Isaiah wrote about the root and the branch. (Isa. 11:1) Jeremiah 23:5 explains that the branch is Christ in His Davidic role. Isaiah 11:10, when compared with D&C 113:6, makes it clear that Joseph Smith is the root, (Isa. 11:10, D&C 113:6) as the father of the last dispensation who gathers all into one. He is rooted in to bring forth the seventh thousand year period. Christ, in His Davidic role, is identified as the branch. The priesthood would seem to be the servant spoken of in Jacob, chapter five, whom the Lord has grafting the branches back into the sacred olive tree that represents the union of latter-day Israel. The bridge is that grafting together of the sixth and seventh thousand year periods, the handclasp between Joseph and David, which brings us to the ancient Jewish and Arabic beliefs in Messiah ben Joseph and Messiah ben David.

Messiah ben (son of) Joseph is an important figure known for thousands of years from rabbinical apocalyptic literature.[117] According to these traditions, Messiah ben Joseph will come prior to the coming of Messiah ben David. Joseph will gather the children of Israel together and reestablish temple worship. He will set up his own dominion, which sounds similar to being a head of a dispensation but will fall in battle. The Messiah ben Joseph will initiate a union with Judah who will be led by Messiah ben David.[118]

We know that the Greek Alpha and Omega are types for Jesus Christ as the beginning and the end. Just like Moses, Joseph Smith holds the double roles as king of his dispensation and also high priest to the Lord in a larger circle. Brigham, who stands in as the high priest to Joseph Smith, is the symbol for the city by the bridge of 2012. Joseph, in his role as high priest to the Second and eternal King David, stands in for the King of kings as the Omega position of this ending round. He grasps the hand of Christ in His Davidic role on the other side of the gulf of 2012, the Alpha of the new round. The overlapping of this handclasp creates stability and protection for the Bride just as she continues to act in a protective veiling role over the king. The interaction between the two creates that sacred light on the hill. The following photograph, taken by Sharon Price Anderson, shows this sacred motif engraven in stone on the Salt Lake Temple. The words above the handclasp, "I am Alpha and Omega", may take on new meaning now.

---

[117] See Sukkah 52 a, b
[118] http://www.freerepublic.com/focus/f-religion/1890301/posts

Photograph by Sharon Price Anderson – Salt Lake Temple

Nibley was well aware of all of this as part of the New Year Rites as he wrote that the famous Shabako document explains that in the coronation rights, the king unites himself with the court. A representative of the court is shown joining hands with the king. This is written as the joining of heaven and earth.[119] We are the court and we must focus our faith and work in tandem with the rightful king to bridge the gap of the crossroads. A knowledge of these principles may help us concentrate and bring to bear a more effective focus as we help bring forth the throne (altar). As we have established, Joseph gathers in the Bride or the court and joins hands with Messiah ben David.

The Maya Hero Twins are all about two sons of God who work together during the 2012 era to bring about the resurrection of their father who was killed by their enemy, Seven Macaw.[120] Who is it they save from the grip of the evil god? It is their father Adam. Each of us must become as Adam or Eve to be saved, thus the Hero Twins, using the Tree of Life, bring the process of redemption to the children of Adam. We will take a closer look at their tale in a later chapter, but we did want to mention them here because after an extensive study of their mythology, we believe they mirror the prophecies of Messiahs ben Joseph and David.

We are piecing together what may seem to be a complicated puzzle in this chapter but we encourage our readers to continue on. Subsequent chapters will clarify and illustrate our points that we are piecing together. Many saints may still be ready for milk only. Others stubbornly demand that we all stick to a strictly milk diet because they fear moving forward. Yes, we must stay on the straight and narrow but we are also supposed to be pressing forward, not standing still. As long

---

[119] Nibley, *Message*, p. 18
[120] Jenkins, *Maya Cosmogenesis*, 56

as we progress line upon line, all Church members should be moving forward in gospel learning.

Joseph Smith struggled to get the saints ready for greater understanding of ancient truths: "Joseph Smith would lament that many Saints were unwilling to accept the glorious things revealed to him from heaven. I have tried for a number of years to get the minds of the Saints prepared to receive the things of God; but . . . [they] will fly to pieces like glass as soon as anything comes that is contrary to their traditions."[121]

How thankful we are that Joseph had a stalwart friend willing to search out and understand the beautiful truths of the Gospel. Joseph shared the priesthood keys with Brigham who took the Bride into the wilderness in the latter-days. There the Bride has been growing and becoming strong until she is ready to fulfill her role of bringing forth the new king.

The High Priest leader has been directing activities of the Bride as she has gone through the process of sanctification, being clothed upon with light and knowledge, preparing herself in her wedding garments, filling her lamp with oil. With the beginning of this new Great Cycle, the time has come for that high priest to hand over the Bride to a servant who acts as the temporary husband (as Josephs often do) over the Bride who will hand over each new initiate through the birth process of the Bride (veil) to the true Bridegroom, who gathers the initiate into His bosom for protection.

The 70th Jubilee

After wandering in the wilderness for forty years, ancient Israel was ready to cross the River Jordan and enter the Promised Land. Forty weeks is the time for gestation of a child. The number four is a sacred number for bringing forth new life from the walls of the womb. Four is the sacred number for creating sacred space for the rebirth. We believe the five-pointed star found on the Salt Lake, and other temples, indicates man being raised from a fallen to a sanctified state through the safety of a spiritual womb. The four walls of the pyramid are a wonderful example of this. The dead king inside (like inside a beehive) rises step by step until he is birthed forth from the capstone at the top of the pyramid like a new sun or a new Urim and Thummim. The all-seeing

---

[121]http://text.farmsresearch.com/publications/books/?bookid=107&chapid=1210

eye coming forth from the top of the pyramid as shown on the back of our dollar bills carries the same meaning. This powerful Egyptian motif is all about the beginning of new cycles. Through the death and rebirth of a king, his kingdom is ordered and organized around him, bringing salvation to his people as God's representative. Why else would millions of Egyptians have spent so much of their time working on those extensive pyramid projects?

Nibley noted that Professor Piazzi Smyth claimed "that the great pyramid was 365.25 sacred cubits on each side; the whole four sides having a hundred 'pyramid inches' for every day in the year."[122] Nibley referred to space and time interchangeably and so will we because this is what clarifies 2012. Before the earth can take her first step up to a terrestrial state, which is a temple state, a sacred space must be prepared. For pyramids and temples it is a plot of ground. Sacred time also creates that purified door to a terrestrial state. We are living in an era of very sacred time. Recent research by LDS Astronomer, John Pratt suggests that the evening before Monday, April 6, 2009, was the 3,430th anniversary of the miraculous crossing of the Jordan River at spring flood by the children of Israel. That day was also the anniversary of Isaac's birthday on four sacred calendars.[123]

The Jubilee year was celebrated by ancient Israel as the anniversary of the crossing out of the wilderness through the birth of the waters of Jordan, into the Promised Land. Every 7 times 7 (49 years) brought Israel to the fiftieth year when they were to celebrate this Jubilee. Slaves were to go free and ownership of land could be affected with lands of original inheritance going back to the original owners. A blast from the ram's horn, the shofur, announced this important Sabbath year. In fact, 'Jubilee' means ram.[124]

Many years later, during the captivity of Israel in Babylon, the Lord indicated that their seventy years of exile were to make up for neglected and uncelebrated Sabbath years. Dr. Pratt believes that 2009 marked the 70th Jubilee for Israel.[125] When blended with the Mayan teachings, and other 2012 indicators, and of course through the lens of prophecy, it seems that 2009 was a very good time to separate ourselves from spiritual Babylon. Seventy is a number of completion.

---

[122] Nibley, *Message*, 249

[123] http://www.johnpratt.com/items/docs/lds/meridian/2005/tsunami.html

[124] http://en.wikipedia.org/wiki/Jubilee_(Biblical)

[125] http://www.johnpratt.com/items/docs/lds/meridian/2005/tsunami.html

After a group of Israelites were allowed to leave Babylon, what did they do? We learn from the Old Testament book of Nehemiah, that they rebuilt the four walls of protection around Jerusalem. Their enemies tried desperately to stop them but with God's help, they completed the job. Nehemiah found old writings of the Law of Moses and had parts read to the people. They were surprised to learn of the law of holding the Jubilee to celebrate the Jordan crossing into Israel.

The idea of the Jubilee crossing dramatically underscores the ideas we are sharing. As we continue forward, bear in mind the story of the Israelites crossing the Jordan and recall that the first thing they did was build an altar (with 4 sides obviously), then also remember the Jews leaving Babylon and first building the 4 protective walls before rebuilding the temple and tie this motif into 2012. Instead of 4 walls of protection, we had 4 years of protection before winter solstice 2012 when a sacred space was created to bring forth the new sun (ark, temple, king).

2008: Baptism of Water

Certain astronomical alignments indicated to us that 2008 symbolized a water year and also death. Baptism is a death and rebirth from water. Israel crossing out of the gates of worldly Egypt (Babylon) through the Red Sea is a perfect type for baptism. As Nephi taught, after entering by the gate of baptism to the strait and narrow path, there is more. We have to press forward and endure.[126] So after emerging from the Red Sea of baptism, Israel entered into their wilderness experience yet all but seventy failed to ascend the mountain to a higher spiritual level. Latter-day Israel is not failing to prepare herself to come before the Lord. Instead of waiting forty years to cross into the Promised Land, a people have already been prepared. With the 70th Jubilee of 2009, endowed and faithful saints prepare the four walls of sacred space. Converted into time instead of space, that would be four years, that brought forth the fifth year into the higher state at winter solstice 2012.

The four years from 2009 through 2012 equate with the four cardinal directions. Jacob, chapter 5, illustrates the servant of the Lord of the vineyard gathering all the good fruit into the barn, the sacred space protected by four walls/years, in preparation for the end. We like to think of the barn as an ark, (Facsimile 2, figure 4 sunship) carrying the sanctified Church to a new spiritual birth.

---

[126] 2 Ne. 31:20

Some ancient cultures taught that there were four sacred days that brought forth the New Year. They believed that a type and shadow for this was the fact that every year at winter solstice, the sun appears to stand still for four days, and then begins moving up on the fifth. [127]

After baptism in the temple, the next step takes place within four booths representing, among other things, the four corners of the earth, the four sacred walls to create sacred space for the sacred birth at the end of 2012. Let us look at each of the four years that correspond to four walls of the temple or pyramid. These years/walls symbolically bring forth the sun like the golden ball beneath Moroni's feet as he sounds the trump announcing the birth of the new, exalted king.

Comprehending the concept of the 4 sacred years of space/time may be difficult for some, so in order to facilitate understanding, we will introduce a nutshell of the four years that follow the 2008 baptismal year, then we will discuss each year in more detail. This process should be seen as an interaction between a Zion people progressing to act as the Bride, and the King symbolized by the sun. The old sun will die and be reborn as a new King. The year 2009 corresponds to the baptism of fire when the initiate (specifically the earth in her spiritual progression) is purified with fire. Then the year 2010 represents a gathering into the Body of Christ, the unity of the fold. With 2011, the initiate is lifted to a higher priesthood state and then 2012 is when the Bride is organized on that higher level to bring forth the new king at the end of that year, Dec. 21, 2012. After the new King is raised to a higher level, He will begin to work to bring His bride up to His level. This process is symbolized by the new sun crossing the galactic plane to a higher level, bringing with it this earth, as a type for the Bride. Thus the earth begins her journey back to a terrestrial place. Now we will break down and clarify the process.

The initiate is cleansed by water in 2008, just as baptism takes place at eight years of age and as Joshua (Yeshua) led Israel through the waters of Jordan. The 70th Jubilee year then begins, celebrating the initiate's entrance into the Promised Land. In 2009, he/she is placed in the foundational sacred space. We have to be individually cleansed by the baptism of fire, purified so that in 2010 the initiate could be gathered in and grafted into the olive tree of Israel as depicted in Jacob, chapter five. Moses brought the keys of the gathering of Israel to Joseph Smith. How is Israel gathered in the latter-days? It happens through the temple ordinances. This temple unity organizes the sancti-

---

[127] C. Scott Middleton, General Ed., *Mythology*, 89

fied members into a city set on the hill of Mount Zion. Working as saviors on Mount Zion, they work with those on the other side of the veil to unify the dispensations.

A further strengthening of Zion comes in 2011, as we focus on supporting Church leaders. This masculine year seems to symbolize the high priest position of watching over the Bride. Messiah ben Joseph stands as the pillar on this side of 2012 to steady the ark as one authorized and works with Messiah ben David of 2013 so a successful turning of the new cycle takes place. This is the year where heroes emerge, moving further from Babylon and lifting others around them. Finally, 2012 is the year of the Bride, a true oneness of heart solidifies sanctified members all over the world into a prayer circle of power that brings forth the throne at the end of the year and on into 2013.

The Bride, or bridge (Brigham) is the birth canal, the rainbow bridge or path that brings forth the next Great New Year cycle. Now a little more about each year:

2009: Baptism of Fire

This was a year of purification, trial by fire, and a day of decision. We watched in sadness during that year as many issues embittered some of the members of the Church and caused division. Others seemed to grow more loyal to the Church. It appears we are now in the day where we cannot live on borrowed light.

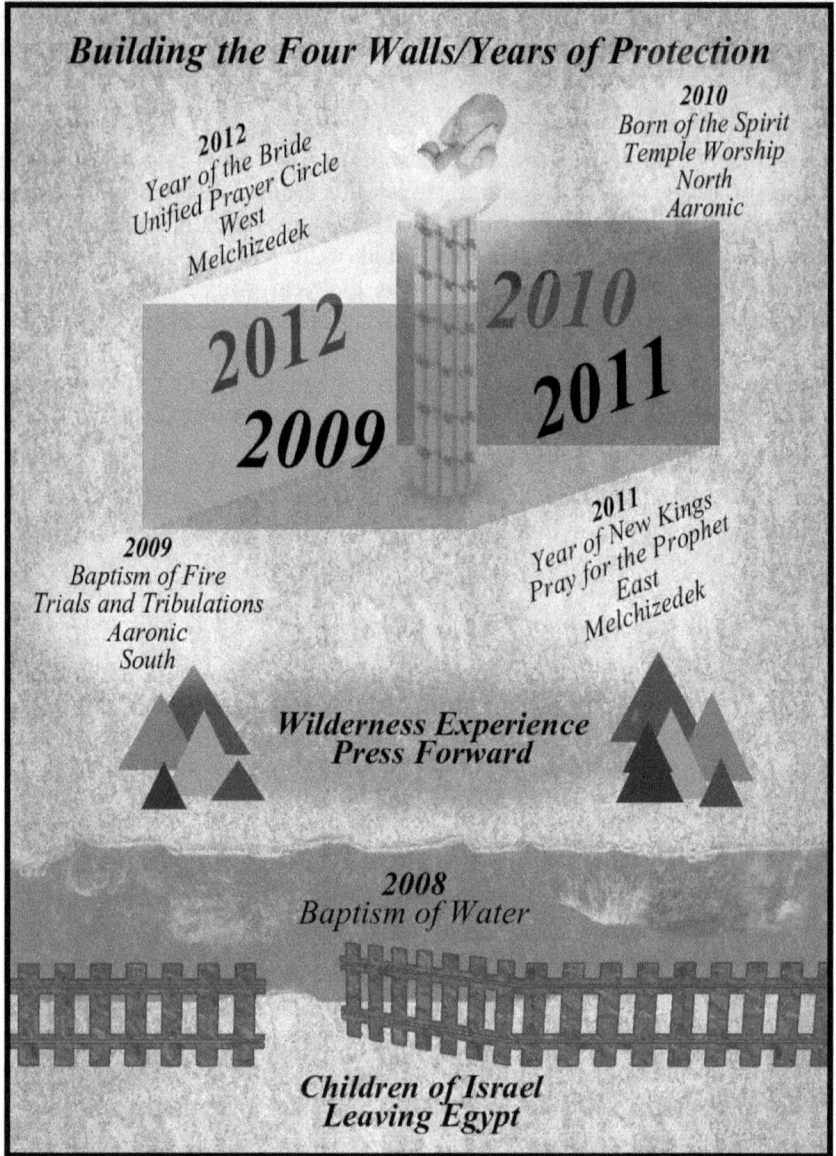

Building the Four Walls/Years of Protection

2012
Year of the Bride
Unified Prayer Circle
West
Melchizedek

2010
Born of the Spirit
Temple Worship
North
Aaronic

2012
2010
2009
2011

2009
Baptism of Fire
Trials and Tribulations
Aaronic
South

2011
Year of New Kings
Pray for the Prophet
East
Melchizedek

Wilderness Experience
Press Forward

2008
Baptism of Water

Children of Israel
Leaving Egypt

2010: Born of the Spirit

In *The Book of Mormon*, baptism is often delineated into 3 aspects: water, fire and spirit. In 3 Nephi, chapter 11, the Lord teaches about baptism. In verse 35, He says that after baptism, they will be visited with fire and with the Holy Ghost. Being born again of the Holy Ghost rarely happens in an instant but is a process. We sanctify ourselves by the power of the Holy Ghost until we come to a point where we are deemed worthy of justification.[128] This makes it less surprising when we learn that the *Sefer Yetzirah* refers to three baptisms: water, fire and the spirit. The year 2010 seems to be a type for the third aspect of baptism, that of the Spirit. We feel this could signify being gathered into the temple. Recall that the *Sefer Yetzirah* teaches that the earthly state is cleansed by water from below, fire from heaven and then comes the cleansing of the breath of life, the wind/spirit in the middle of the other two that seems to be the temple state where the initiate is preparing for a triumphant rising like the sun.

The oil of the olive tree, like Lehi's white fruit, can be seen as an endowment of light, a definite step up the ladder. The winter solstice of 2012 would then be a type for being born from the womb of the temple, with Moroni standing as a witness and blowing his trumpet to signify a crossing into the Promised Land.

Isaiah's words now make more sense to us as they did to Abinadi: "How beautiful upon the mountains (temples) are the feet of him that bringeth good tidings."[129] The next verse talks of the watchmen singing with one voice. We feel those watchmen are symbolized by 2011 and the singing with one voice is like a prayer circle of 2012 to "bring again Zion". Verse 10 explains the Lord making bare His arm. Zion will be brought with power, like a bolt of lightning or a pillar of fire. Verse 11 warns us that this will be the time when we must leave worldliness behind and touch no unclean thing. Each person brought forth from that sacred womb is considered a new king or queen, beneath the holy title of Christ, the King of kings. This birth of new kings happens at the winter solstice of 2010 and is another step in preparing sacred space to bring forth the Davidic kingly role in a higher level in 2012.

Let us take a moment to look at spiritual rebirth in light of that basic ordinance of baptism. There is one baptism, as there is one God but the Godhead has three parts, as does baptism. The ordinance is performed in the name of the Father and the Son and the Holy Ghost. In the economy of the Lord, any number of things can be taken care of at once. It is much more efficient. For example we do not need to spiral up through four levels with four different veils in the temple endowment when the job is done thoroughly with a shorthand version. Mem-

---

[128] See Rom. 2:13
[129] Isa. 52:7

bers should never be disturbed by improved efficiency in completing temple ordinances.

2011: The Year of New Kings

The number '1' was taught by the Egyptians to denote the staff of authority. The scepter of righteousness of the King is contained within the staff that holds all potential life. The number 11, with two staffs side by side, shows that the initiate made king, is still subject to the head King and his staff is brought forth and sustained by the authority of the King of Heaven. As Moses opened the path through the Red Sea through the authority of his staff, so did the Father open a path through the primordial waters of chaos for His children to organize a new creation. He who holds the staff of authority, as authorized by Jesus Christ, to head this final dispensation is Joseph Smith. He is over the winding up scene, the autumn of the Great Year, often depicted as the west, the going down of the sun on this day. The autumn equinox of 2011 brought astronomical events and symbols establishing Messiah ben Joseph in his important role as great high priest to watch over the Bride as she gave birth in 2012. It was the year of the Great High Priest being made a king in his own right.

During 2011, those who had stepped up the spiritual ladder should have begun to seriously feel a peace that from then on can only come from God and cannot be found in the world. Those who choose not to unify with the Saints, the prophet and especially Heavenly Father, will be left without peace in a quickly darkening world. The initiate leaving the darkness of earth was symbolized in the rare lunar eclipse on winter solstice 2010. Just before dawn, the moon was birthed forth from the dark shadow of the earth.

Israel, the latter-day grafted in tree of life from Jacob chapter five, brought forth fruit in the form of leaders in 2011, a masculine year. This was a time to begin unifying further by strengthening our tie to our leaders, starting with Heavenly Father and His Son. Our living prophet is the physical center place we need to orient around as God's representative on earth and the man who holds the keys. How do we do that? In Conference of 2009, both President Monson, and President Packer asked us to pray for the prophet. We felt this was a very important request. At this crucial time in history, the prophet, as the priesthood center of the physical kingdom, needs protection and strength. We can help strengthen the canopy of light over him. This action of protection was needed for 2012 and will be needed continually as the winding up scenes play out. But this is not all. The more we pray for him, the stronger that priesthood power will return to us as our own canopy of protection. The more saints who actively sustain and pray for the prophet, the stronger the Bride and more effective she (the Church) is in fulfilling her role and feeling peace from its only source. Then we take this right on down the line to each of our leaders, sustaining, loving and praying for them…and not expecting perfection; no backbiting.

Winter solstice of 2012 is only the center of the door that leads into a crucial future where we are needed as events unfold. The information in this book will not become obsolete after that date. What is inside the room behind that door is a subject that should concern all of us.

2012: The Year of the Bride

As we have seen, 2012 was the year the higher form of the Bride, the unified dispensations as symbolized by the Pleiades, joining heaven and earth to bring forth the new cycle as shown by Venus acting in the role of morning star, the throne of David. The Second David, is the Second Adam[130] on a higher level. Paul wrote that "first man" (Adam) is of the earth and the second man is of heaven.[131] So these four years or a forty year period, etc. were types for the four steps or covenants a person goes through to complete bringing Adam back into the presence of God and/or transfiguring him into a king beginning his own creation.

With the strong bonds formed by those who were willing to unify with and strengthen their leaders in 2011, the Bride was then ready in 2012 to create spiritual energy and bring forth the branch of David that would pierce the veil, connecting heaven and earth. The sacred midnight sun was the dawn only for those ready to move high up the spiritual mount of Zion. All others were left in a darkness that has grown more profound. Now we do not claim that these specific years are when each of these principles must be lived exclusively. They are simply a type and shadow of the pattern as shown in time and an illustration of the earth beginning her journey back from a fallen state, a process the early Mayas were well aware of.

---

[130] See Rom. 5
[131] 1 Cor.15:47–48

The Four Walls of Time

Creating and maintaining sacred space for the protection of the throne, the political kingdom of the Seventh Seal, will be no easy task and will be overseen by the armies of the Lord of Sabaoth. The Bible Dictionary says there are two parts to that protection; heavenly and earthly. Ten is a number long connected with armies. When modern Israel came across the plains, they were organized into units of ten. We learn from the Bible Dictionary that "The Lord of Sabaoth" was a title of Jehovah; the hosts were the armies of Israel[132] but also included the angelic armies of heaven."[133] When the armies of earth and of heaven are combined, a very real protection is in place. Some will still die, but this should be seen as a transfer from one regiment to another, with full honors and pay.

Doctrine and Covenants section 95 describes the Saints' failure to speedily build a temple as walking in darkness at noon. The temple blessings are what bring us into the light, brighter and brighter as we progress. The Lord explained one of the reasons the early Latter-day Saints needed a temple: "And for this cause I gave unto you a commandment that you should call your solemn assembly, that your fastings and your mourning might come up into the ears of the Lord of Sabaoth, which is by interpretation, the creator of the first day, the beginning and the end."[134]

As we study the subject of Lord of Sabaoth and follow all the scriptural footnotes, we can see that the kings being brought forth, past and present, as symbolized by 2010 bringing forth 2011, are those who assisted the Savior in the creation of a new first day. This is done by the overlapping of the beginning and the end, alpha and omega. This council of heaven is being called forth and organized to fulfill the same general role, bringing forth another creation cycle. Some will fail to heed the call, as Jesus taught us in the book of Matthew.[135] Others, the meek and lowly came forth to take up those vacant positions for a perfect prayer circle, focusing upon the Lord to bring forth the New Great Year. They were birthed forth by the third aspect of baptism, the Spirit, the white fruit of the tree, being clothed upon with the wedding garment. Some people will always attempt to crash a wedding party but

---

[132] 1 Sam. 17:45
[133] Bible Dictionary, p. 764
[134] D&C 95:7
[135] Matt. 22:8

they will not have on the right garments and will be taken away.[136] All of this is a part of ancient New Year's rites and 2012 winter solstice was a major New Year, involving the renewal of a multitude of cycles. The majority of the ancient cultures attended those yearly ceremonies to help reestablish the king as year by year, he spiraled up the ladder of spiritual ascension.

Returning to our place in the council of heaven, but on a higher level, should be our goal. Nibley wrote that: "the goal [of the ancient civilizations was always] to restore the primal community of Gods and men or as we would say, to achieve atonement."[137] The New Year Rites of most of the major ancient societies was all about enthroning and em-powering the king so he could bring about a state of organization and oneness in the community he ruled but before the foundation of a community can be stretched out, a center place has to be established through the power of the priesthood and as we have explained, this is the sunthrone. Again, Nibley explains:

At hundreds of holy shrines, each believed to mark the exact center of the Universe and represented as the point at which the four corners of the earth converged [the middle omphalos] - the navel of the earth [the umbilicus] one might have seen assembled at the New Year - the moment of creation, the beginning and ending of time - vast con-courses of people, each thought to represent the entire human race in the presence of all its ancestors and gods.[138]

The years 2009 and 2010 can perhaps be seen as a type and shadow for the offices of the Aaronic Priesthood, and 2011 and 2012 can represent the Melchizedek Priesthood, four steps in all. We should look at each of the four walls or years, as an adding upon and not a leaving behind. All of the offices of the Priesthood and every member of the Church who is trying to follow the Savior, has a role to play in the last days and is needed. We are all in the process of spiraling up-ward, step by step, year by year.

The year 2010 was very important and we want to take a closer look at her symbolism. Five days after the summer solstice of 2010, when the sun appeared to begin its descent, there was a full moon lunar eclipse. This is an eclipse in which the moon is covered by the earth's

---

[136] See Matt. 22:11–13
[137] Nibley, *Temple and Cosmos*, 400
[138] Ibid 156

shadow. What made this extremely unusual was a rare planetary alignment called a Grand Cross.[139]

2010 is a feminine year. The **Zohar**[140] teaches that odd numbers are masculine and even numbers are feminine. Many cultures, including the Romans, saw the summer solstice as a celebration of the Bride. Remembering that the moon is the scriptural symbol for the terrestrial kingdom, it is interesting to note that five days after the summer solstice of 2010 the moon may have been representing modern Israel as she moves from an earthly sphere to a higher lunar sphere, symbolizing the birth of the Spirit. Temples are considered terrestrial states and are the epitome of creating sacred space here on earth. The Grand Cross opens a door of transition for this rebirth.

Six months later, there was an even rarer complete lunar eclipse on the winter solstice. It has been almost 26,000 years since such an alignment has occurred. The earth, moon, sun and galactic center were all lined up in a role similar to what happened later during winter solstice 2012. Only the 2010 event is the Bride bringing forth the initiate into a Zion unity in 2011. Astronomically, this can be seen as the high priest over Israel bringing forth her children as kings in 2011. There need be no confusion about kings and David's throne, nor which year is the significant one. As we will see more clearly as we continue, is that the new creation is proceeded by a council of kings and priests who assist in the work of bringing forth the Davidic throne and the new cycle. The year 2011 simply is a symbol of the raising of initiates to kingship. "And hath made us kings and priests unto God and his Father; to him be glory and dominion for ever and ever."[141] Under our dispensation leader, Joseph, the unity of latter-day priests and kings is something that has seldom been seen on such a scale and at such a time.

Earlier examples of this kind of Zion unity were found with the City of Enoch, also Melchizedek's city of Salem and in the Americas after Christ's visit. Yet, never in the history of the world has there been a spiritual gathering of a nation of kings and priests that cover the earth and was necessary to help lift her from her fallen state.

---

[139] A Grand Cross is said to occur when four planets are all separated from each other by Square aspects (90 degrees apart). See http://en.wikipedia.org/wiki/Grand_cross_(astrology)
[140] This is an ancient Rabbinical work.
[141] Rev. 1:6

Each of the four years beginning with 2009, represent-
ed a wall of the temple, pyramid or fortress and corresponded to one of
the four cardinal directions. This sacred space, oriented to the Cosmos,
made the paths straight for the emergence of the new David from the
starry Milky Way mother.

(The goddess Nut, or the Milky Way, protecting the king in preparation for his new birth.)[142]

2012 is the midnight, sable coat of the female panther, holding within
her the seeds, or stars of the kings from all the ages who have united to
act as the Bride of the Pleiades, lifted high in the night sky to birth forth
the new sun king, as depicted on Apocalypse Island. Representing the
Bride is the great high priest who bridges the dangerous gulf by the
priesthood organization and temple work. Deseret had the job of bringing the hidden king out of the protective beehive of night into the new
day of 2013. Yet, since the new king will need time to grow and
strengthen, Deseret will continue her job of protection on a higher level. Remember, Christ went back to the protection of his parents even
after He was twelve. He went about His Father's business but not yet in
a public manner.

All Have a Place

If the moon represents the terrestrial state and the sun represents the celestial state, then why do we keep saying 2012 was about
bringing fallen earth into a celestial state? The answer is that the terrestrial level comes under the influence of celestial law, not the full law
but the basic law of opposites as represented by the male/female positive tension instead of the law of opposites in the telestial world between good and evil. We are taught that the moon reflects the light of

---

[142] © Richard Deurer – http://www.egyptartsite.com/myth/nut.jpg

the sun and likewise, the terrestrial state reflects the laws of the celestial light.

Those who have faithfully kept their temple covenants are standing in a holy terrestrial state and are members of the armies of Sabaoth. As such, they can enjoy the refreshing influence of the Celestial Room. A purified people, the armies of the Lord of Sabaoth on both sides of the veil, open the door and bring forth the sun. The moon will no longer be needed after the actual Second Coming, because Jesus Christ will be the light of the world.

For those who do not feel this book applies because they may not feel they are in a sanctified state, it is important to note that all who desire to follow God are needed, be they members or not. Members of all spiritual levels are needed as long as they have a desire to follow Christ. A top rung of a ladder is no good without a supporting cast. Heavenly Father needs us, the prophet needs us. All it takes is a repentant heart and a desire to truly leave Babylon and come to Zion, from the humblest deacon or primary child, every voice, every heart can be bound together in love and worship to help bring about unity.

Oh Ye Gates

Psalms 24 begins to make more sense in light of the things we have been learning. Keep in mind doors, gates, and veils and our part as the Bride to encircle, bring focused energy and veil the sacred birth. In preparation for this momentous time of Alpha and Omega, the Church has built many temples, the hills of the Lord, so members can first be lifted up to stand in a holy place with clean hands and a pure heart. Then they can assist in lifting others up, acting as doors (gates) to a higher state, becoming saviors on Mount Zion.

Unlike Israel in Moses' day, modern Israel is the generation that will not reject the Lord's call to ascend the mountain and seek His face. Israel will qualify as doorkeepers. These doors may seem as flimsy as veils but they are as impassable as locked gates, keeping out those not prepared but parting for those who are. Then together, on the top of this hill, similar to the events on the Mount of Transfiguration but with the reformed and redeemed Creation Council in attendance, the King is lifted (birthed) to an even loftier rung on the ladder, that of David's throne. The Lord of hosts with His armies of Sabaoth, have begun a new creation cycle and as always, they will be challenged so they are prepared in battle formation. Now let us carefully read the following verses from Psalms 24:

3 Who shall ascend into the hill of the Lord? or who shall stand in his holy place?

4 He that hath clean hands, and a pure heart; who hath not lifted up his soul unto vanity nor sworn deceitfully.

5 He shall receive the blessing from the Lord, and righteousness from the God of his salvation.

6 This is the generation of them that seek him, that seek thy face, O Jacob. Selah.

Lift up your heads, O ye gates; and be ye lift up, ye everlasting doors; and the King of glory shall come in.

8 Who is this King of glory? The Lord strong and mighty, the Lord mighty in battle.

9 Lift up your heads, O ye gates; even lift them up, ye everlasting doors; and the King of glory shall come in.

10 Who is this King of glory? The Lord of hosts, he is the King of glory. Selah.

King David's words above, prophesying the coming forth of the Second David, describe the latter days when the Lord comes in power to save Israel, as the first David saved Israel from the Philistines. This coming with power will not be seen by the world in general until a later time. For now, the sacred throne, or political kingdom, will be kept veiled by the Bride as David grows and spreads His kingdom. During the dark and dangerous crossing of the gulf, Joseph and David reaching through from either side, stabilized the ship of Zion on its journey. Only authorized individuals can reach out to steady the ark as it is birthed first through the Jordan. The light of the Urim and Thummim held within, is the only place light is found. Isaiah in chapter 60 wrote of the symbolism of the dawning light of a new day or cycle:

1 Arise, shine; for thy light is come, and the glory of the Lord is risen upon thee.

2 For, behold, the darkness shall cover the earth, and gross darkness the people: but the Lord shall arise upon thee, and his glory shall be seen upon thee.

3 And the Gentiles shall come to thy light, and kings to the brightness of thy rising.

The Fortress of God

Endowed in the wedding garment of light, the Bride was prepared for the sacred wedding at midnight. Again, the city (Bride) is not a specific place but a spiritual state of being, the preparation for a future actual city: "And I John saw the holy city, new Jerusalem, coming down from God out of heaven, prepared as a bride adorned for her husband."[143] If this marriage is to be eternal, no corruption can enter in to introduce telestial entropy (the breakdown of matter). The ceremony had to take place in a sacred space, a fortress, and it must be hid from the eyes of the world. The four years preceding winter solstice 2012 created this purified time. Death of the old, birth of the new and the sacred marriage at midnight all follow one another immediately because we are not talking about literal events, but covenant symbols.

It takes both male and female to create the protection necessary for the birth and marriage. As noted earlier, the Egyptian Bride goddess Isis wears a throne as her crown. She works with her spouse Osiris who was murdered by his brother. Together they work until Osiris is brought forth into his higher state of Re, the sungod. They represent the female and male aspect. In sacred geometry, a triangle is the representation of a soul. Blending the male and female triangles together, creates the six-pointed star, or shield of David.[144] They are father and mother, joined together to bring forth man into a different state from the center or seventh spot during this, the seventh dispensation. Nibley wrote that the Zodiac can also be divided into male and female. The joining of male and female, may perhaps be illustrated by the masculine Urim as the head, and the feminine Thummim as the heart. Joined together they create a great star, light, protection, door, and new spiritual birth.[145] "Nevertheless neither is the man without the woman, neither the woman without the man in the Lord."[146]

A few years ago I had to present a memorized speech in Hebrew for a class at BYU. The assignment made me nervous because I was older than the other students and felt a little out of place. To make the challenge more interesting, I decided to use a portion of the *Sefer Yetzirah*. According to Nibley, Abraham received this creation document from his personal seer stone (Urim and Thummim?).[147] I was very

---

[143] Rev. 21:2
[144] Nibley, *One Eternal Round*, 625
[145] Ibid, 453
[146] 1 Corinthians 11:11
[147] Nibley, *One Eternal Round*, p. 510

surprised to find that none of the many translations I looked at matched my own translation that I was required to do for my speech. I questioned my translation but found that it fit perfectly with Nibley's assertions about the book and also aligned well with our research of the pattern of creation. As discussed before regarding the *Sefer Yetzirah*, the three mothers (baptisms) bring forth the initiate, cleansed, shaped and purified, and finally made fit to become a stone in the fortress of God.

Peter wrote that we can be spiritually reborn as a newborn, and made a living stone in the spiritual house, a holy priesthood.[148] This temple fortress brings forth sacrifices acceptable before God. This fortress is the heart of the city set on a hill to give light to the world. Enoch sanctified his people and prepared them to be a holy city. The idea of Zion, a sacred city has persisted throughout time. The Book of Chronicles declares: ". . .Zion, which is the city of David."[149]

Both Bethlehem and Jerusalem are referred to as the City of David but the spiritual city of David is Zion, a people presently scattered physically but not spiritually. Noah was thought to be born the year the city of Enoch was lifted to a terrestrial state. This was both the ending of a cycle that began with Adam and ended with the city being taken up and the beginning of a new cycle with Noah acting as a new Adam. In fact, the long-count Mayan calendar began on 3114 B.C. and this could easily have been the year these events transpired. Indeed, Gabriel (Noah) has played an important role in moving forward the Plan of Salvation.

When the throne of David symbolically comes forth as a new sun to begin a new cycle, is it too late for members to become a part of this? No, even after Zion was taken up in Enoch's day, whenever an individual completed the requisite covenants, they also could be taken up to the terrestrial city. How does an individual do this? Just as we outlined the process above in the years 2009 through 2012, it begins with baptism. For those already baptized but who have not continued to fully live those covenants, there is the weekly sacrament to begin again. Then there is the baptism of fire where we become born again, as Alma described in Alma, chapter five. We have a new heart, a new countenance and lose the desire to do evil. After this, we enter into the temple covenants wholeheartedly, become sanctified and become grafted into the olive tree of Israel. Once these covenants are kept so well that Heavenly Father judges we are ready, we can become justified, receiving the promise of eternal kingdoms. One of the requisites for this step

---

[148] 1 Peter 2:5
[149] 1 Chr. 11:5

is being faithful to Christ and always staying true to Him as the king of kings and likewise, fully sustaining His authorized church leaders. This binds us very tightly together like electrons around atoms. Finally, we are ready to put all the pieces together into becoming a true Zion people.

To review, each unit (family, ward, stake, dispensation), from smallest to largest, brought together in perfect order and united with all the dispensations into one cluster, is symbolized by the Pleiades Star Cluster. This is the priesthood (mother goddess aspect) order that brings forth the initiate in the sunship to a terrestrial state, to become a part of the spiritual City of David, the Heavenly Jerusalem.

Thus, we have only to live the Gospel as our prophets have laid it out for us...but oh how exciting it all is when we can see the bigger picture and understand the unprecedented place in history where we now stand. In the latter-days, we will not have a flood wipe out most of mankind. Instead, we will have a rainbow bridge, all the seven dispensations working together to assist Messiah ben Joseph and Messiah ben David, to lift the whole earth into a terrestrial state so we will not be burned by fire at the coming of the Lord.

Spiritual Zion will be under constant threat but we need not fear. The Lord told us in the book of Doctrine & Covenants: "For Michael shall fight their battles, and shall overcome him who seeketh the throne of him who sitteth upon the throne, even the Lamb."[150]

What we want to do so badly is to say that all will be well as we move further into last day prophecies but this simply is not the case. That is what so many people want to hear. What we will do instead, is lay the foundation of cycles in this book.

To downplay the intensity of what is coming would be unfair because it would make it unimportant to learn the principles of protection that are found within the pattern of the Gospel. It is only through living those principles that we can go forward without fear. The perspective brought through understanding what is happening around us will help us wade through tribulation with hope. The black panther on Apocalypse Island will do her job in protecting the sungod. Whether we will be one of those stars on her velvety black coat is up to us.

As we cross with Yeshua into the Promised Land of the Seventh Seal, as Israel crossed the Jordan with Joshua into the Promised

---

[150] D&C 88:115

Land, there is still a determined enemy in possession of the land. We will need, as did ancient Israel, a pillar of fire by night and a cloud of protection by day. It is the union of the Bridegroom with His Bride that creates this sword of fire and veil/canopy. It is time to build and gather into this fort of protection, as the Nephites, at times, had to build and gather into their cities for protection. The good news is, even knowing the enemy would come again, even after devastating losses, the Nephites described that time as one of the happiest periods in the history of the Nephites.[151] How could this be? It is simple. Nothing on earth can touch the sweet peace that comes from uniting with fellow saints in a valiant cause, and more importantly, becoming one with our Heavenly Father and His Blessed Son.

We can all feel the increased tension in the world. The opposite of that is what we desire, which is peace. We truly feel that only unity with God and with other believers will bring that gift and bring the comfort necessary to successfully deal with what is coming. This will enable us to assist in spreading the kingdom of God, to help in redeeming the earth, and in unifying struggling loved ones. This kingdom will grow until it bursts forth in view of the whole earth with the Second Coming of Jesus Christ, and those who are His at His coming.

In the midst of the dark storm that is brewing in the world, the way to find light and comfort is to gather around the hearthstone with those we love, and learn to love better those we should love. If we sit shoulder to shoulder and keep our eye on that life-giving fire, then we can actually experience a cozy comfort even while hearing the piercing winds outside. If we all help build up that fire together, then seekers who desire to come out of the darkness and cold, will see the light and gather with us.

---

[151] Alma 50: 23

Chapter Four: The Three Pillars of the Gospel

One of the Churches I attended as a child had a very large cross behind the pulpit. I can remember sitting there aching for the day when I would turn 18 and be allowed to attend the LDS Church. What relief I felt when the day came that I no longer had to sit looking at a giant cross. This attitude made it hard for me to have an open mind later in life as I began to stumble across a pattern found within the symbol of the cross. With time, I have come to appreciate the perfection and importance of this sacred geometrical shape. No longer do I judge other Christians for holding the cross in such esteem, although I still strongly support the LDS position of not worshipping the instrument that was used to kill our Lord. Though many people have told me they do not worship that symbol, their actions indicate otherwise. It is so easy to begin idolizing the process instead of God. If we look at the cross as the basic form for the structure of the universe, then we can appreciate the pattern and not be concerned with inappropriate worship of that symbol.

The latest fad dismisses patternism as antiquated thought. Dr. Nibley studied this subject at Cambridge, but it has now passed out of vogue. When we hear things like this, we think of the patterns held within the Three Pillars of the Gospel. The temple endowment is found in various forms and pieces throughout the ancient world and proves a very definite pattern. Without discovering and understanding the temple pattern, Egyptology is indecipherable but with it, their teachings are beautiful and inspiring. We have a plethora of quotes by General Authorities about this subject in the Gospel, insisting that "the Lord gives patterns in all things.[152] Neal A. Maxwell especially used that word numerous times.[153]

The word pattern is sprinkled throughout scripture and is so obviously a part of the Gospel plan that we just cannot fathom scholars having a problem with this concept. Here is one of the many scriptures invoking this idea: "And again, I will give unto you a pattern in all things, that ye may not be deceived; for Satan is abroad in the land, and he goeth forth deceiving the nations—"(D&C 52:4) *The Book of Mormon* especially is full of patterns and some of them are often discussed in the Church, like the "pride cycle". That book was written for

---

[152] Elder William R. Walker, "Presidencies Part of Gospel's Pattern" Published Saturday, April 12, 2008
[153] Neal A. Maxwell, "Brightness of Hope", Ensign, Nov. 1994

our day because Mormon, who was shown our day, saw that we would fall into many of the same patterns that his people fell into and also teaches the positive patterns found within the Plan of Salvation. One of the beauties of this idea is that once we have fit enough of the puzzle pieces into place, we can more easily decipher truth by how it fits into the pattern.

We feel there would be little that would better please the adversary than to throw out the works of Hugh Nibley. It would be ironic if Latter-day Saints reject the teachings of a man who has tried to show the truth of LDS doctrines through ancient manuscripts while the world rejects him because he did it so effectively. Our enemy does not want us to understand the temple because knowledge is power. Nibley was well respected by Church leaders. As we are relating how we feel these writings of Nibley can be applied in the latter-days, it becomes apparent that faith is certainly the key. The intense mental focus that he wrote of so often will be the salvation of the Church through the unfolding events we are passing through. Was he a prophet that we should follow his teachings? No but a prophet of God suggested to us that we study his works and since he was often brought in to share his knowledge with the prophets of the Church, perhaps we should listen.

It is our personal belief that Hugh Nibley, a very meek and self-effacing man, is one of many examples of fulfillment of a verse in D&C 128. The theme is the welding link between heaven and earth, followed by these words: "And not only this, but those things which never have been revealed from the foundation of the world, but have been kept hid from the wise and prudent, shall be revealed unto babes and sucklings in this, the dispensation of the fullness of times." (D&C 128:18) Why would I refer to Nibley as a babe if this verse can be applied to him? Let's look another scripture that mentions 'babe': "At that time Jesus answered and said, I thank thee, O Father, Lord of heaven and earth, because thou hast hid these things from the wise and prudent, and hast revealed them unto babes" (Matt. 11:25). A footnote to the word 'babes' says this means the innocent. This certainly describes Hugh Nibley. He was a man of great virtue and humility. According to Alma, the word 'babes' does not only signify youth but also can apply to men and women (Alma 32:23). It appears that the term "wise and learned" could imply the proud scholars who set themselves up as a light to the world. This kind of priestcraft is not only discussed many times in *The Book of Mormon* but is found in the stories of the doctors of religion who fought against Joseph Smith and the Pharisees and lawyers who mocked Christ. The meek and humble, even if they have PhD's, are the babes who we should listen to. This includes Nibley.

The incorrect philosophies of men are going to be shown for the counterfeit they are. New Age teachings are seeping into some of the members of the Church. Many of those teachings are beautiful and fit with the Gospel but some are polluting members with deception. Nibley's writings help us avoid these pitfalls and at the same time stretch our narrow minds to see there is still a great deal for us to learn. Perhaps *The Book of Mormon* coming forth is not the only fulfillment to the verse in 1 Nephi chapter 13 that tells of the Latter-day coming forth of truth. The many manuscripts that have been unearthed in modern times have not only confirmed the truth of *The Pearl of Great Price*, but have also helped clarify the powerful basics of the restored Gospel. No one has had a greater hand in translating and explaining these manuscripts than Hugh Nibley. Nephi wrote of the Bible and then continued:

39 And after it had come forth unto them I beheld other books, which came forth by the power of the Lamb, from the Gentiles unto them, unto the convincing of the Gentiles and the remnant of the seed of my brethren, and also the Jews who were scattered upon all the face of the earth, that the records of the prophets and of the twelve apostles of the Lamb are true.

40 And the angel spake unto me, saying: These last records, which thou hast seen among the Gentiles, shall establish the truth of the first, which are of the twelve apostles of the Lamb, and shall make known the plain and precious things which have been taken away from them; and shall make known to all kindreds, tongues, and people, that the Lamb of God is the Son of the Eternal Father, and the Savior of the world; and that all men must come unto him, or they cannot be saved. (1 Ne. 13:39–40)

Brother Nibley most certainly used many newly revealed manuscripts to establish the truth of all of the scriptures. In addition, that knowledge helps restore missing pieces that expound upon the plain and precious principles of the Gospel. Some of the information does not seem simple but that is because this knowledge has been lost and is outside of our experience. Joseph Smith struggled to teach the Saints simple truths that were so outside their traditions that they simply could not open their minds to them. It would be a mistake to believe Joseph Smith revealed everything. He did not and was sorry the Saints could not accept more at that time. And according to what we read above in D&C 128, there are many hidden things to yet be revealed in the Latter-days. We are not saying that Nibley has the right to add new revelation to the Church but when he brought forth ancient writings that tie in with the Gospel, then this seems to fulfill the prophecies of plain and precious truths being restored. We also feel that the above verse in Section 128 can apply to all of us together as we, the Bride of Christ, help through study and prayer, to spread the light and mission of Latter-day Israel.

The Sacred Space of Four

The time has come in the history of this world to deepen our discipleship, as reported in the Ensign in 1992: "And then as Elder Neal A. Maxwell has so eloquently described, also included are those ' 'honorable' members who are skimming over the surface instead of deepening their discipleship and who are casually engaged rather than 'anxiously engaged.' "[154]

All right then, how do we deepen and apply what we have been learning? Again, it goes back to the basics for this is where the power of the Atonement is manifest. We have been baptized but we must come to the altar of sacrifice every Sunday in the attitude of a renewal of those baptismal covenants. We repent of our sins, take upon us the name of Christ and rededicate ourselves to our Heavenly Father's commandments. That bread and water, taken properly, purify us so there is no spiritual corruption, thus we do not burn up when the severe trials fall upon us.

Coming out of the waters of baptism or its renewal, we must create sacred space so that we are standing in holy places. Now that we are living in the day when this earth is moving from the telestial to a terrestrial condition, there is only one way to bridge that step safely and that is by standing in a holy place. Being redeemed from the fall, purified and qualified, we put on the armor of God, stand on a firm foundation above the waters of chaos and progress through the steps of the endowment until we are clothed upon with a canopy of light. It is the joining of these lights that creates the exponential power and protection of Zion. Perhaps it will not be until we, as a Church, are purified enough to be bound equally, heart to heart, that we will qualify to receive the protection of the cloud by day and the pillar of fire by night as Isaiah wrote about the latter-days: "And the Lord will create upon every dwelling place of mount Zion, and upon her assemblies, a cloud and smoke by day, and the shining of a flaming fire by night: for upon all the glory shall be a defense." (Isa. 4:5)

---

[154] Ensign, Nov. 1992, p. 65

There is an actual scientific process behind the spiritual qualification for receiving this pillar of fire and cloud of protection which we will continue to explore. The unity of Zion is the key to that qualification. When two or more are gathered in His name, He promises to be there in our midst.[155] The Lord seems to be the representation of the pillar of fire, with the righteous saints unified around him and being in tune with the Holy Ghost. When that Zion body is overshadowed by the Spirit, the effect is like a cloud. The joining of heaven and earth draws down the dews from heaven upon the heads of the faithful and virtuous members as they focus on the King of righteousness.[156] Without the purity of virtue, that Zion body has corruption and cannot qualify to be in the sacred space necessary for the joining of heaven and earth. So before the unity is enacted, each individual must go through a process of purification and endowment to prepare for the prayer circle where the dews of heaven distill as a cloud.

Life can be such a struggle for each of us. Many times we find ourselves in conditions that make it difficult to feel the Spirit. Often we wonder how we can live the unity of Zion with others who seem to feel no desire for that unity. This is why the first law of the Gospel is to love God with all that we have. This relationship is the most important key. If we give equal importance and dedication to loving those around us, then the binding of our heart is sideways and our eye is not single to His glory. Many have a spouse and/or children who lack strong devotion and it is sometimes the tendency to wait for them to join us before we step forward. If this is our choice, then we are not standing in holy places. Without that spiritual endowment, we not only lack peace, we also are not drawing upon the Spirit in a way that will bless them also, whether they are aware or not.

Then what are the four spiritual walls of our sacred space? What makes a temple sacred? It is the covenants we make within its walls. These walls of safety are represented by many things including the sheepcote. The shepherd lays down his life for his sheep. Indeed he is the very door of the sheepcote, lying across its opening at night to protect his sheep from lion and bear. And now our Good Shepherd, having lain down His life, lifts up His sheep to the spiritual place of safety through the Atonement. As we have referred to before, the Savior gave the purpose of His travail on earth in 3 Nephi 27:14. He was lifted up so that He can lift us up. He is the door of that higher sheep-

---

[155] See Matt. 18:20
[156] See D&C 121:45–46

cote that brings us back into the Spiritual presence of the Father. This reversal of the fall is our subject here. So now let us consider how we are gathered into that higher sheepcote.

Found throughout the ancient world, including among the Jews, the concept of four deities (or angels) who preside over the four cardinal directions is a primal doctrine.[157] The Egyptian Four Sons of Horus represent many things including spreading the dominion of the Pharaoh who is their representative of God upon the earth. All three of the facsimiles in *The Pearl of Great Price* depict these figures so they hold great import not only for the ancient world but also for us. What do they represent and how would that apply to us? We will try to explain this in the following section of this chapter.

If we keep our covenants, the four winds can represent the spiritual energy necessary to help us climb each step of sanctification. There are four covenants we must especially keep; first, we must bring forth a broken heart and contrite spirit as a sacrifice. Second, we must live the principles of the Gospel. Third, we need to be true to our marriage covenants and also to the Bridegroom by not whoring after other gods. Fourth, for now,[158] to pay generous tithes and offerings and to help those in need with a spirit of charity will help us have a Zion heart. Those covenants can either lift us or destroy us. A two edged sword can cut us free from the chains of a fallen earth and it can open the way for the initiate to ascend higher. But if we fail to keep our covenants, or use the principle of repentance, then the sword comes back around to cut us back down. We need to be mindful of the power of words and covenants as the Lord has said: "Behold, I am God; give heed unto my word, which is quick and powerful, sharper than a two-edged sword, to the dividing asunder of both joints and marrow; therefore give heed unto my words." (D&C 6:2)

In Egyptian scenes depicting the four sons of Horus, they are usually standing before a throne or an altar of sacrifice. They are like the four cardinal directions of a circle which help to bring the faith and energy, like a wind. This swirling wind helps to create a vortex that allows a prepared initiate to be brought forth to higher spiritual births at the center place, which is the altar or throne. Even after one has progressed rung by rung up the ladder until reaching exaltation, there are still further rungs as the initiate moves from exaltation to exaltation. Each step is as if it were a new day with the rising sun announcing a

---

[157] Nibley, *Book of Abraham*, 312
[158] Eventually the law of Consecration will be required of us if it is not already.

new year, a new first day. There are many allusions to these four offices in their various aspects in the scriptures:

And after these things I saw four angels standing on the four corners of the earth, holding the four winds of the earth, that the wind should not blow on the earth, nor on the sea, nor on any tree. (Rev. 7:1)

And before the throne there was a sea of glass like unto crystal: and in the midst of the throne, and round about the throne, were four beasts full of eyes before and behind. (Rev. 4:6)

Nibley stated that those four figures tie everything together, the Four Sons of Horus stand upon the lotus before the throne of God[159] "As far as the Egyptians were concerned, the four quarters of the earth were people.[160] Where does the throne ultimately lead? It would appear to be a series of doors (or veils) to the celestial light. One cannot ascend through those doors without passing by those who require words of power. First, we spiritually ascend and then eventually, we will be physically gathered for the resurrection. Nibley wrote: "Adam's remains, composed of the four elements, were believed to be scattered to the four winds. Gathering them together again for the resurrection is symbolized by the four sons of Horus."[161]

The Egyptians also believed the four regions of the universe had four gods in charge of them. Nibley wrote that they planned the creation of the universe.[162] We do not want to go into the details here since there is already so much food for thought already but we would suggest four individuals as a possibility for these four positions. All of them would come to this atonement earth to be tried and tested and give leadership to this key planet. In chronological order, they are Adam, Abraham, Christ (with Peter often standing in for him) and Joseph Smith. We would never suggest that the other three are on par with the Lord. He is far beyond any other man and is in fact, the holder of all the major offices. The Egyptian god, Wepwawet, is the Opener of the Way mentioned earlier. Christ is first in all offices except that of the Father and He will always be subject to Heavenly Father in the order of things.

For a smaller circle since the flood and the re-creation, there would possibly be Noah (Gabriel) and then the three who brought keys to Joseph Smith at the Kirtland Temple; Elias, Moses and Elijah. Per-

---

[159] Nibley, *An Approach to the Book of Abraham*, 296
[160] Ibid
[161] Ibid, 297
[162] Ibid, 302

haps each dispensation also has place holders for those four offices, working its way down to individual families. However the organization, we can know that perfect order exists in our Father's kingdom.

Nibley wrote that the four sons also represented kings and the four main stars of the Big Dipper.[163] Thrones gather us in as beneath the waves of the sea of chaos like a fountain of purified water...or like protective wings of a hen and lift us higher. At times the four sons of Horus were depicted on thrones, each son with an X on them like the X on figure one of Facsimile 2.[164] The initiate must be born of each office before stepping through to a brighter light. Later in this chapter, we will see how this concept of 4 offices leading to the throne agrees with facsimile 3.

Paganism

Perhaps we can begin to see why ancient cultures turned to paganism. They came to worship this amazing ascension process that brings the initiate to a higher spiritual state, assisted by the bride concept; the mother goddess. The Christians were careful to fight against such blatant paganism but did they fall into any traditions that patterned this paganism? Yes, the worship of Mary as a kind of mother goddess figure, saints as intercessors between us and Heavenly Father and also the worship of the cross, whose deeper meaning, the Atonement, is about the process.

The sun aligning with the galactic center is referred to by the Mayas as the Cosmic Cross, so in the following section we will study the cross on Golgotha with its four directions. We live in a day where many are rejecting both paganism and Christianity, so does modern man have anything that equates to the worship of the mother goddess or the cross? Indeed we do. It is called Secular Humanism and even some in the Church are falling victim to this push to arrogantly believe we can save ourselves. With the spread of this religion, the sophisticated modern person no longer believes good and evil are cut and dried. Many people believe they are a better judge of right and wrong than is God and His representative, the prophet. Humility is out of vogue and without it, no one can become a Zion person and in fact without it, no one can be cleansed by the Atonement of Jesus Christ.

Secular Humanism, according to its own manifestos, is "a philosophical, religious, and moral point of view."[165] So do not be fooled by those who maintain that this movement is simply an absence of reli-

---

[163] Ibid, 298
[164] Ibid, 299
[165] http://www.christiananswers.net/q-sum/sum-r002.html

gion, merely wanting to keep religion out of the public venue. A mixture of paganism and humanism is growing in popularity. New Age teachings about the spiritual ascension process, blended with the idea that mankind can use this process on their own without a god to believe in, will continue to grow along with the pride of the world (The Tower of Babel). Many eastern religions like Taoism, do not focus on a god but they believe they have the power within to save themselves. At least they are usually humble about this and there is much to admire within the eastern religions. Humanists, on the other hand, promote pride and power and make it very difficult for those steeped in their ideas to humble themselves enough to accept the Gospel. They believe that we are gods and we do not need an outside source.

The answer to this confusion is the same simple message that Ammon gave to King Lamoni. There was a creation and then a fall. Because of the fall we cannot return to our Heavenly Father without help. This brings us to the Atonement. In mortality we cannot fully understand the process of how the Atonement works but we can learn more about this subject. As we continue to study this process we may need to consciously be careful to not fall into that age old curse of focusing solely on the role of the Bride instead of keeping our eye single to the glory of God in the center place.

Throughout time, history has shown that pure religion always gets to the point where some version of the forms remain but the true understanding of God Himself is lost, along with the priesthood. Thus we have so many pieces of temple rites sprinkled throughout the world. The ascension process of the temple endowment is a function of the priesthood in its feminine role of rebirthing initiates. When symbolized by the mother goddess aspect as the process of helping mankind return to God, the symbol is kept and worshipped (Isis, Venus, Athena, Mother Earth, Inanna, etc.) instead of the focus being on God.

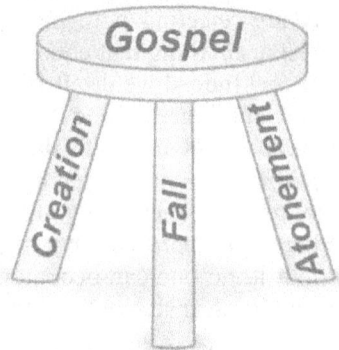

Some of the points we will be making in this section repeat previous discussion, as in the above paragraph but we feel there is great value in looking through the lens of the Atonement itself as we study the Plan of Salvation.

The Pillars and the Cross

Bruce R. McConkie wrote extensively about the Three Pillars: "God himself, the Father of us all, established a plan of salvation whereby his spirit children might progress and become like him. It is the Gospel of God, the plan of Eternal Elohim, the system that saves and exalts, and it consists of three things. These three are the very pillars of eternity itself. They are the Creation, the Fall, and the Atonement."[166] With each new day, year, or cycle, principles of a new creation are put into place. This can be illustrated by new growth after a death-like winter or flowers opening to a new sun after a dark night. Creation is the first pillar and is crucial as Elder McConkie taught us: "The Lord expects us to believe and understand the true doctrine of the Creation—the creation of the earth, of man, and of all forms of life. Indeed, as we shall see, an understanding of the doctrine of creation is essential to salvation. Until we gain a true view of the creation of all things we cannot hope to gain that fullness of eternal reward which otherwise would be ours."[167]

The Three Pillars of the Gospel given above by McConkie, are the foundation upon which the pattern of the Plan of Salvation rests. As we have begun to show, this pattern can be identified in cycles of time. Although there are numerous cycles that are all coming together at this time like cogs in a wheel, they are beyond the scope of this work. There are a number of significant steps within the different cycles, one of which we have been discussing, the precession of the equinoxes which is shown in the Central American Maya and Toltec temple complexes.

We assisted Jehovah and Michael in the original creation of the universe. Each of us takes part in the fall when we are born into this telestial sphere which necessitates an atonement to reinstate us back into the presence of God. Our research strongly indicates that the 2012 Winter Solstice marked the point in time when the earth began transitioning from a fallen telestial state back to a terrestrial state. The earth must be purified and made ready, becoming sanctified by the power of the Holy Ghost, a temple-like process that will spiritually prepare her for the physical baptism of fire at the Second Coming.

Remembering that the 2012 date was believed by the Mayas to represent the Tree of Life, a door and a cross, let us look at how these tie in together. The Tree of Life represents the binding together of heaven and earth. It is a very common motif in ancient American beliefs. Adam could not partake of the fruit of the Tree of Life until he

---

[166] Bruce R. McConkie, "Christ and the Creation", LIAHONA, Sept. 1983, 22
[167] Ibid

had been cleansed through the power of the Atonement and was ready to be reclaimed from the Fall. The sacrifice on the cross opens the door to lifting fallen man from a telestial to a terrestrial state and is represented by the temple, which in turn represents the Atonement of Christ. The keeping of temple covenants reverses the effects of the Fall. The Lord, through the sacrifice of the Atonement, is the only door to return to Heavenly Father.

It is through sacrifice that the center place of salvation is established that lifts the repentant sinner to the sanctifying embrace of the Savior. The arrested sacrifice[168] we make in the temple means we do not have to go through the literal wounding process that Christ did but through the covenants that are made, the repentant supplicant can achieve the reward of that sacred embrace. We cannot go into detail about the arrested sacrifice because of the sacredness of this subject and the covenants we make not to reveal them. The Atonement and temple ceremonies are inseparable.

As discussed previously, temple comes from the word 'templum' which is an instrument that cuts. If an instrument cuts through space and time, it can facilitate the movement from one place to another. Alma taught that the Atonement cuts through space and time, covering all of God's children from the beginning.[169] Because of this blessing we will all be resurrected but what kind of glory we receive depends on how determined we are to progress and our willingness to be challenged along the way.

The temple is known as the omphalos (navel) within almost all ancient cultures, which means it can be seen as the umbilical cord that ties heaven and earth. This crossing of heaven and earth is symbolized and actualized by the Man on the cross at Calvary. It was not the wooden Cross that is the door of the sheepcote, (temple, or place of safety and rest) Jesus Christ himself acts as the door.

When I was five, I was asked by my Sunday School teacher to stop chastising her for teaching that we should worship the cross. I tried to obey but every once in a while I could not stop myself from suggesting we worship Jesus instead of the cross. After a few months of this, the minister asked my father to talk to me. He did and I obeyed...for a time. Finally my father was told to keep me with him in adult Sunday School and shortly after that, we stopped attending that church.

---

[168] An arrested sacrifice is one that does not have to be completed as with Abraham offering up his son.
[169] Alma 34:10

We believe from our studies of ancient apocryphal writings, that there were deep teachings about the process of salvation as depicted by the cross. Because of these teachings the cross itself became an object of worship, instead of the man. The wood of that cross is simply a symbol of the Tree of Life, who is Jesus Christ. The at-one-ment brings fallen man back into the presence of God through repentance and authorized ordinances. This meeting of heaven and earth creates the door that effects both spiritual sanctification and the resurrection.

http://forum.prisonplanet.com/index.php?topic=184101.80

The four arms of the cross represent many things including, the four cardinal directions which gather in all who will come from the four quarters of the earth. They also represent the four quarters of the year, gathering in and organizing initiates into the body of Christ from each dispensation and/or cycles of time. As shown in the last chapter, we also believe the years 2009 through 2012 represents a gathering in for a higher birth. Nibley writes that the form of the cross represents sacred ordinances. He goes on that "the four wooden extremes spread out reaches the four utmost regions of the earth."[170] (Typically, spring, or east is depicted on the right side and west on the left.)

The winter solstice, the southern point of the cross, can represent fallen man, Adam. He can only be saved through the sacrifice of the Lamb. The eastern point, the spring equinox can represent being born of the Spirit by keeping the commandments and becoming a Son of God. The north, the summer solstice, can represent being gathered into the Church of the Firstborn, becoming unified as part of the Bride of Christ. For this aspect, it is important that we keep our covenants, be faithful to the Bridegroom and not go whoring after other gods, as ancient Israel so often did. The western arm of the cross, the autumn equinox can represent gathering all into one on a higher level in preparation for the resurrection and being established as a creator, a father or mother of eternal lives, ready to be placed in the center heart position

---

[170] Nibley, *Message*, 524

and begin our own creation. That does not mean the initiate literally begins his/her own worlds at this time but that they are qualified to do so. The seed of that future kingdom actually begins here. It is here that Zion must fulfill her role.

Facsimile 3 from the Book of Abraham

The Center Place, the Heart

The year 2012 represented the Bride beginning to establish that center place at the heart of the cross, the door that joins heaven and earth and gathers in all who will be His at His coming. The fifth directional point is the heart or throne of God, and is represented by the sacred and seldom discussed Second Endowment. Nibley wrote that the heart is the center of gravity.[171] A new creation begins with the center place like Kolob, creating the necessary gravity to order the cosmos around it and provide the stability needed to hold everything together in its orbit. It is like the altar in the center of a prayer circle, the umbilical cord, door or conduit to heaven. Another type would be pharaoh in the heart of the pyramid to order his kingdom around him. In our opinion, the thousands of workers who helped build those pyramids understood enough of the ancient New Year Rite and its eternal purposes so that they gladly gave their labor. Of course they erred in that the pharaoh did not possess the true priesthood and thus had no power to help

---

[171] Nibley, *One Eternal Round*, 252

Heavenly Father organize and order the priesthood and family lines for eternity but the general concept was sound.

Facsimile 3 from the Book of Abraham, in the illustration on the left, helps us understand the four steps or covenants that bring us to the center place on the throne. Although there are many explanations and symbols entailed in this facsimile, we will suggest one aspect to illustrate the four covenants of the endowment. First, figure 6 can represent fallen man, Adam with the yoke of slavery in a telestial world. Figure 5 is the next step up, a messenger and important assistant to the king, freed from the yoke of bondage himself. He is there to assist in freeing fallen man from the yoke. Figure 4 is the prince, the Son, who dressed in feminine clothing is standing in the role of the Bride (Venus in evening star office). Passing through the veil as represented by figure 3, where we can see Abraham reborn into a higher state as the king of his dispensation. Figure 2 is Pharaoh, the father of his people, dressed also in a feminine role, acting as high priest to birth forth the new king from the throne. It is the work and glory of the Father to bring forth every person who is qualified as a future father or mother in heaven, a king in his own right. Adam, the Holy Ghost, the Son of God and Heavenly Father, all stand ready to lead the initiate, step by step in our return journey to the presence of God. Righteous priesthood holders can act in those offices to assist in the work. At each crossroads there is a challenge but at the last one, the center place, the challenge is greatest of all because it brings us to a showdown between the true king and the false king for possession of the earth itself.

To start that process, we each must begin as if we were Adam or Eve. Fallen man is often depicted by a serpent, and the wings of a bird, like the Phoenix, is a symbol for the spiritual power to return to God. The winged serpent is the symbol of Quetzalcoatl. The Maya showed the crossroads as the human heart of the serpent, standing with outstretched arms.[172] Isaiah often depicted the Lord as patiently standing with hands or arms stretched out.[173]

Facsimile 2 in the Pearl of Great Price, shows a cross over the heart spot on figure 1 and we believe this represents the throne, the portal to rebirth. The Maya taught that the "sacred ruler does not just sit on the throne symbolizing the cosmic center and crossroads; instead he *is* the crossroads."[174] For the Mayas, Quetzalcoatl had "a king-sun-cross association" with 2012 that was "literally a doorway between

---

[172] Jenkins, *Maya Cosmogenesis,* 177
[173] For example see 2 Nephi 19:21
[174] Jenkins, *Maya Cosmogenesis.* 177

worlds."[175] Thus, Christ is the door to the higher birth and symbolizes the birthing throne which will bring the earth back from her fallen state. This preparation is important to prepare the world to be in a state to receive the resurrected beings which will be a part of the winding up scene and for the Millennium itself. For us to personally be a part of stepping up to a higher spiritual state, we must be born again through the Atonement of Christ.

Confusion often comes as to the exact role of the Savior and others. The key is to remember that there are offices and a person can act in one office, then in others, depending on the time and situation. Christ can act in the office of Father as the center place and so can Adam, the first physical father, as can one who becomes as if he were an Adam through covenant keeping. By the sacrifice of Gethsemane, Jesus Christ earned the right to birth the repentant initiate into a higher state, thus becoming their father/mother. When we are born again through Jesus, then He becomes our spiritual father. *The Book of Mormon* often refers to the Savior as our father, which anti-Mormons love to point out. We have a Father in Heaven who is also the father of the Lord. But, Christ is both the father of creation and the father of the spiritually reborn. We can be both a child of our parents and also parents of others. Having just one permanent role would rule out the concept of eternal progression.

So how do we become born of God? After being cleansed by Gethsemane's blood, we offer our purified sacrifice of a broken heart and a contrite spirit on the altar (cross). Death and rebirth (in a spiritual or symbolic sense) into a higher form is the result of that sacrifice when properly performed. The initiate is clothed upon with light and glory. In other words, the level of sanctification we reach determines the glory to which we will be resurrected. That light is represented by the idea of the pillar of fire and cloud of protection. We needed to be clothed upon with that protection for ourselves, our families and communities as we passed the crossroads of Dec. 21, 2012 and will continue to need that protection as we head into the final decades of testing and preparation before the Second Coming. The Church is fulfilling her part. It is up to us to stand with her. Thankfully, if we have come short or fallen behind, our feet can always be placed back on the path through sincere repentance.

The age old battle of heaven has raged across the 2012 time barrier as Satan pursues his claim of being god over this earth and over

---

[175] Ibid, 177

those brazen enough to want to spiritually leave his telestial realm. This meeting place between heaven and earth is not celestial exaltation yet. It represents the terrestrial sphere and we know that in that realm, the old serpent still gets his last chance to tempt and to try. Only through perseverance does the initiate reach the point where the Adversary is cast out on his behalf and he is sealed up to eternal life. Remember, when Lehi's people reached the tree and partook, there was still a time of testing as spiritual Babylon mocked and clamored for attention.

The Tree of Life can be seen as a door to another state of being. The ancient Egyptian city of Heliopolis was the city of the sun god. At winter solstice, the Egyptians would split a sacred tree, "freeing the dead as the sun at the solstice", and then the New Year would follow with the classic depiction of the fight between light and darkness.[176]

In our opinion, we believe the Mayas were right and the resurrection will begin in greater earnest and the peaceful, terrestrial state of the Millennium will begin as a seed, hidden in rich soil and nourished with Living Waters. The keys for bringing about this resurrection and the endowment in preparation for it, were restored to Joseph Smith. The Church sheltered and nurtured this process of rebirth for decades. With the transition to the Seventh Dispensation, the Church will continue to act as protector and nurturer as the new kingdom begins to spread. There will be differences as we move through this transitional time. It now becomes crucial to be gathered, in a spiritual not physical sense, as one body in a true Zion state. As we keep repeating, creations and recreations begin spiritually, then physically. Becoming empowered with spiritual understanding of the process will help keep fear at bay and should ease our journey as we focus intently upon the Savior who will be actively working to rescue His bride from the false Pharaoh, to bring her up out of Egypt (Babylon) and into a place of refuge and safety.

---

[176] Nibley, *Message*, 291

Chapter Five:
The New Year and the Suffering King

This writer remembers being four years old and deciding that New Year's Day was the most boring of all holidays. When I heard someone mention that it was a holiday, I got very excited with my memories still fresh from the colorful and gift filled Christmas the previous week. I ran to my mother and asked her what kind of a holiday it was. I assumed it would not be exactly like Christmas and my mind raced with vague memories of earlier celebrations called holidays. Weeks before, on a cool dark night, children roamed in crazy costumes clutching bags of candy and at home gooey caramel apples waited at the end of the evening. A long time before that holiday, there was another day with a parade on a sunny morning, lots of good food and ending with bright sparklers lighting a warm night.

"Today we celebrate a new year," my mother informed me.

"But what do we do?" I asked excitedly. Remembering something about bunnies and pastel colored eggs I looked around for tell-tale signs, decorations, anything to give me a clue. Not even a boring turkey was in site. I then noticed that Mom was looking a little uncomfortable. Hesitating, she thought for a moment and then said, "well, on New Year's Day we make a lot of noise to celebrate another year." She then disappeared into the kitchen and I heard banging and clanking. She returned with two pots and two large metal spoons. She then had my sister and me go out and sit on the front porch steps and bang on the pots and yell "Happy New Year's." We lived on a farm. No one heard us and I was glad.

I know my poor mother gave it a good effort but I remember sitting there feeling stupid, banging on an ugly pan and looking up at a steel gray sky. It took thirty years for me to ever show any real interest in New Years and that was because of Hugh Nibley. When I learned that this holiday was the major festival of the ancient cultures, filled with fun, feasting, boat trips, etc., I felt like I had been missing the boat, so to speak, for many years. Hopefully, with this chapter, we can all get on that New Year boat (metaphorically) and have a good trip learning how important this celebration really is. The ship of Zion is definitely heading down that Milky Way River, gathering all who love the king.

Chaos of the New Year

One of the subjects of study in this book is the concept of "order verses chaos." The goal of ancient cultures was to continue the traditions of the fathers which they believed had been handed down from the dawn of creation. They felt this was the way to keep chaos at bay, establish a stable society and have peace. We are now in the middle of a world-wide movement to overthrow established society. Gadianton robbers come in many forms. Most of us have been confused about the purpose of groups such as we saw a few years ago who were occupying Wall Street and many other cities around the United States and in other countries. As it turns out, one of the groups most responsible for organizing that multi-national movement is The Zeitgeist Movement. Reading from their website we learn:

The Inaugural 2011 Zeitgeist Media Festival Global Event set, which enabled a socially conscience Arts and Media platform across 20 countries, accessing about 10,000 people in person and almost 200,000 through free live Webcasts, was a notable success. Organized by The Zeitgeist Movement, a global, non-profit sustainability advocacy group seeking to change the current social order, this unprecedented concept has generated a resonance that is expected to grow every year as it continues its development. [177]

The Zeitgeist newsletter for June 2011 uses the teachings of Karl Marx to explain their beliefs.[178] What is the origin of this new socialist movement and what is their motivation? The Zeitgeist movement began as a rejection of traditional Christianity, insisting that Jesus Christ was not a real man but a myth. To prove their point, they quoted from many ancient sources to show that the whole idea of an atonement and also some of the details of the life of the Savior were much older than 2,000 years. It seems obvious to many people that there is no way the story of Christ could be original and must have been stolen from earlier accounts. This would be true if there were no such things as prophets.

One of the major points of focus for Zeitgeist has been the Ancient New Year Rite. The suffering king was an obvious depiction of

---

[177]http://www.thezeitgeistmovement.com/press_releases/ zeitgeist-media-festival-2011-12-000-meals-raised-via-40-events-in-20-countries

[178]http://www.thezeitgeistmovement.com/uploads/upload/file/4/tzmjuneenglish.pdf

the Atonement of the king of heaven. Instead of weakening our testimony, as has happened with so many Christians, a study of the New Year Rite in light of the Gospel does nothing but strengthen and amaze us.

The chaotic New Year's Eve tradition may have stemmed from these ancient traditions with the night of chaos preceding the rising sun of the new day. The old king renews himself and then organizes his kingdom anew. There is still a period of suffering for the new king and a coming battle as we shall see, but the citizens of the kingdom know that their new king will be triumphant and overcome chaos.

Nibley on the New Year Rite

Why study 2012 and the New Year Rite? It is actually quite simple. If we want to learn more about increasing the spiritual protection for our families, we need to learn more about and implement temple teachings. Nibley taught that the New Year Rite stems from the teachings of and meaning behind the temple. The 2012 cycle is the most perfect example that we know of to illustrate the New Year Rite.

A friend recently asked if my book was going to be simple to understand. When I answered that it would take effort and thought for many of the readers to grasp these ancient concepts, there was a look of disapproval until I reminded this good member that if we are ever to be prepared to receive the sealed portion of *The Book of Mormon*, we need to begin making more progress in understanding the meat of the Gospel. Instantly her face cleared and she said, "You are right". It also made sense to her that if Christ commanded us to search the words of Isaiah[179] and since so many members do not even understand that it is a temple text with deep explanations of the process of redemption, then we obviously need to move beyond the first layer and begin searching the scriptures, deepening our discipleship as Elder Maxwell asked. To those who believe it is wrong to study deep eternal truths, please consider the following quote by Elder Winkel in General Conference: "The temple is a place to know the Father and the Son. It is a place where we experience the divine presence. The Prophet Joseph Smith made this

---

[179] 3 Ne. 23:1

plea: "I advise all to search deeper and deeper into the mysteries of Godliness." And where shall we search? In the house of God.[180]

A second reason is also simple. Heavenly Father brings about righteousness through an interaction between His children and the Godhead. We had a part to play in the successful turning of the Great New Year Cycle and that part has not ended. In God's time, the opening of a door takes a great deal of time. More faith means less chaos. It is not only the 2012 that is a focus. The opening of the Seventh Seal takes years to swing open and the principles we are writing about will never cease to be pertinent and necessary. We can help gentle the turning of this era so that massive destruction will be held at bay (but not stopped, for prophecy will be fulfilled). What we want to see is that the rioting upheaval of the Great New Year turning will be less devastating than it would otherwise be without our help. We can each do our part as we move through the era of this great New Year Rite. These next chapters will begin to unfold more about how we can do that.

The scriptures are clear that the Atonement was "prepared from the foundation of the world for all mankind, which ever were since the fall of Adam, or who are, or who ever shall be, even unto the end of the world." (Mos. 4:7) We must go through the steps of the same process in the creation of our own eternal kingdoms. This has been the pattern from the beginning. The prophets from Adam have been given this pattern and so it is no surprise that the concepts of The Three Pillars of the Gospel were well documented before the advent of Christ upon this earth to enact the saving ordinances which overcome time and space and go back to the beginning to empower the creation.

Anciently, the great New Year festivals lasted for days. Nibley identified several common elements of these festivals:

1) A dramatic representation of the death and resurrection of the god, king, sun, year, cycle, etc. The old year dies and is reborn. In 2012, the 26,000 year cycle dies and a new one begins.

2) A recitation or symbolic representation of the myth of creation. As the new cycle repeats, it is time to begin sketching plans for the terrestrial creation for the future Millennial reign of King David and spiritually putting this into motion.

3) A ritual combat, in which the triumph of the god over his enemies was depicted. The new sun is seen as defeating the old

---

[180] Richard H. Winkel, The Temple is about Families, General Conference Sept. 2006

sun...also there will be combat between Satan and the Lord over possession of the Bride after the center place is established in 2012.

4) The sacred marriage symbolizing the joining of heaven and earth at winter solstice 2012 represents the marriage of the king (male aspect) or sun on the throne, with the female aspect of the priesthood (prayer circle); also, the council of Adam-Ondi-Ahman seems to fulfill various aspects of this sacred marriage.

5) The triumphal procession in which the king played the part of the god followed by a train of lesser gods or visiting deities [This often happened on a boat trip] (Second Coming).[181]

So we can see that this all began even before 2012 and gradually moves from there to the Second Coming. Nibley explained that "the all-important timing of rites and festivals required close observations of the heaven." He also explains that Eden is supposed to surround the temple.[182] Thus, we help establish the center place, the temple, then as smaller, less glorious trees of life, we surround the main tree of life to begin the new Edenic condition. All who qualify to be a part of the new cycle "must be registered in the Book of Life opened at the Beginning of the World."[183] So the New Year takes us back to when we helped create Eden. The creation cycle is on-going.

According to Nibley, the New Year Rite and the hypocephalus contain the whole plan of salvation within these repeating cycles. He goes on to explain that *The Pearl of Great Price* brings all the dispensations into one.[184] Joseph Smith, as the dispensation gatherer, will present the unified dispensations to the Lord. Temple work brings the living and the dead together, filling in the Book of Life with the names of those on both sides of the veil.

It is not up to us to decide whether or not we can enter into the sacred place. Nibley further explains: "[We are] challenged by the lion, the messenger proposes to prove his ties with the All-Highest by uttering the secret word: 'Horus has repeated to me what his father said to him at the [Egyptian hieroglyphs] (the partition or veil -a woven screen) on the day of his burial.'"[185]

---

[181] Nibley, *One Eternal Round,* 123
[182] Ibid, 125
[183] Ibid, 126
[184] Ibid, 130
[185] Ibid, 139

Nibley goes on to say that the messenger descends to the feminine earth to raise the sleeper up. He lies in a "horror of great darkness" and is rescued by the lion (David's lion throne) and birthed up into the lighted world of heaven by Hathor the cow.[186] The underworld can be said to describe both the spirit world where spirits await the resurrection and also mortality where we are spiritually dead until rescued from the fall. We move from a funerary situation on the lion couch, to a re-birthing situation on the lion throne.[187] Heavenly order is restored and the balance between the patriarchy and matriarchy is restored[188] to its Edenic condition.

This whole process is supposed to help us comprehend the structure of the universe[189] and in the next chapter, we hope to help our reader do just that. Once we can do that, we should be able to clearly see the significance of 2012, the New Year Rite and how to apply that in our own personal lives as the ever repeating Three Pillars of the Gospel point the way to exaltation.

The Hebrew word for 'year' is 'shanah' and means; repeat, to do again. Giving examples from scripture and history, Nibley calls this repeating pattern a 'new age.'[190] This can make us balk and back away from these powerful truths because we do not want to be associated with the New Age Movement. We should refuse to give the stage to the counterfeit just because they happen to have many pieces of the truth. Elijah did not give the stage to the 400 priests of Baal but went ahead and gave the true sacrifice necessary to bring about the refreshing rains that brought life to Israel. It is the true priesthood that will create the acceptable sacrifice that will bring about the cleansing water as we move toward the constellation of the man Aquarius who pours out the water of life (refreshing rains) from the jug on his shoulder.

As we gather around our prophet who holds the keys of the priesthood and stands in the king position, we will help this process. This reminds us of the Egyptian Pharaoh who stood as a representative of God on earth "receiving the strength and wisdom that is part of the victory motif of the year-rites rather than to the cold facts of history."[191] We can see examples of one acting as a representative of God in our temple while the Bride (sanctified members) sustain and support him around the altar. The greatest high priest in mortality, one who holds

---

[186] Ibid, 140
[187] Nibley, *One Eternal Round,* 141
[188] Ibid, 142
[189] Ibid, 138
[190] Ibid, 167
[191] Nibley, *Approach to the Book of Mormon,* 176-78

the keys, is our prophet and our sustaining of him, especially at this crucial time in history is necessary in order to draw down strength and power as the Lord makes bare His arm to protect His Bride.

In this latter-day, an international spiritual nation of kings and priests are becoming empowered by Heavenly Father, beginning their own eternal kingdoms like Pharaoh, receiving strength and wisdom as they are born again as a new-year sun, a new Adam. Gathering their families around them, they then in turn join the unity of a larger circle around the focal point of the prophet, under the direction of Jesus Christ. Only in this manner will there be enough protection to navigate the dangerous challenges coming our way.

In the mythology of ancient Egypt, the organization of the priesthood is shown working together to hold up the great sky goddess. Nibley wrote a great deal about Hathor the cow, the sky-goddess who births forth the sun. As the womb/river/ocean of the Milky Way, the new sun passes through her body during the night and is reborn every new day. Nibley taught that the birth refers to "the eternal rebirth of the sun"[192] to show the recurring cycle describing the ascension process. Remember, the Mayas believe that Quetzalcoatl, with his symbol of Venus the morning star, would rise to establish his political kingdom at the end of their long count calendar on December 21, 2012. Perhaps the modern-day Mayas were disappointed to not see this long-awaited fulfillment just as the Jewish followers of Jesus were disappointed when He did not bring forth the promised political kingdom of Messiah. Sometimes important things happen right beneath the noses of unsuspecting believers.

This rebirth process, symbolized by Hathor the sky-goddess, represents "the resurrection of the dead, the glorification and deification...which is certainly a central element of our own temple ceremony."[193] We can see how so many cultures mixed up types and shadows and began to worship the sun. We do not worship the symbol but we also should not reject it as a powerful metaphor. Nibley insists the sun is a representation of the connection of heaven and earth[194] but the connection is not made without Hathor, the womb of the priesthood that uses ordinances to bring about rebirth.

---

[192] Nibley, *One Eternal Round*, 325
[193] Ibid, 327
[194] Ibid, 424

What is Old is New

The celebration and traditions of the New Year have been so prevalent throughout history that it is amazing more scholars do not wonder at the significance of the elaborate ceremonies. The similarities between the ceremonies of the ancients should make one think there is something to all of this instead of bundling them all into a pile to discard. The meaning of the New Year is all about the ascension process. The celebration of the New Year is the oldest festival we know about. The Egyptians were far from alone in holding onto sacred pieces of ritual. Babylon was one of many cultures that held massive festivals for their celebration of the New Year: "Such celebrations were closely tied in with various gods and goddesses and creation myths popular among ancient nations, and involved rites and ceremonies expressing jubilation over life's renewal, which is the essence of the New Year festivals."[195] According to scholars, these celebrations: "Represented a remembrance or repetition of creation myths on the symbolic anniversary of these events in order to strengthen the bond between gods, cosmos and human communities and therefore to preserve the cosmic order essential for the survival of human life."[196]

In the Babylonian New Year Rites, the creation story would be enacted by men, women and the general of God's army, Marduk would overcome the enemy, Tiamut. Order would be brought out of chaos. Also, the Babylonian king would:

Go through a ritual of humiliation, by removing his royal insignia by the high priest. He would spend time praying and asking for forgiveness at the major temple. By repenting his sins (and those of his people whom he represented) he would reappear again and claim his royal insignia. Ceremonies followed to ensure that nature would support the king and therefore the community during the coming year.[197]

Our own New Year's Eve traditions may have arisen from the ancient New Year practice of wild, chaotic celebration to begin with, allowing chaos to rule for a while, until the ritual battle was won and order was restored during the end of the festival.[198] The following comes from the Iranian New Year traditions:

Once the material world was created the Hostile Spirit saw and wanted light and attacked the good world. He crashed in through the sky, plunged down into the waters and then burst up through the centre

---

[195] http://www.cultureofiran.com/newyear_celebrations.html
[196] Ibid
[197] Ibid
[198] Ibid

121

of the Earth. The Earth was shaken and broken causing the appearance of mountains. The ocean was disturbed and rivers flowed. With the hostile spirits invading, help was needed. The struggle between the good and evil had started.

The struggle continues for 12,000 years. There are four periods, one for each 3,000 years. During the last phase, several saviours come and the last one, Saoshyant, will save the world. When he comes there is resurrection, all dead people are resurrected and will walk over the Chinvat Bridge (Sarat Bridge in the Quran) and this is when the last judgment occurs. We recognize this figure as the Time Lord (Imam Zaman) in Iranian version of Shi'ite Islam.[199]

For years, we have been calling the bridging of the sixth and seventh seals, the Rainbow Bridge. Aboriginal Australians and many other early cultures made mention of this idea of a rainbow bridge spanning the gap between heaven and earth. We were not surprised to see a rainbow bridge depicted in the movie *Thor*. Recall that we earlier discussed Brigham and the meaning of his name stemming both from 'bride' and 'city by the bridge'. There is a great deal of food for thought here.

Included in the ancient Babylonian festival was homage to the seven creations. There would be seven feasts of obligation. "Six are known as Gahambars, feasts of obligation. The seventh and the most elaborate was No Ruz, celebrating the Lord of Wisdom and the holy fire at the time of spring equinox."[200] This is especially interesting to us because 2012 marked the ending of the 26 thousand year precession when the spring equinox, as the marker, has completed a full circuit around the zodiac. This is the time of year that the Atonement took place. It may seem confusing to mix the significance of the winter solstice and the spring equinox when discussing 2012. They work together as two offices to bring about the desired results. The winter solstice means we are at the end of a cycle and ready to begin a new one. The spring equinox represents the Atonement of Christ and the promise of the renewal of life. So they both count as a birthday. In our opinion, the winter solstice is the birthday of creation being put in order, and the spring equinox is the birthday of spiritual rebirth through the Atonement. The new center place came forth like the birth of a new king from the altar/throne/Kolob/sun on the winter solstice.

---

[199] http://www.cultureofiran.com/newyear_celebrations.html
[200] Ibid

As previously stated, at the winter solstice, the sun appears low on the horizon and seems to stand still for about five days. Ancients believed that it took the faith and united voice of the people in celebration to sustain and support this new birth, thus the festival. Then the new king begins to order his kingdom and overcome chaos. This is a process. The sacrifice of the Savior during the spring equinox brings about the literal power that puts all things in motion. The seed that was planted, the faith that was put into effect by the new king now bears fruit and can be seen by all the world in the renewal of life.

It is during the spring equinox that a shadow snakes down the pyramid at Kulculcan at Chichen Itza in the Yucatan Peninsula and appears to descend into the well of souls. The well represents ritual sacrifice.[201] The return of Kulculcan (Quetzalcoatl/Venus), at the end of the 26,000 year precession of the spring equinox around the zodiac, marks the time of the resurrection. As a reminder, one of the main themes of 2012 is resurrection. The groundwork is being laid during this era for the resurrection to take place in a much greater way.

In early Babylon history, the sacred marriage was also a part of the New Year Ritual. The king would spend the first night of the New Year with a young virgin.[202] Obviously, we do not condone this practice. It is another example of a pattern of symbolic meaning being taken too literally. For us, we understand that the marriage of the Lamb is symbolic and fulfills a legal requirement for eternal order, as we have discussed previously.

Babylon has become Iran and modern Iranians celebrate the New Year for 13 days. They bath and cleanse themselves in preparation for donning a new garment that represents newness of life. Their New Year is celebrated during the spring equinox. These kinds of symbolic festivals persist throughout the world because they were so deeply ingrained anciently. We also believe that the human spirit reaches out to the deeper meaning behind the outward acts.

In traditional Iranian families, the father and the firstborn son walk about the home with a mirror and a small candle and they ritually bless the physical space. Then they leave the candle burning.[203] This correlates with the new sun born at the end of every fifty two weeks and the Maya/Aztec Fire Ceremony when every fifty two years all of the light in the kingdom must be extinguished and then ritually relit. [204]

---

[201] Maya Cosmogenesis, John Major Jenkins, 71
[202] http://www.cultureofiran.com/newyear_celebrations.html
[203] Ibid
[204] Ibid

A new cycle needs a newly born sun. This earth on a higher level is that new cycle now and Venus, as the bright and morning star of Christ (Star of David), represents that new day.

We are now living in the seventh thousand year period. The Iranians equate the number seven with the celebration of the New Year as noted before. In their feasts they place seven different items on their table to represent the seven creations and seven holy immortals that protect them. Could that be the seven heads of the dispensations? According to an Iranian culture website, Zoroastrians (mostly Iranians): "Have the ritual of growing seven seeds. Ancient Iranians also grew seven seeds as a reminder that this is the seventh feast of the creation, while their sprouting into new growth symbolized the festival's other significance as a feast of resurrection and of eternal life to come."[205]

Returning to the Babylonian New Year Rites, Nibley wrote that the king had to disappear each year in order to show that he could overcome death. He would enter an underground vault, where he would be humiliated. A priest would slap his face until the tears ran down; he would be clothed in a mock robe and crowned with a crown of weeds. A reed would be put in his hand. Then the Lord of Misrule, the false king, took his place for three days."[206] Afterward the king would come forth from the tomb triumphant to show that he had overcome death and now he was fit to rule for a new year. To assist him in coming forth, the people, representing all the inhabitants of the earth, would sing the great hymn, the Enuma Elish. Nibley wrote that "they were repeating what had happened elsewhere, before - the pattern on which this particular earth was founded."[207] Since Nibley makes it clear that this is the pattern established when the universe was created and also for this particular world, one is left to wonder if there is something different about the history of this earth compared to other creations. Many points of science and mythology lend credence to the idea that the conflict at the beginning of all creation in this universe was repeated and is still ongoing on this, the Atonement earth.

The one crucial point that was understood anciently was that the New Year festival gave a sense of stability in an unstable world:

> Inasmuch as it was celebrated annually in many places with the same rites and theme enacted for the same purposes, whether the divinity was Tammuz, Marduk, Ashur, or any other vegeta-

---

[205] http://www.cultureofiran.com/newyear_celebrations.html
[206] Nibley, *Temple & Cosmos,* 161
[207] Ibid

tion god. This continuity in the myth and its ritual established a harmony with nature in perpetuity, when the renewal of life was the most urgent need of the moment.[208]

---

[208] From www.mindspring.com/~mysticgryphon/bitakitu.htm: On the evening of the fourth day, the Enuma Elish, or the Epic of Creation, was recited in its entirety, for each New Year shared something with the beginning of times, when the world was created and the cycle of seasons started. A recital of that triumphant achievement increased the power of all favorable forces to overcome the hazards which had led to the incarceration of the god of natural life. In later stages of the festival, Marduk´s battle with Chaos was actually represented in the ritual, but on the evening of the fourth day the recital of the Epic was only an interlude in the general preparations for the atonement.

In the city, people were disturbed. The king, the shepherd of the land, had been robbed of his splendor, of the protection of the royal insignia and reduced to a minimum of power which corresponded to the low ebb in the life of nature, to the "captivity" of the god and also to the state of chaos preceding creation. Five days of sacrifice, atonement and purification culminated in the king´s degradation and reinstatement.

The commentary says that "Marduk was confined in the mountain", and it is a Mesopotamian formula for the death of a god, characterizing the point from which the festival took its start. Death here means the suffering of the god, and here we have a clear allusion to the Descents of Inanna/Ishtar, who descended, were wounded, died and were reborn. Similarly, it is said of Marduk at the New Year´s festival that "Into the house of bondage, from the sun and light, they caused him to descend".

And more: "people hasten in the streets, they seek Marduk saying, ' Where is he held captive?'" We assume then that much of the commotion centered around the temple tower, the ziggurat, the man-made mountain that links the Underworld to the Realms Above.

With these words, the gods put all the power of which they dispose in the hands of Marduk. Marduk´s destiny is now declared to be unequaled, for he actually commands the consolidated power of all the gods. It is in the Epic that this power is given so that Marduk can command all threats of annihilation to existence, and this is also the meaning of the ceremony of First Determination of Destiny. All gods´ powers are conferred to the liberated god, who then is ready to lead the battle against all powers of darkness, death and chaos that could affect Babylon in the coming year.

The harmony referred to is created by the balance of the male/female bond. This is a crucial factor in the stability necessary to successfully turn a new year.

What should interest us is the ritual meaning of the sacred marriage at the beginning of these new cycles. It is the interaction between the Bridegroom and the Bride that ensures the abundant harvest of the New Year. The harvest we will reap is the resurrection of the dead. How is the resurrection effected? How do we overcome the veil that separates the realm of the dead from the living?

Cutting Through Space and Time

"The first thing which emerged from the primordial waters was the temple, from which point creation spread in all directions, specifically this earthly creation, for the temple was actually transplanted from a preexistent world created long before."[209] This statement by Nibley explains how so many truths from the temple have found their way into very ancient traditions. Why was the temple believed to mark the exact center of the universe and is that important?

At hundreds of holy shrines, each believed to mark the exact center of the Universe and represented as the point at which the four corners of the earth converged [the middle omphalos] - the navel of the earth [the umbilicus] one might have seen assembled at the New Year - the moment of creation, the beginning and ending of time - vast concourses of people, each thought to represent the entire human race in the presence of all its ancestors and gods.[210]

We continue to cover a lot of the same ground because we have been told that since these ideas seem new, they take repetition to grasp them fully. Also, the examples we give shed light on different aspects of the pattern and we hope that helps our readers.

---

[209] Nibley, *Temple & Cosmos,* 72
[210] Nibley, *Temple & Cosmos,* 156

The creation of earth followed the pattern that began with the creation of the universe, beginning with Kolob. The center spot, like an altar, was where it all began but it did not happen without the participation of the faithful. Nibley wrote that the function of the New Year was to repeat and continue this cycle. He repeatedly made the point in his writings that this was associated with the birth of the sun when all things were put into motion. Since our sun was lit by Christ,[211] it is clear that Kolob came first as the central sun/star/planet.

What we do in the temple is a crucial part of the continuation of the ordering process of the ongoing creation: ". . . we must all participate in the revival of a new year and a new age, in bringing things to life again and make our new oaths and covenants for a new time."[212]

As we have established, the center place around which all things revolve is the first step. In the New Year Rites, the people raise their voices in acclamation for the new king, much as we sustain our prophet in General Conference. The king is enthroned and then orders his kingdom around him so that chaos is kept at bay and the New Year will succeed. When a person has kept his temple covenants to the point of receiving the promise of eternal life, he/she is ready to be rooted in as a new Adam/Eve for their own creation. They assist their family in ordering their unit and progressing together. These smaller units come together in a Zion manner around the prophet and then in a higher level around the Lord as the Body of Christ, gathering in all that is good to the ship of Zion. Christ brings us to the Father, where all things are presented in order and perfect love and faith. The sealing power of Elijah binds us together into a powerful heavenly and mortal army of the Lord of Sabaoth. This sacred space, like a prayer circle around the central altar, is the seed of the millennial terrestrial condition and will grow until it fills the whole earth. The strength of that union will be what

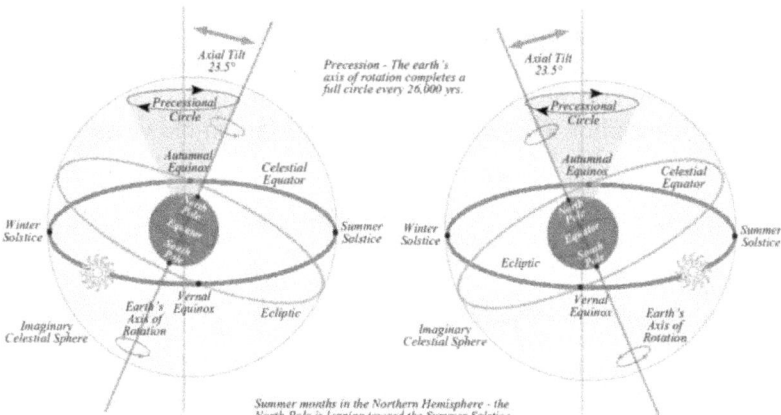

Summer months in the Northern Hemisphere - the North Pole is leaning toward the Summer Solstice.

Winter months in the Northern Hemisphere - the North Pole is leaning toward the Winter Solstice.

brings to pass the Second Coming.

Since time as we know it is only relevant to this earth and because we also understand that space is not a barrier to higher beings, it will be helpful if we can see the integral message in Nibley's book *Temple and Cosmos*: the temple can overcome time and space to bring us symbolically back to the point of all creation, the beginning of time itself. He wrote: "The New Year was the birthday of the human race and its rites dramatized the creation of the world; all who would be found in the 'Book of Life opened at the creation of the World' must necessarily attend."[213]

Nibley wrote often of the treasury where all knowledge is found, 'the treasury of light', which can be approached only by those who have passed through all the eons and all the places of the invisible God. We return to obtain it, bringing a lot of experience."[214] No wonder so many prophets make it sound as though heaven is all about a prayer circle and constant hymns to God who is at the center. These prophets, taken to the treasury of all knowledge, are brought to not only the place but also the time where it all began. It is this experience that the temple and the New Year rites repeat and continue.

As noted before, 'temple' comes from the word 'templum' which is an instrument that cuts. If an instrument cuts through space and time, it can facilitate the movement from one place to another. Nibley wrote: "It's the same thing as the outer court of the Greek temple, the temenos, which means 'temple,' 'to cut' - the point at which the two lines intersect. All space comes together at this absolute, theoretical, perfect point. It is the center of everything. It puts us into the picture of time and space."[215]

So what made the cuts necessary to bring us to the time and place for the rituals? Nibley taught that Christ opened the way. "That's why we call him 'the way, the road, or the gate.'"[216] Since the cross ties together heaven and earth and is the symbol of the Atonement, the center of the cross would be significant. Yet, hopefully we will not make the common mistake of thinking it is the cross itself that holds the significance but will recognize that the Man on the cross would be the focus.

---

[213] Ibid, 157-8
[214] Nibley, *Temple & Cosmos*, 234
[215] Ibid, 144-5
[216] Ibid, 294

The Mayas taught that the first sun is symbolized by the cross.217 This cross is the door from the old to the new and is a New Year's Day.218 That crossroads of a new day was also called the sacred tree.219

(Facsimile 2, figure 1)

The X is the door from the lower underworld to the higher world. It is time again to repeat one of our favourite scriptures that helps us keep our focus on the center place, showing some of the many facets of the Atonement: "14 And my Father sent me that I might be lifted up upon the cross; and after that I had been lifted up upon the cross, that I might draw all men unto me, that as I have been lifted up by men even so should men be lifted up by the Father, to stand before me, to be judged of their works, whether they be good or whether they be evil— (3 Ne. 27:14)

Another example of an ancient concept of a center place is the orphic bowl, which is an ancient alabaster bowl that depicts God as: "A winged serpent coiled around the World Egg. The praying figures encircling it are witnessing the miracle of creation. Whatever the form, the powerful idea of a tangible sacred center to the cosmos always fascinated the ancient world."220 The men and women in the prayer circle depicted within the orphic bowl are shown in a very sacred pose, assisting the process happening in the center point where the serpent is shown in death around the egg. His sacrifice was not in vain however, for creation was now in motion. This reminds us of the plumed serpent, Quetzlcoatl. Once the serpent, representing the fall, is overcome through rituals, then he is reborn with wings to lift him aloft. Perhaps we can see this as the good serpent regaining the limbs that were lost in the fall. Yet this time, instead of arms, through the Atonement and the sacred priesthood, the arms are upgraded to wings. The plumbed serpent lifts the initiates as upon eagle's wings, overcoming the fall.

The Ordinances

Repeating the pattern of the creation is certainly instructional but why is it necessary for us to continually do the same thing? Why

---

217 *Ibid*, 90
218 Ibid, 94
219 Ibid, 106
220Nibley, *Temple & Cosmos*, 160

the cycles? Nibley quoted the poet Yeats in explaining that: "Things fall apart; the center cannot hold; mere anarchy is loosed upon the world". Nibley goes on: "Our civilization is collapsing, falling apart, because there is no center, everything is loosened."221

The early apostles had the knowledge of how to continue to bring order out of chaos. This gnosis was partially revealed and understood from the beginning but the full package was given to the twelve. Nibley wrote that these things were "given to them as a special blessing to make that dispensation complete.222 He went on to say that those ordinances were described in great detail and that we could almost go through the whole temple ceremony from the writings scattered throughout the ancient world. The difference, he said, was that "the authority remains in one church."223

Many church members reject a further understanding of sacred knowledge because they feel other sources are polluted and they do not want to receive knowledge from anywhere other than the Church. That is very sad since this is the dispensation of the fullness of times and so many wonderful things are being uncovered that have been hidden. If the source is evil that is one thing but if it is only misunderstood by its adherents, then we can benefit by sifting the good from the bad. A word of caution here; If the source is deeply evil, even if what they offer is true, we feel very strongly that it is wrong to accept the fruit. Knowledge of good and evil should be given when the Lord determines and not when we decide to push for it and thus partake from the wrong source.

Patience is hard when we want to know now or want power now. Satan offers a counterfeit of those things freely if we only accept him as the giver. But we must remain firm and wait for those authorized by God to teach us. I am not talking about general knowledge but the mysteries are dangerous when given from the wrong hand. We try to follow Brother Nibley's example to be subtle and also to use ancient sources to hint about deeper understandings. We will not directly give away those things we have been counselled to not share. We each should have those understandings revealed when the Holy Ghost determines our readiness.

---

221 Ibid,140
222 Ibid, 296
223 Nibley, *Temple & Cosmos*, 160

Many ancient writings including the Pistis Sophia224 make a strong case that one of the main purposes in this life is to learn to determine which source a particular piece of knowledge stems from. As we seek to determine the source of this knowledge the adversary will tempt us and try to fool us into taking knowledge from him. We must not settle for the philosophies of men but seek to get the gift of discernment so we can separate kernels of truth from sources that have become polluted with worldly doctrines. Those who qualify for the Celestial Kingdom must be solidly plugged into the correct source in order to not pollute that sacred place. The seventh chapter of Moroni explains that everything good comes from the Lord and everything evil comes from Satan. There is no middle ground…no gray area. Which source we plug into is crucial. Knowledge is power, so what we must learn is if that knowledge is transmitted through the true priesthood or the false priesthood.

Aside from the blatant give away of deeply sacred mysteries, we can learn much from many sources both ancient and modern. If we learn the pattern found within the Three Pillars of the Gospel, we can detect counterfeits and misconceptions. For instance, the early Gnostics in the Christian Church became confused about matter being evil but they also recorded many truths. To reject what we can learn from them because of their errors would be short sighted because most of them had honourable intentions and were making efforts to learn truth. Nibley told us where the term gnosis came from: "That's what gnosis is: the knowledge of what the Lord taught the apostles after the resurrection."[225]

It all begins with the Atonement: "Adam in the presence of God is the quintessential atonement."[226] Since Adam and Eve experienced spiritual death, which was separation from God, their purpose after being cast out of the garden was to return to God's presence. The Atonement makes that possible. The temple, a symbol for the Body of Christ, is the organizing force for the eternities that makes it possible to return to the Father and become joint-heirs with His Son. We know that mortal man cannot bear the presence of God without being overshadowed by the Holy Ghost. The temple process, followed with full intent, slowly prepares the initiate to receive an endowment of light necessary to be safe and comfortable with the Father where He lives in Eternal Burnings:

---

[224] The Pistis Sophia is purported to contain teachings of Christ after his resurrection to his disciples.
[225] Nibley, *Temple & Cosmos, 221*
[226] Ibid, 383

You have got to learn how to be Gods yourselves, and to be kings and priests to God, the same as all Gods have done before you, namely, by going from one small degree to another, and from a small capacity to a great one; from grace to grace from exaltation to exaltation, until you attain to the resurrection of the dead, and are able to dwell in everlasting burnings and to sit in glory, as do those who sit enthroned in everlasting power.[227]

The Egyptians believed the temple was the primeval mound from which the sun god emerged to begin cosmogony (the creation of the universe). It is all about sacrifice and rebirth of the individual and the unity and organization of the eternal community, the Church of the Firstborn. It always comes back to the Atonement and being born of God:

For if you keep my commandments you shall receive of his fullness, and be glorified in me as I am in the Father therefore, I say unto you, you shall receive grace for grace. And now, verily I say unto you, I was in the beginning with the Father, and am the Firstborn; And all those who are begotten through me are partakers of the glory of the same, and are the church of the Firstborn. Ye were also in the beginning with the Father; that which is Spirit, even the Spirit of Truth. (D&C 93: 20-23)

"The goal [of the ancient civilizations was always] to restore the primal community of Gods and men, or as we would say, to achieve atonement."228 The New Year Rites of most of the major ancient societies were all about enthroning and empowering the king so he could bring about a state of organization and oneness in the community he ruled but before the foundation of a community can be stretched out, a center place has to be established. Facsimile 1, the lion couch scene, gives the story of the establishment of the center place. Facsimile 2, fig. 1, illustrates the next step. He who has been sacrificed (or has gone through the authorized re-enactment) himself through death and rebirth then begins to organize his own family and stewardship. Anciently, before the new kings could complete their coronation, they would have to symbolically go through the sacrifice that brings about life.

Druids, Romans and other cultures looked upon the year as a complete age, beginning with the winter solstice. This is when the king would be symbolically born along with the sun. His complete life cycle would be over in one year and then his death and rebirth had to be re-

---

[227] Teachings, 346-47
[228] Nibley, *Temple & Cosmos,* 400

peated. Each year or cycle is seen as spiralling so that progression is made. It is the blood of the Atonement that powers the ascension.

The sun appears to stand still for a few days after the solstice. Some cultures believed it would not move for twelve days. These were days that needed united celebration, prayer circles and gift giving to bring about the energy necessary to help get the sun going. This would also be the time that the Egyptian goddess, Isis would hide her new son, Horus in the swamp until he was old enough to defend himself. When we remember that Isis wears a crown shaped like a throne, we understand that she represents the Bride who brings forth the new king in an upward birth. Thus the crown is on her head.

Although 2012 is in the past, the new symbolic king or the concept of the political kingdom of David, is still in its infancy and must be hidden and nursed until a later time. Christ at twelve years old (priesthood age) went to the temple and established Himself as the authority of truth and announced to Mary that He must be about His Father's business. We feel that this was a part of the pattern. The claim is made at the center place, the authority is stated but the youth must still be protected and cared for until He is ready to come forward at a later date to publicly do his work. Until then, things proceed quietly.

Adam

Although the titles of the gods were fluid and should be thought of as stations or offices more than people, it is clear that Horus the hawk (or falcon) has many traits in common with Adam, as does Marduk in Babylon. Father Adam leads out in the celebration and the organizing work of the temple. He does this under the direction of the Godhead as shown in this quote from Nibley:

> Almost always when the plan is mentioned something is said about its glad reception, 'WHEN THE MORNING STARS SANG TOGETHER, AND ALL THE SONS OF GOD SHOUTED FOR JOY' (Job 38:7). The great year-rites, common to all ancient societies, are a rehearsal of the Creation, usually presented in dramatic form; invariably the rites end with a great and joyful acclamation: so all the gods and all the spirits came together to hail God upon his throne and they rejoiced before him in his temple, the source of all good things. The word poema, meaning literally creation, owes its prominence, as Walter Otto has shown, to the circumstance that the first poets were all inspired people who sang one and the same song, namely the Song of Creation.

The whole purpose of the book of Jubilees is to show that the great rites of Israel, centering about the temple and the throne, are a celebration 'which had been observed in heaven since the creation'. The thing to notice here is that man shares fully in these heavenly jubilations; the poet is simply intoxicated with the assurance that man, a mere speck of 'wet dust,' is allowed not only to know about the secret councils of the beginning, but actually to share in them, not only as a participant but as one of the directors![229]

We normally think of beginning our creation far in the future but as stated, the seeds of that creation are begun here for those who have the opportunity of receiving the ordinances and living up to those promises. Each one of us can follow Christ, as Abraham has shown us and begin a center point, a foundation and an eternal family. That was what the ancient kings were doing. The king symbolically went through the atonement, assisted by the faith of his people who considered him their father. The king was given rebirth and then he assisted his people to achieve rebirth, to become a feather in his cap, a jewel in his crown, a star on the evergreen tree of life; a Urim and Thummim which then becomes the foundation for the new god's creation. This was all done through the power of Christ and without His priesthood, the forms mean nothing. "Like the offering table and the lotus flower, the Savior has offered His all on the altar and through that offering, new life has burst forth like the seeds from the pod of the lotus plant to take root in new soil, 'a tree springing up unto everlasting life.'"[230]

The Lord, just like all of us, will be given the opportunity to move on to being a Heavenly Father. Just as we must begin our eternal kingdoms by rooting into this fallen earth, He also establishes his political kingdom here. Earth will become His footstool, the heavy gravitational lodestone that is necessary to hold all things in place, where he has put his enemies beneath his feet. An example of this is the black hole at the center of our galaxy which is necessary to maintain the structural integrity of the galaxy. The fall was necessary. If this is truly the last creation in this larger universal round, as the scriptures indicate (Rev. 21:1) then now, near the end, Christ will bring forth His Davidic throne and put all enemies beneath His feet, thus establishing the heavy, gravitational foundation upon which the next universal round will be founded. This is a process and does not happen overnight, but in celestial time, it will seem but a moment.

---

[229] Nibley, *Temple & Cosmos*, 192–193
[230] A Study Guide to the Facsimiles of the Book of Abraham, 81

The Divine Union

Indeed, the renewal of nature in spring, at the New Year's festival, was conceived as the marriage of the Goddess with the liberated god. Their union took place in the temples and the change in nature and the temple ritual constituted the Divine Union, being the two events inseparable and equivalent. The king was then made the Divine Bridegroom, and the High Priestess was his Divine Consort, the Goddess incarnate.[231]

With the establishment of the throne of David at the end of 2012, the Bridegroom will fight for and eventually win His rightful Bride. As stated above, we believe that the sacred events that are to take place at the council of Adam-Ondi-Ahman will bring about the completion of one fulfilment of the symbolic marriage ceremony. It began with 2012 but just as a corrupt pharaoh took Sarah from Abraham, Satan will not give up dominion of this earth and its inhabitants until conditions become so desperate that he fears complete destruction of his kingdom. Then, as when Laman and Lemuel finally agreed to release Nephi in order to save the ship from destruction, Satan will release his claim on the Bride.

Like Sarah being returned to Abraham, the rightful husband, the earth and her children will return to Christ. No more will the enemy gain power over the saints from that time. The Millennium will have a canopy of protection, as we read in 2 Nephi: "And the Lord will create upon every dwelling-place of mount Zion, and upon her assemblies, a cloud and smoke by day and the shining of a flaming fire by night; for upon all the glory of Zion shall be a defense." (2 Ne. 14:5)

The good news…indeed the crucial news, is that we can have this protection to a degree now and this power will increase as we progress through the last day challenges. The process of how to do this is the subject of this and following books. Laying out all of the pieces takes time but begin we must. And DO NOT listen to those who tell you not to learn any more. Yes, we must be careful and boil things down to fit properly into the basic principles of the Gospel but do not be satisfied with how you understood those basics in Primary although they must not contradict Primary teachings. Joseph Smith revealed these words from the Lord in D&C 130:19: "And if a person gains more knowledge and intelligence in this life through his diligence and obedience than another, he will have so much the advantage in the world to

---

[231] www.mindspring.com/~mysticgryphon/bitakitu.htm

come." It must start here for all who have the opportunity. Heavenly Father needs us to make the difference.

We do not have to wait for specific callings to help strengthen Zion. Heavenly Father told us in the Doctrine and Covenants: "For behold it is not meet that I should command in all things; for he that is compelled in all things, the same is a slothful and not a wise servant; wherefore he receiveth no reward. Verily I say, men should be anxiously engaged in a good cause, and do many things of their own free will, and bring to pass much righteousness;" (D&C 58:26–27)

Help us spread the message of Zion. We must circle around the prophet, sustaining him with faith and prayers as he acts as God's representative on earth. At the same time, we work on our personal relationship with God so that we are endowed with light and power from above. In this manner that light combines and joins with all who are born of the Spirit and together, joined with the prophet, a cloud of protection forms around the center place to protect the altar that joins heaven and earth. Then, when necessary, in the moments of our greatest need, the Lord makes his arm bare like lightening in the midst of that cloud and a pillar of fire protects the encircling army of the Lord of Sabaoth, the Bride of Christ. This sacred union is the key for the renewal of life, energy and power as we walk through the valley of the shadow of death in the winding up scene.

In Celtic beliefs, the king in myth is 'married' to his kingdom in a ceremony at which a libation is offered him by his bride, Sovereignty. The Sovereignty of Ireland may appear as an ugly hag, symbol of the desolate and bloody kingdom. However, when kissed by the rightful claimant to kingship, she becomes a beautiful girl who reveals herself as a goddess.[232]

We can now more easily see the meaning of the parable of the Bridegroom and the ten virgins. This parable is so important in a legal sense. The Church of the Firstborn is the Bride of Christ by law so that those who participate in the symbolic Sacred Marriage can receive all the rights that would pertain to Christ by being His legal spouse. Thus we become joint-heirs and can receive all that the Father has to offer.

The Suffering King as the Center Place

---

[232] World Mythology, 186

As stated before, to begin a new creation, the first thing we need is the center place. This is symbolized by the throne, lion couch, Kolob, sun, etc. It is the point that pierces the veil like the point of a spear to claim a new territory…new space. It must be established. Facsimile 2, fig 4 represents the sun and also a boat, the firmament and 1000. We are gathered into Christ, encircled by His robes of righteousness and protected. As a part of the body of Christ, we can be lifted above the fall, escaping the spiritual grasp of the devil and the effects of the fall. We can enter into the presence of the Father spiritually, even though our feet remain in mortality.

To illustrate how this works picture the crystal throne sitting on top of the waters of chaos. Our foundation is Jesus Christ. He is the center place and His Atonement is the sacrifice. In order to set up an electro-magnetic field of protection, according to Pierre Curie, the discoverer of the piezo-electric effect, a force must be brought against the crystal quartz in the center. He, his brother Jacques, and his famous wife Madam Marie Curie, experimented with magnets placed at a distance around the quartz. The magnetic field produced a force that pressed against the quartz at the center, which pressure distorts the crystalline structure of the quartz. The crystal then releases voltage which interacts with the electro-magnetic field around it, creating a plasma field. This is the same process that creates our atmosphere. This is the breath of life which is a subject dwelt upon a great deal in ancient writing. It is the process of creating atmosphere. We do not have room in this book to explore all of the science behind this but we do assert that the temple does hold the framework of how to become a god/goddess and to create worlds.

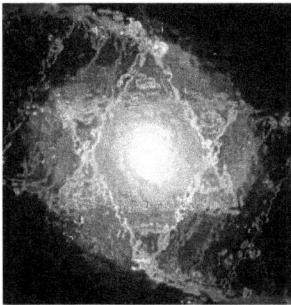

Let us take a metaphoric look at the Atonement in the Garden of Gethsemane. Christ had to suffer for our sins, taking them upon Himself like a great olive press. Encircled by olive trees, as the center place of the sacred garden, He is the one who was pressed. The other trees can also become a tree of life eventually as they stay centered around the Lord. Although those trees (representing those seeking sanctification) will also have fruit that will be pressed, they will not have to bear the full weight of that press. Theirs will be an arrested sacrifice so they will not have to suffer even as He did. The pressure of that force against the Lord's physical body caused the capillaries in His body to burst and blood seeped from every pour. Like the finest virgin olive oil that comes from the fruit of that sacred tree being pressed upon, energy is released, and the Father's anointed one becomes the center place, the crystal throne around which we circle. There is an exchange of energy, like the circle of electro-magnetic force around quartz to cause the piezo-electric effect. A cleansed and purified sacred space is established and a shield of protection like a cloud by day around a pillar of fire comes from the altar.

Star of David logo[233]

The Star of David according to Nibley is the union of two triangles representing the Bride and the Bridegroom as well as the visible and invisible world.[234] He also equates the Star of David with the throne and the shield of Solomon as an instrument of protection.[235] This illustrates the concept that the male aspect (sun/altar/throne) and female aspect (Milky Way river of energy around the sun) work together to form a protection. The pillar of fire and the cloud worked together to protect Israel.

It took the Son of God, coming in physical form, to offer Himself in righteousness and purity to take up His place at the center and become our new and higher foundation. As we reorient ourselves toward Christ, we are lifted above this fallen earth and the waters of chaos and we are rooted in like palm trees around the waters of life that come from that central position at the altar. Olive trees describe some aspects of this process and palm trees describe other aspects. Waving our palm branches high, we give voice to our testimonies that here is where the weary world can find refuge from the parched wilderness to partake of that water necessary for eternal life where we never thirst again. Come to the temple of the Lord, a spot of ground redeemed from the fall where we gather around Christ in great energy and faith. Like Brigham Young and Heber C. Kimball upon Ensign Mountain, let us raise our banners and wave to the world so they may enter the sacred gates and be lifted up. As the world darkens, the weary and thirsty need our help, so as saviors on Mount Zion we must reach out to them and pull them into spiritual safety where they can be refreshed with the waters of life: "Lift ye up a banner upon the high mountain, exalt the voice unto them, shake the hand, that they may go into the gates of the nobles." (2 Ne. 23:2)

---

[233] (used by permission. The Star of David logo was designed by Contois Reynolds of Hamlin, WV, and is protected worldwide by copyright)

[234] Nibley, *One Eternal Round,* 625–626
[235] Nibley, *One Eternal Round,* 626

The ongoing power of the Atonement centers us on that higher level of the Mountain of the Lord's House. If we press forward and continue our journey up Jacob's ladder of sanctification, we will be rooted in like a new tree of life and join in Zion unity around Jesus Christ. Then how beautiful upon that mountain are our feet, cleansed from the waters of chaos, anchored around the center place with hearts unified in love toward each other. With Zion focusing inward toward the altar, the interaction between that circle, representing the Bride of Christ (cloud) and the Bridegroom at the center (pillar of fire), then the Lord will make His arm bare. When done in perfect faith and unity, it can bring about an energy that opens a vortex to Heaven and our beloved Heavenly Father. Then dear brothers and sisters, we are standing in holy places . . . temples ourselves. This endowment of power clothes charity upon the initiate. This bright grace, when unified in a Zion unity, is that city on a hill that gives light to the world.

The 12th chapter of *The Book of Ether* illustrates this process in a sacred and powerful manner and brings us back to the basics of the Gospel, showing that they are indeed the true mysteries of the Gospel. It may be interesting to read the whole chapter after studying these next few paragraphs. Those verses have taken on a new meaning to us since we have learned the pattern that Nibley identified.

First, we must unify together in great faith, reflecting upon the Atoning sacrifice that was made for us that we might not have to suffer as He suffered. Then, as one we use that faith to concentrate on Christ as the center place and unite and focus our hope like a laser beam. Like King Benjamin making covenants before God for the assembled people or the Jewish high priest who voices the feelings in the hearts of the people yearly on Yom Kippur, the Day of Atonement, we unite through the voice of the great high priest here upon the earth. This is the prophet who holds the priesthood keys or one authorized to act in that office. We hope for good and specific things, calling upon the Father to bless us and those who need help.

The energy of a circuit that is unbroken, spinning in a clockwise manner produces current that spins, creating a vortex in the middle like spinning a bucket of water. Christ is the door and it is He who brings us before the Father when we are ready but we can have a taste of that now. The power of the Atonement can bridge heaven and earth and if we do our part, the interaction between our faith and hope in Christ will open an effectual door so that we can then be clothed upon with charity, which is a gift from God. If we do all else in our own power to be saved, lifted to a higher level of sanctification but we have not charity, then Paul's words apply to us: I am become as sounding brass, or a tinkling symbol (1 Corinthians 13:1) it is all for naught.

Why? Because if we are clothed upon with charity, then this is the witness that heaven and earth were indeed joined on our behalf through our faith and hope so that we received the reward of that effort which is the grace of God which we cannot earn but is given as a gift.

There is a perfect blending of works and grace in this process. If we bring forth fruits with a pure heart as did Abel and not in resentment as did Cain, that action results in our qualifying for the grace of God, a gift we cannot earn but is freely given. Our part is to do those things necessary to be cleansed from this fallen earth so no corruption will be introduced into heaven. In this manner we are prepared to be a smaller circle of the pattern with our own eternal creations as we stand as the center place for our families. Thankfully, the lion throne at the center is a gift of God given without us having to endure the lion couch of suffering upon which our Savior was stretched out in agony in Gethsemane and upon the cross. All depictions of the Suffering King at the New Year Rites go directly to the Lord and His Atonement which is in effect from the foundation of the universe, overcoming time and space. **Praise be to the Son who finished the work and drank the bitter cup, becoming the sweet waters of life for all who love and serve Him.**

The blood of sacrifice becomes the pure water that cleanses us from filth. The seed of corruption brings about the Second law of thermodynamics, as Nibley explained so well throughout the first chapter of Temple and Cosmos. The natural breaking down of all things is due to corruption. The Atonement of Christ cleanses us through His blood so that we can be redeemed from the fall and rejoin the Father and the Son for all eternity. We do not have to wait until death to enjoy the fruit of this process, which is peace, security and stability. We must remain humble and realize that after all we can do, it is not enough and takes the intercession of Christ to make up the difference: "For we labor diligently to write, to persuade our children, and also our brethren, to believe in Christ, and to be reconciled to God; for we know that it is by grace that we are saved, after all we can do." (2 Ne. 25:23) We cannot save ourselves. We must leave the natural man behind and step onto the sure foundation in that sunboat of Facsimile 2 so we can escape the chaos:

15 And now I, Jacob, am led on by the Spirit unto prophesying; for I perceive by the workings of the Spirit which is in me, that by the stumbling of the Jews they will reject the stones upon which they might build and have safe foundation.

16 But behold, according to the scriptures, this stone shall become the great, and the last, and the only sure foundation, upon which the Jews can build. (Jacob 4:15–16)

According to the **Sefer Yetzirah**, the interaction between the heavenly fire and the earthly water brings about the center place in the middle. This intermediary position is where air, the breath of life, is created from that interaction and a place of safety and cleansing set up. It is the door which allows those prepared for heavenly fire through being clothed upon with light and glory, to receive the presence of God without danger. It is a temple, or terrestrial condition.

There are a few passages in **The Book of Mormon** that have confused us through the years that only made sense in light of the pattern of the Three Pillars of the Gospel. It would seem that this sacred book is saying that Jesus is both the Father and the Son. It is easy to see the confusion of the early Christians in light of the following concept. The Savior is the Father of creation and the representative in authority and voice for Heavenly Father here upon the earth. He is also the Son because of the flesh. We feel that means that the office of the Son of God requires the physical presence of the anointed one (Messiah) so that He, the Great Suffering King, can offer Himself to be pressed as are olives, in order to bring forth the power of cleansing and healing protection necessary for salvation. We read in Mosiah:

2 And because he dwelleth in flesh he shall be called the Son of God, and having subjected the flesh to the will of the Father, being the Father and the Son—

3 The Father, because he was conceived by the power of God; and the Son, because of the flesh; thus becoming the Father and Son—

4 And they are one God, yea, the very Eternal Father of heaven and of earth.

5 And thus the flesh becoming subject to the Spirit, or the Son to the Father, being one God, suffereth temptation, and yieldeth not to the temptation, but suffereth himself to be mocked, and scourged, and cast out, and disowned by his people. (Mos. 15: 2-5)

So brothers and sisters, as Joseph wrote:

Brethren, shall we not go on in so great a cause? Go forward and not backward. Courage, brethren; and on, on to the victory! Let your hearts rejoice, and be exceedingly glad. Let the earth break forth into singing. Let the dead speak forth anthems of eternal praise to the King Immanuel, who hath ordained, before the world was, that which would enable us to redeem them out of their prison; for the prisoners shall go free. (D&C 128:22)

Shall we not do our part as the Bride that surrounds the holy altar of our God, the great throne of sacrifice? Through the power of the Bridegroom, we can help bring forth the faith and focus that will distill the powers of the priesthood upon our souls as the dews from heaven. (D&C 21:45) If we do this, our tree is watered and will grow into a Tree of Life. Standing in holy places, as an effectual temple of God, we can thus invite our loved ones to shelter beneath our boughs as they press forward in their own efforts to climb Jacob's ladder which is the process of sanctification. Even many of our loved ones who reject those efforts will find themselves gathering for emotional support as future events unfold.

Lifting our voices as spiritual Zion, the congregation of the north will be that city set on the hill by the Rainbow Bridge to give light in the darkness, so we must not fear the world but be watchmen and sing together as the cloud by day so that in times of darkness the pillar of fire will be our defense as the Lord makes bare His holy arm:

29 Yea, Lord, thy watchmen shall lift up their voice; with the voice together shall they sing; for they shall see eye to eye, when the Lord shall bring again Zion.

30 Break forth into joy, sing together, ye waste places of Jerusalem; for the Lord hath comforted his people, he hath redeemed Jerusalem.

31 The Lord hath made bare his holy arm in the eyes of all the nations; and all the ends of the earth shall see the salvation of our God. (Mos. 15:29-31)

The king had to suffer in order to be planted as the foundation of his people but he did not have to suffer to the degree the Chief Cornerstone of that foundation did. The Bride will go through great trials but never on the scale of the Bridegroom. Nibley quoted from the Acts of John:

You must see Me as I suffer, what I suffer, who I am, and then ye shall know that I go hence. Then he gave them certain signs, and he took their hands and said, 'Know my suffering and thou shalt have the power not to suffer. I will be crucified so that you won't have to be. You will merely be in token,' he says.

'That which thou knowest I myself will teach thee.'[236] The cycles of the seasons teach us about death and resurrection. Here the mountain becomes the symbol of these things:

---

[236] Nibley, *Temple and Cosmos,* 315

Autumn Offering

Crowned with sun disk
yellow as September aspen,
the dying mountain
bleeds crimson leaves
across its back.

Red flows down
canyons and ravines
to valley floor where we
glean golden fields.

In fading light
we build a hedge against
dark winter nights
dreary as Golgotha, grateful
for Nature's annual offering
that guarantees us spring.

© Sharon Price Anderson

Chapter Six: The Firmament

As the Oregon rains would drizzle down the school bus window, I would count the drops as I was first learning my numbers. It was a long trip to the farm and I had plenty of time to practice. That began my love for numbers and math in general. All that good feeling abruptly left in eighth grade when we began studying algebra. What were those letters doing there and why use parentheses? Strings of mystical formulas made my head spin.

Raising my hand, I asked the teacher to explain what the purpose of algebra was. His answer was to wait a few years and it would all make sense. I tried again. What are the letters for? Another obscure answer…you will understand some day. The sad results; my brain immediate shut off like a switch had been flipped.

Years later, when I needed algebra for college, I told my husband about this incident and that my brain seemed to work in a certain way that was not conducive to algebra. I needed to see the bigger picture…a general framework before I could fit the pieces in and make sense out of a subject. Understanding this about me, he patiently showed me a number of applications for algebra, then he demonstrated the purpose of the letters. I could almost hear the hum of the gears beginning to move in my head as the switch flipped on after years of being dormant when it came to math. Suddenly math made sense again and I did well in my algebra classes.

In pondering how to share the information in this chapter on the firmament, I was reminded of this story from my life and felt I should use the same principles for our readers. Studying dry details about the formula of creating a firmament would not appeal to many. Therefore, let us share the reason we are about to break down this subject. The application of this knowledge is what we need to know in order to create a bubble of protection around ourselves, our loved ones, the Church and eventually the whole earth. Indeed, this is the very knowledge necessary to help us eventually create worlds. We can use this information this very day to reap fruits of peace. Winds may swirl around us but if we stand within that place of protection, we will not "reap the whirlwind," unless we are in one of the necessary Gethsemane moments. But even then, we need to understand that if we are standing in holy places, even those Gethsemane moments are sacred and the bounds are set so the enemy cannot cross a certain line.

Throughout the ages, scholars and sages have pondered and debated the meaning and purpose of the firmament. For most people, the firmament holds little interest and is usually believed to be simply the atmosphere between space and the earth. While this may answer one aspect of the definition, there is enough information sprinkled throughout ancient writings to suggest that the complete meaning of 'firmament' is far more complex and mostly remains a mystery. We believe the time has come for the mystery of this illusive concept to be understood and used since it is time to create a new, spiritual firmament, as we once helped create the first creation under the direction of the Lord and Father Michael. That means we must study. This information cannot be spoon fed to us as if we were babies but must be chewed on as meat. Once we do this and learn how perfectly 2012 fits into the idea of a firmament of time, we begin to see confirmation everywhere we turn. This pattern is attested to by every discipline of study we have examined to the point of being overwhelming.

We will attempt to establish the definition of a 'firmament' as a sacred space and time, set apart and protected either for the sanctified living or for the dead. Showing a number of motifs, especially a ship, we will attempt to explain what the firmament is and also its purpose.

Although gaining greater insight to any possible hidden meaning behind the firmament may seem to some readers to be an interesting factoid, many would probably question the pertinence of such information in their life. The possibility that the answer could actually hold vital keys to understanding the LDS temple endowment may seem a stretch yet this is just what we hope to accomplish. The firmament is a key of spiritual protection for us and our loved ones. To begin, we will take a look at some scholars' general idea of the firmament. The final chapter of this book will tie in the concepts we are sharing and show how to use these principles specifically to protect our families.

Some may question how it is we can protect loved ones who have chosen not to live the Gospel. Lehi and his children provide a very good example to help us understand. If our loved ones doubt the Gospel or have weak testimonies but they trust us enough to have some unity with us, they can come under temporary protection. Laman, Lemuel and other rebellious members of Lehi's family did get into that boat to the Promised Land. If we think of earth's transition to a terrestrial condition, we know that it will take time to cleanse and separate the righteous from the wicked. It was not until Lehi's family had been in the new land for a while and Lehi had actually passed on that there was a physical separation. So, it would seem that eventually our friends and family will have to choose one side of the fence or the other but for a time, there may be protection in the ship of Zion for them if they make some effort to avail themselves of the Spirit that attends those who stand in holy places.

Order verses Chaos

The firmament may be shown in many types and shadows from something as flimsy and ethereal as a cloud, to the most solid dome of gold but in all the different concepts, it is considered a barrier that is impassable unless one is authorized to enter. Thomas O. Lambdin, a Hebrew scholar, wrote that the firmament has been "apparently considered as a solid barrier by the cosmographers of Genesis."[237]

The firmament seems to represent the process of bringing order out of chaos. The creation of the firmament, according to Susan Brayford, a professor of religious studies, was not a moment's work, but was a process in which, "creation then takes place by giving things order, function and purpose." [238] "The word *cosmos*, attributed to Pythagoras, meant originally 'Order'... This idea was developed as the correspondence between the Macrocosmos (the World) and the Microcosmos, or Man, with sometimes the Temple as link... again the basic quest of religion, to establish a 'link' between mortal man and the imperishable worlds."[239] If the firmament represented order, it was the sea that was a symbol for chaos.[240] This idea is also found in the Babylonian Talmud which declares, "the sea represents an element of chaos."[241]

---

[237] Thomas O. Lambdin, *Introduction to Biblical Hebrew*, Harvard University, Darton, Longman, & Todd, 1973, 74

[238] Susan Brayford, *Genesis, Septuagint Commentary Series*, Brill 2007 Leiden, Boston, Mass., 156

[239] Nibley, *One Eternal Round,* 267–8

[240] *Dictionary of the Old Testament Pentateuch*, Editors: T. Desmond Alexander and David W. Baker, InterVarsity Press, Downers Grove, Illinois, Leicester, England, 2003

[241] In Babylonian, Canaanite and Egyptian literature, the sea represents an element of chaos. The Mesopotamian sea is personified in the Akkadian deity Tiamat (though the god determinative is not used with her name in the theogony of Enuma Elish). The Egyptian chaos-ocean is personified in Nun, who has neither cult nor temple, and the Canaanite sea is personified in Yam, the enemy of Baal. In the creation account in Genesis, the sea (tehom) is a primordial element but is neither deified nor personified. The tehom represents chaos only as a disorder, not as a threatening, combative enemy (as Tiamat becomes in Enuma Elish),

Many scholars believe that while some parts of the creation were formed quickly, the firmament was something to be established in a process. This fits in perfectly with 2012 being the seed of the new firmament that has its completion at the actual Second Coming.

The Firmament was once believed to have a hard protective covering that separates the atmosphere from the waters below and above. To most ancient Hebrews, firmament or expanse "suggests a firm vault or dome over the earth. According to ancient belief, this vault, which held the stars, provided the boundary beyond which the divine dwelt." [242] Even with scientific advancements, this old idea will not die and enters into much of modern discussion.

Susan Brayford describes the firmament as the "generative power" that separates the water. Until the firmament is created, the water is all one body. It takes strength and firmness to keep the water separate and this is where Brayford believes the idea of a solid structure stems from.[243] For us, this is where Zion and the priesthood power (with man and woman joined in faith) come in to create the strength denoted by a firm dome.

The most prevalent belief found among modern scholars regarding the firmament is that it is simply a description of the expanse above the earth. Biblical Commentaries are heavily leaning toward using 'expanse' in place of 'firmament' in biblical translations and discussions with many simply calling it 'sky.[244] When discussing rituals involving the firmament, it is usually thought that they are simply an elaborate way to describe the sky.

Firmament-Representing Ritual

Michael D. Rhodes, professor of ancient scripture at BYU, stresses the ritual aspect of the firmament or expanse, especially leaning on *The Book of Abraham* and the facsimiles. In fact, he appears to indicate that Facsimile 2 (the hypocephalus) is describing a firma-

---

nor as the source from which creation emerges, as in Egypt. *The Babylonian Talmud, Seder Mo-ed Vol. IV, Rosh Hashanah*, Editor, Rabbi Dr. I Epstein, The Soncino Press, London, published 1938, 2.3 Sea, 158

[242] *The Torah, A Modern Commentary*, Edited by W. Gunther Plaut, Union of American Hebrew Congregations, New York, 1981, 18
[243] Brayford, *Septuagint,* 210
[244] Plaut, *The Torah,* 18

ment.[245] Rhodes ties the Apocalypse of Abraham[246] to the Book of Abraham and the hypocephalus, describing the vision showing the firmament. Rhodes also defends Joseph Smith's description of the firmament in Facsimile 2, figure 4.[247]

Creation is a teaching aid to help Latter-day Saints' instruction. Nibley illustrated the point that the structure of the creation should be viewed in light of temple teachings. He says each level of the firmament is a concentric circle, and each level reflects the others. "The king is a revelation of the godhead he incorporates."[248]

Then what is a firmament? It is a safe habitat for life. In one of my Hebrew classes at BYU, my professor was discussing the illusive concept of the firmament and how it has been the topic of mystery throughout known time. I admitted that I was doing a paper on it and he asked what I had concluded. When I suggested it was a temple state, a terrestrial condition of protection from chaos, he said that from his studies, he believed I had it right.

From the book *Temple and Cosmos*, recommended by Thomas S. Monson, we learn more about why we must become temples. We are living at the exact time when we must have temples to bring order out of chaos, and this means both the buildings and the human type.

Within the respected apocryphal work *Ascension of Isaiah*, we can see that through the principle of divine investiture, each of the seven firmaments had a throne in the middle upon which was a representative of Christ, surrounded by angels in a prayer circle singing praises. Each firmament was brighter than the one immediately below it. Why only seven and not eight? Seven firmaments are seven heavens which are reflections of the great heaven above where the Father resides. We believe that the level above seven reflects the various branches as initiates are qualified to become eternal fathers and mothers and spread out into space to begin their own creations or have the promise of that future capability. The Abrahamic Covenant would seem to explain this concept. A future promised land of our own, and eternal seed is that high goal.

There are many ancient traditions that reflect the concept of seven heavens. The idea of a rainbow bridge that joins the highest

---

[245] Michael D. Rhodes, *The Book of Abraham: Divinely Inspired Scripture*, FARMS Review: Volume-4, Issue – 1, 1992, 120–26

[246] This is an ancient religious work attributed to Abraham but is regarded as pseudepigrapha (falsely attributed).

[247] Rhodes, *The Book of Abraham*, 120–126

[248] Nibley, *Abraham in Egypt*, 415

heaven and earth is one we have touched on. The Australian Aborigines, the Japanese Shinto religion, the seven days of the week, the seven tones of the major scale, the seven stars of the Pleiades and many other examples help illustrate the point. The idea of joining heaven and earth is also found within Nibley's teachings on the Facsimiles.

The Facsimiles

First, let us look at the Facsimiles from *The Book of Abraham*, beginning with facsimile 1. It may be natural to suppose that the gap in lines of the river in Facsimile 1 was purposeful in order to write the number 12 for which the following explanation is given: "Raukeeyang, signifying expanse, or the firmament over our heads; but in this case, in relation to this subject, the Egyptians meant it to signify Shaumau, to be high, or the heavens, answering to the Hebrew word, Shaumahyeem."[249] An assumption that the gap for '12' was not a purposeful part of the facsimile and only a convenience for writing the number would presuppose that firmament was synonymous with water, river or sea. This would not coincide with the account from Gen. 1:6–8:

6¶And God said, Let there be a firmament in the midst of the waters, and let it divide the waters from the waters.

7And God made the firmament, and divided the waters which *were* under the firmament from the waters which *were* above the firmament: and it was so.

8And God called the firmament Heaven. And the evening and the morning were the second day.

The scriptural account affirms that the firmament is not the water but a place within yet separated from the water. Facsimile 2 also suggests that the firmament is not the water but a place of protection provided within the water. Figure 4 depicts a boat but not just any kind. Like the Ark of Noah, and the Ark of the Covenant and the barges of the Jaredites, this is a closed vessel to protect those within, not only from the waters below but also from the waters above. Joseph Smith's explanation of figure 4 in Facsimile 2 expresses the idea of a firmament: "*4.* Answers to the Hebrew word Raukeeyang, signifying expanse, or the firmament of the heavens; also a numerical figure, in Egyptian signifying one thousand; answering to the measuring of the

---

[249] The Pearl of Great Price, 28

time of Oliblish, which is equal with Kolob in its revolution and in its measuring of time."[250]

The focus is on the ship. Thus, it may be logical to view the space within the water in Facsimile 1 as the firmament Joseph Smith is referring to. That space would need to be a sort of bubble of protection from the water and also from the crocodile within the river. The blood-thirsty beast makes a good analogy for the need for the initiate within the ship to be cleansed from the blood and sins of his generation[251] so that he/she does not attract unwanted attention. The role of the crocodile is crucial to the process. It is his job to keep unclean things from crossing the river and entering the portals of heaven.[252]

The story of Moses and Israel applies to this concept of 'firmament'. If Egypt is seen as a symbol for the world under control of the counterfeit ruler, then Israel escaping that telestial place through the Red Sea could be seen as a type for baptism. The wilderness is not their ultimate goal although it brings a measure of safety and for our purposes could be seen as a terrestrial state. The Ark of the Covenant, if seen as a symbol for a boat carried upon its staves, could help us envision the desert experience as a river to cross to reach the Promised Land, returning to the place of their fathers, which could symbolize our ultimate return to Heavenly Father and the Celestial Kingdom.

Israel did not take a straight course to the Promised Land but instead followed a circular path, circumambulating about the Ark of the Covenant, which could typify a prayer circle around the altar of the temple. The forty years in the wilderness recalls the 40 week gestation time for a new birth. Israel completed her tomb/womb journey and was reborn into a higher condition. The firmament, a temporary place for the weary to sojourn and progress, meets with many of the types of Israel's wilderness experiences. Moses stood as a representative of Christ, a 'Sent One', and Israel was organized around him. When the time came for the final crossing up into the land of Promise, it was not the representative, but Yeshua himself who led Israel. Indeed it was not the actual Savior but the name Joshua would seem to suggest this type.

In Figure 4 of Facsimile 2, and also on the Ark of the Covenant, protective wings are placed over the ship or ark as a powerful protection from enemies. The ship itself may be seen as a tomb or womb, carrying the sacred dead. Christ referred to the role of protective wings: "O Jerusalem, Jerusalem, which killest the prophets, and stonest them

---

[250] The Pearl of Great Price. p. 36
[251] See D&C 88:85
[252] Facsimile 1, figure 11; pillars

that are sent unto thee; how often would I have gathered thy children together, as a hen doth gather her brood under her wings, and ye would not!"[253]

Facsimile 2 from the *Book of Abraham*

A sacred city of light set on a hill could be another example of the idea of 'firmament'. A city of the sanctified is protected by wings of a mother figure or a winged sun disk in many Egyptian motifs. In their mythology, the sun disk spreads its winged over the solar boats on their travels.[254] Anubis takes the initiate by the hand and guides him into the presence of the throne where his heart is weighed in the balance. If his heart weighs more than the feather of truth, then he is devoured by the god of pharaoh waiting in the Nile River.[255]

---

[253] Luke 13:34
[254] Tomb of Ramses VI (c. 1150 B.C.)
[255] Willis, *World Mythology*, 55

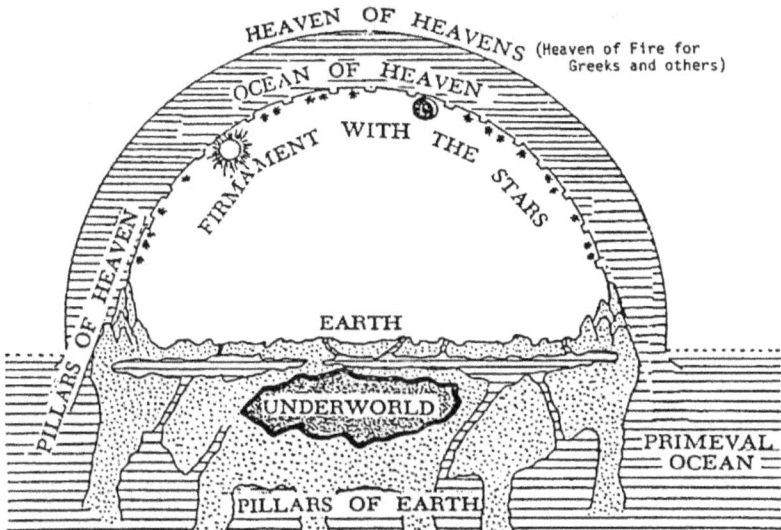

The Inuit Native Americans equate feathers and stars together and show them as the boundary about the Cosmos.[256] Feathers, stars, as well as similar symbols seem to represent the protection which comes from the unification of sanctified individuals acting as gate keepers. The only initiates who would be allowed to enter in are those who have the name and countenance of Christ. I would suggest that the endowment of light and power is the key that unlocks entrance into the higher firmaments. The crown of light upon the head of the king is the birthing place as the initiate is reborn in an upward direction. A king gives birth to new kings as jewels in his crown or for Native American chiefs, as feathers in his headdress. This upward birthing sheds more meaning on the Psalmists words that we mentioned before but hopefully have more meaning now: "Lift up your heads, O ye gates; and be ye lift up, ye everlasting doors; and the King of glory shall come in."[257]

Facsimile 3 is one of a myriad of examples in Egyptology that show either wings covering the hidden sacred space or a line of stars accomplishing the same purpose. Thus, the stars of the firmament are the boundaries of protection for the initiates within, as are the feathered wings of various birds who cover and watch over the sanctified. This process is also described in a different way by the Egyptians, using the ancient Hermetic teachings. Purity of heart, prayerfulness and other virtues are necessary after passing through the gate and traversing the path.

---

[256] Mythology, *The Illustrated Anthology of World Myth and Storytelling*, General Editor C. Scott Littleton, 497
[257] Psalm 24:7

The idea of a set apart place for the dead is familiar to those who study mythology. Valhalla, Odin's Hall from Norse legend is not the part of heaven where God resides but somewhere in between.[258] The same is true for the Egyptian teachings of the Hall of Osiris or Hall of Maati. A ship is a good symbol for the state of being where one is separate from this mortal world and in a place where they progress and travel back to the presence of the Father.

The Sefer Yetzirah

It is time to tie the idea of the firmament into Abraham's ancient book. The clue to unlocking a deeper understanding of the firmament is found in the **Sefer Yetzirah.** It is the earliest mystical writing that has been handed down and is believed to be the foundation for many of the rabbinical writings and especially the kabalistic doctrines. Jewish tradition holds that it was written by the hand of Abraham, some believing him to have received the information through means of a seer stone.[259]

Nibley makes it clear in his book **One Eternal Round** that the hypocephalus (Facsimile 2) is all about creating a firmament of protection. He also states that there is a group of documents to which the hypocephalus surely belongs and the oldest and greatest of them all is the **Sefer Yetzirah**.[260] Although it is clear that Nibley understands this mysterious and sacred writing, he says that the **Sefer Yetzirah** remains a sealed book[261] and from our studies, it does seem that its pages remain a mystery. We are convinced that Nibley's writings hold the key to unlock that mystery. It is a blueprint for creation, thus a temple text.[262]

The firmament is a series of concentric circles, one above the other. (Concentric: Of or denoting circles, arcs, or other shapes that share the same center, the larger often completely surrounding the smaller. Concentric does not describe the diagram below. Instead of concentric could it be said "The firmament is series of circles oriented on the same axis.") Nibley goes on to say there are seven chambers in the universe and above the seventh is a sapphire stone with the great

---

[258] Littleton, *Illustrated Anthology*, 280
[259] http://www.wordiq.com/definition/Sefer_Yetzirah
[260] Nibley, *One Eternal Round*, 504
[261] Ibid, 505
[262] Ibid, 507

ETERNAL PROGRESSION
UP HIGHER DIMENSIONS

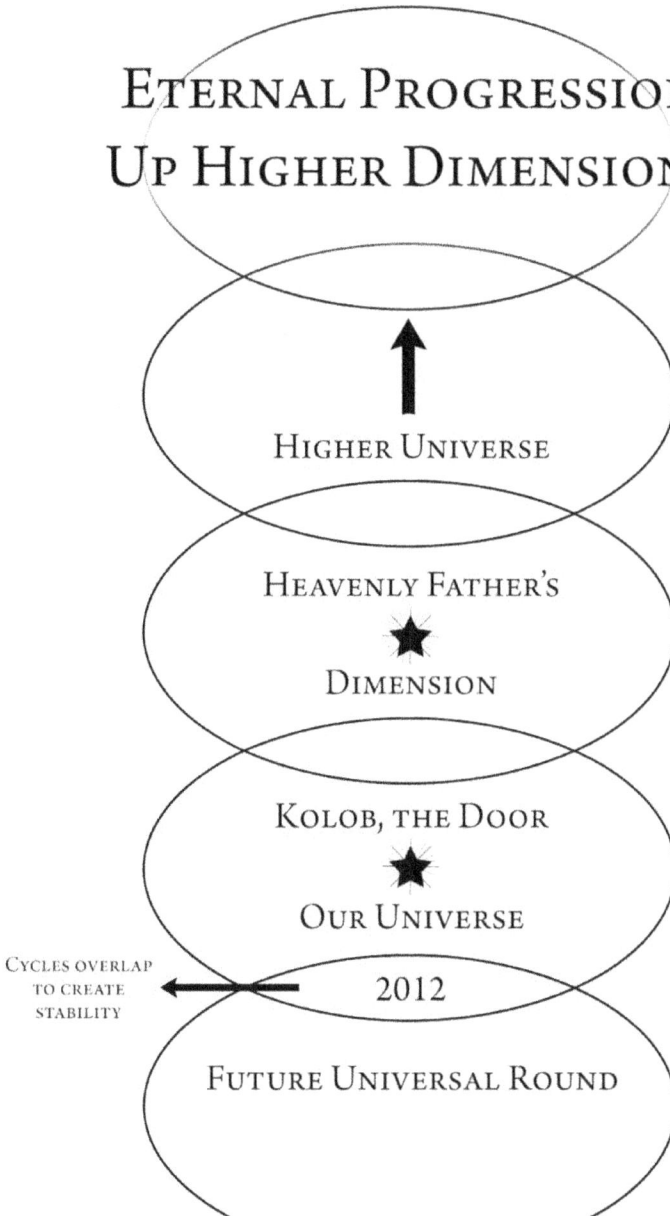

HIGHER UNIVERSE

HEAVENLY FATHER'S

DIMENSION

KOLOB, THE DOOR

OUR UNIVERSE

CYCLES OVERLAP
TO CREATE
STABILITY

2012

FUTURE UNIVERSAL ROUND

throne above that.[263] The creation accounts of the firmament say there are waters below (waters of chaos) and waters above the firmament. This would seem to support that idea that there is a veil-like separation of the universe above which Heavenly Father lives. We know that Jesus is the door to the Father, so it would make sense that Kolob is the door to the higher realm. Nibley explained that the **Sefer Yetzirah** is a science book about the fundamental make up of the Cosmos.[264]

When each universal round is completed and there is a new heaven and a new earth, it appears that everyone who is faithful moves up one dimension...thus there is eternal progression, even for those already perfected. Centuries ago, Rabbi Rava[265] stated that from the **Sefer Yetzirah**, we have knowledge to be able to create our own worlds. In the book, Abraham describes three mothers and their role in preparing a soup, or initiate to come back to the presence of God. The following is from chapter three of the **Sefer Yetzirah** in its original Hebrew:

שלש אמהות א, מ, ש: יסודתן כף זכות וכף חובה ולשון חק מכריע בינתים.

שלש אמהות א, מ, ש סוד גדול מופלא ומכוסה וחתום בשש טבעות ומהם יצא אויר ומים ואש ומהם נולדו אבות ומאבות תולדות.

שלש אמהות א, מ, ש ומתן כרעם: אש למעלה שא רוח אויר תולדות, מים האראצ תולדות, מים שהמיס.

שלש אותיות דוסי, שרושתו ותישם עשרים:
ש, מ, א שלש פשוטות ב יו תכולות ושבע אמות

צח ב"חקק ןצבה ק"יצר ן הקלש"ן
צלר: העתיד וכל ריציה פנש בהו וצו רימהו צרפ"ו שקל"ן

My translation of Chapter 3, above is as follows:

Twenty-two signs are the foundation, three mothers, seven doubles, and twelve singles.

[263] Nibley, *One Eternal Round*, 510–511
[264] Ibid, 512
[265] Ibid, 513
[266] http://www.hebrew.grimoar.cz/jecira/sefer_jecira.htm

Three mothers, namely; aleph, mem, shin. The history (make-up, or attribute) of heaven is fire, the history (attribute) of earth is water, the history of the light of the air or spirit.

Fire ascends, water for a staff (rod) and air a binding covenant made.

Three mothers, aleph, mem, shin. Mem is silent and still. Shin is whistling or hissing, aleph is a binding covenant made.

The three mothers, they are the foundation. Purity and innocence are balanced and weighted in the palm of the hand, obligation and duty are balanced in the palm of their hand, and with the spoken language is the binding covenant made.

Twenty-two signs are the foundation, engraven on stone. Each soul is hewn, weighted, refined as metal, redeemed and formed, created, prepared and destined to be a stone in the rock fortress.

Relating the above translation to 'firmament', the water below would be the fallen, telestial world. The waters of baptism draw us as a lotus or a reed-like staff out of the condition of spiritual death and birth us into a new life. The baptism of fire would equate to the heavenly state of fire that continued the process of purification. The mother in the middle, that of spirit or air is where the initiate is weighed and balanced and through temple covenants is prepared to be a stone in the fortress of the firmament.

The idea of being a part of a fortress was familiar to the prophet Peter. He wrote of the process of being quarried as a stone in the temple on that foundation rock: "Ye also, as lively stones, are built up a spiritual house, an holy priesthood, to offer up spiritual sacrifices, acceptable to God by Jesus Christ."[267]

Nibley was saddened by the LDS community's inattention and outright hostility toward the *Sefer Yetzirah*.[268] This writer had experience with the same attitude when I shared the above Hebrew selection in a scholarly setting. It was then that I realized I would never be accepted by the scholarly community and was glad that my path had diverged from the planned PhD. I would never have been allowed to study the things Heavenly Father wished for me to learn about and expound upon.

---

[267] 1 Peter 2:5
[268] Nibley, *One Eternal Round*, 514

Feast of the Tabernacles

The Feast of Tabernacles has all the aspects of the above verses in the ***Sefer Yetzirah***. The water from below is drawn up and purified by the burning altar of sacrifice. Covenants made by individuals and by Israel as they circumambulate in the courtyard make a strong typology for the prayer circle which brings the energy and faith to bring light, as the city on a hill, for the entire world to see. Through the power of the sacrifice, initiates can be spiritually born again through these covenants, receiving the breath of life as a newborn babe. This air is a crucial part of the creation of a firmament or a sacred space. Just like the Jaredite barges opening at the top for air whenever the boat would resurface, the sacrifice is a joining of heaven and earth, allowing an opening for sacred air to symbolically flow into the temple.

Much of the subject of creating sacred space deals with the theme of the protection that comes from becoming a temple of God and indeed, the tremendous power and necessity of uniting with others who are in that sanctified, Zion state in order to help bring to pass the Second Coming amid tremendous opposition.

The ascension process is the series of steps necessary to return to the presence of God. As the solar boat from Facsimile 2, figure 4 ascends through the opening of the cross at the center up to heaven, the initiates become purer and are clothed upon with a greater endowment of light until they are prepared to stand in the presence of God. Comparing the above selection from the ***Sefer Yetzirah*** to the Feast of the Tabernacles can help us put many of the ascension pieces together to begin seeing the bigger picture.

According to the many sources we examined, the Feast of the Tabernacles (booths or sukkot) seems to represent the binding of heaven and earth, creating a sacred space of protection for the righteous and the penitent to stand in holy places. The sukkot, as a symbol for the Tree of Life, is a door for the dews of heaven to distill upon the booths.[269] If enough people are righteous, their booths, as a collective forest of trees of life create a cloud of protection as representatives of the true and living water; Christ. Nephi, in interpreting the dream of the Tree of Life, freely exchanged that tree with a fountain of pure water.

---

[269] D&C 121:45

"And it came to pass that I beheld that the rod of iron, which my father had seen, was the word of God, which led to the fountain of living waters, or to the tree of life; which waters are a representation of the love of God;"[270]

The Book of Mormon, in a number of places, describes baptism a little differently than the Bible. Baptism is broken down into three parts; baptism of water, of fire and the Holy Ghost. These can be seen as three mothers who bring forth the initiate into a higher rebirth. Three baptisms in one could be seen as shorthand for three separate, major rebirths. We read in 3 Nephi the particulars of the breakdown of the baptism of fire and of the Holy Ghost. "And ye shall offer for a sacrifice unto me a broken heart and a contrite spirit. And whoso cometh unto me with a broken heart and a contrite spirit, him will I baptize with fire and with the Holy Ghost, even as the Lamanites, because of their faith in me at the time of their conversion, were baptized with fire and with the Holy Ghost, and they knew it not."[271]

Baptism of water happens in a moment after a period of preparation. Baptism of fire seems to be a process of purification. These correlate to the two mothers from the *Sefer Yetzirah*, water and fire. The last is the covenant in the middle or temple covenants. Being born of the Holy Ghost comes after the baptism of fire. With the firmament of protection (created by water and fire) completed, the initiate is ready to be born of the Holy Ghost within the enclosed sacred space in the middle. Perhaps it could be symbolized by the initiate being born from the temple, now becoming a temple him/herself, so that they are a representative of Christ, a Tree of Life, a booth of protection for their loved ones.

The above process brings to mind the trial of Shadrach, Meshach and Abed-nego, who refused to worship a golden image as a god and were thrown into a very hot furnace.[272] Their spiritual state is made very clear since they not only are not singed but also have the presence of the Lord to attend them. For the initiate to be prepared for a celestial glory, which is eternal burnings, they must be refined as gold, brought forth from the solar boat and clothed upon as a sun.

Book of the Dead

---

[270] 1 Ne. 11:25
[271] 3 Ne. 9:20
[272] See Dan. Chapter 3

The Egyptian *Book of the Dead* gives many examples that appear to illustrate the idea of a firmament and a return path to God. Among others, one of the symbols used for a sacred, set-apart space is an egg: "Hail, O egg! I am Horus who liveth for millions of years, whose flame shineth upon you [lightning bolt] and bringeth your hearts unto me. I am master of my throne...I have opened a path."[273] Fac. 2, fig. 4, is the sun-boat filled with initiates. The tightly sealed egg is another symbol for the sealed boat with the sun safely inside and is equated with the egg in The *Book of the Dead* as shown in the following quote:

The chapter of giving air to the scribe Ani in Khert-Neter. Ani identifies himself with the Egg of the Sun, which was laid by the great god Keb. As the embryo inside the shell obtains air and grows to maturity, so the embryo of Ani's spirit-body breathes, and lives and grows inside the tomb, which takes the place of the shell of the Egg. Ani also identifies himself with the god Utcha-aabt of whom little is known. The "dweller in his nest," and "the babe," are, of course, himself.[274]

People have mistakenly believed that the *Book of the Dead* and the land or Hall of Osiris was only for the physically dead. It is also for the living who die as to the things of this fallen world which is everyone born into mortality. The initiate becomes an Osiris. Referring to the judgment throne of Osiris in the Hall of Osiris which is a type for the firmament, the *Book of the Dead* says, "...all sorts and conditions of men and spirits, both living and dead come before him, and bow down in homage before him...And naturally the best kinds of offerings shall be made to him, and he shall be supplied with an abundance of fresh water..."[275] Both the living and the dead work together in our temple firmaments to prepare those on both sides of the veil for sanctification, resurrection and exaltation.

One of the consequences of the Fall was that we would have to die. Christ's life was given to bring about the Atonement but we each must give our life in order to qualify to be brought back into the presence of God. With baptism, we die to the telestial state and are reborn into a new and higher place. We leave Egypt through the Red Sea and come forth into the wilderness experience. Being dead to this world takes us into the foundation of the firmament.

---

[273] *Book of the Dead*, 612
[274] *Ibid*, 283
[275] *Ibid*, 566

To put it in a nutshell, *The Book of the Dead* may be applicable for a dual purpose, one for the physically dead who enter into the firmament of the Spirit World Paradisiacal state. We know this is not heaven where our Heavenly Father dwells. The other possible application for the *Book of the Dead* is a temple-like condition of the living sanctified initiates.

The firmament is a terrestrial condition where the initiates are no longer under the influence of the serpent. The law of opposites, the tension between good and evil, is the energy that powers the telestial world. Since evil is excluded in the firmament, the law of opposites is manifest differently there, i.e. by male and female, which is the higher law. The city on the hill is a type for this place of safety and is also a type for the Bride of Christ. This brings balance in the middle as described by the *Sefer Yetzirah*, restoring the celestial order by the tension between Bridegroom and Bride.

The Boat of Ra the sun-god is a recurrent theme. Many statements in The *Book of the Dead* say that the boat is a gemstone: Speaking on Ra-sun-boat and the covenants associated with it, the rites continue; "recited over a boat made of green stone (compare to fac 2, fig 4) make a heaven of stars and purify it and cleanse it with natron and incense."[276] Natron and incense are part of the mummification process. Death and life or rebirth, are two sides of the coin. The initiate must die as to the fallen world and be reborn into a higher level. The ordinances put things in motion. The *Sefer Yetzirah* states that water, representing earth, is still and motionless. Fire, representing heaven, puts the water in motion, and brings forth the initiate, lifting him/her to the altar of sacrifice where the broken heart is brought for the purification of fire.

The pool of Siloam, which is used in the rites of the Feast of the Tabernacles, also is known for another yearly event. The waters of that pool were believed to be stirred up once a year and the first into the pool was healed of their infirmities. (St. John 5:7) The *Book of the Dead* teaches that the god is Osiris (god of the dead) when all is still and Ra, the sun-god when the boat is in motion.[277]

As shown in the last chapter, the booths represent an individual temple state for each sanctified person. The *Book of the Dead* explains, "I have built a house for my ba-soul."[278] The temple rites build our own firmament, or booths, and when added together with others, we have a unified firmament, a circle of protection. The branches on the booth

---

[276] *Book of the Dead*, 507
[277] Ibid, 512
[278] Ibid, 517

certainly seem to depict the building of a Tree of Life to protect our family with the trunk of the tree or beneath the bows. This tree is another symbol for this gathering hall. The Egyptians believe the rites give instructions for the establishment of a kingdom or Hall of Osiris.[279]

Within the firmament is the need for air since water is above and below, much like the Jaredite barges needed air. As shown in the idea of the three mothers from the **Sefer Yetzirah**, the water from the lower world and the fire from the upper world, come together through temple covenants to create a sacred space in the middle where there is air for the initiate.

In **The Book of the Dead**, the Hall (firmament) of Maati…is the bridal chamber for the wedding between the heavenly king and his Bride", the sanctified, Church of the Firstborn…all who have become part of the body of Christ. This brings us back to 2012 as the point in space and time when heaven and earth are brought together to begin the symbolic wedding between Christ and His Church. [280] One of our jobs as the Bride is to be in that sacred space, singing (or repeating) praises to the Lord, who tied heaven and earth through His Atoning sacrifice on the tree on Golgotha: "I am Ra who stablisheth those who praise him. I am the knot of the god in the Aser tree…"[281]

The cross and the Atonement (which includes Gethsemane and the resurrection) are what the temple is all about. The cross is the knot in the middle that ties all together. Christ is the ultimate doorway to the sheepfold, which is again, another symbol for firmament where the initiate is lifted up by the Father through the Son. We enter the protective sheepcote through the Atonement.

The name "Amen" or "Amun" is an Egyptian god, means "Hidden One." We do not have space here to go into the interesting subject of the word "Amen", but feel there is a strong connection between many names of the head gods of ancient religions that begin with 'A'. The idea of the Egyptian fertility god and pregnancy to bring forth the initiate is woven in many belief systems. A pregnant belly is one of the ways this concept is explained.[282] The ship of Zion, like the Ark of the Covenant, as a tomb/womb is the place where the initiate is attached to the umbilical cord of heaven for air and sustenance during the

---

[279] *Book of the Dead*, 565
[280] Ibid, 572
[281] Ibid, 607
[282] Ibid, 194

return trip to the Father. The firmament is a place of rest on the journey back to the Father.

Through temple ordinances, we are prepared to come into the Celestial Room, the Elysian fields of rest. It is like the sunboat, the house of the sun. It is not actually the Celestial Kingdom, but is blessed by the light and truth and peace that distill upon the souls of the sanctified in that sacred space. This is truly the land of milk and honey where we can be fed knowledge, feasting upon the word of God. The sacrifice has been given upon the altar, the feast is prepared.[283]

The paradise of the Spirit World would be an example of a firmament. In mortality, the only way to participate in the blessings and protection of the firmament is to spiritually enter into the unity of Zion as a temple. The place of rest is not our ultimate goal but is a meeting place between heaven and earth that affords the weary traveler rest on his journey and protection from the elements. In mortality, this does not mean literal elements but would seem to be protection from the fiery darts of the adversary in a strictly spiritual sense, even though there are Gethsemane moments when those darts are allowed to test us as we come to crossroads of each higher spiritual rebirth.[284][285]

---

[283] *Book of the Dead*, 206

[284] Ibid, 202

[285] Ibid 268 "The Egyptians believed that the country forming the Kingdom of Osiris was divided into districts, or parts, the boundary of each of which was marked by a fortress or stronghold, which was held by a group of servants of the god. They also thought that these forts were used by the souls of the dead on their journey to the "City of God," much as a modern travelers in the Sudan, or Perisa, or Mesopotamia, use the "khans" or inns, or halting-places, which supply the weary wayfarer with shelter and food, and enable him to enjoy some days of rest in security. At one time these forts, or strongholds, or "gates," were thought to be seven in number, and at other times the Egyptians believed their number was ten, or fourteen,"...etc. "The seven forts that formed a chain across Dead-land were called "Arits" (Hebrew for earth) a word which is often translated "Mansions" or "Halls." Each Arit was provided with a doorkeeper, a watcher, or official who kept a good look out to announce the arrival of a traveler, and a herald, who interviewed the visitor and enquired his name, and reported it to his companions. This arrangement is identical with that which has been common in al parts of Africa from time immemorial in respect of the forts that are built at the entrances to towns and villages. In the case of the Seven Arits no soul could hope to gain admission to anyone of them unless it was able to state the names of the doorkeeper and watcher and herald, and to repeat a formula which would convince them of his good faith.

The ***Sefer Yetzirah*** refers to a staff coming from the waters of earth. The reed or lotus coming forth from a pool of water is a beautiful symbol of the initiate rising out of the waters of chaos. The Egyptians depicted the initiate as standing on a reed mat with a lotus on his head.[286] The pure lotus is a symbol of holding the purified initiate within itself and bringing him/her forth from the water into a terrestrial state. The ***Book of the Dead*** describes a human head coming from a lotus that comes out of a pool of water.[287]

The throne of Osiris is set upon a coffin.[288] This again brings us back to the Ark of the Covenant and Facsimile 2, figure 4. The throne is sometimes set upon water (womb/tomb) and a lotus comes up from the lake in front of the throne with the four sons of Horus upon it. Why? To spread the new firmament in the four directions and preparing a creation for those who come after. Here Osiris wears a different crown, one that is used to resurrect the dead.[289] Horus pleads with Osiris to allow the initiates to "be admitted into his presence" and be deified.[290]

Another aspect of the process that the ***Book of the Dead*** expounds on is the concept of the Bride being prepared for the sacred wedding. Another name for this sacred, set-apart place is the Hall of Maati, goddess of truth. This place is the holy bridal chamber for the wedding between heavenly king and his Bride, the sanctified, Church of the Firstborn. [291]

The holy hill of Zion is also used as a type for temple and an idea that seems to perfectly describe a firmament. "Homage to thee, O thou who dwellest in the Holy Hill of Amentet![292] Pyramids, with the sepulcher inside, are a very powerful type for the holy hill, a firmament. Our eternal kingdom is founded upon Christ and the Apostles. Each smaller circle is also founded upon those who have qualified as a representative of Christ. For Egyptians, the foundation is Osiris. The pharaoh, as an Osiris, organizes his kingdom and is the foundation stone. I believe that all the time and resources that were spent in preparing a pyramid were a reflection of the Egyptian understanding of a firmament. Pharaoh, standing in as a representative for the Son of God,

---

[286] *Book of the Dead*, 245
[287] *Ibid*, 310
[288] Ibid, 239
[289] Ibid, 242
[290] Ibid, 241
[291] Ibid, 572
[292] Ibid, 365 Appendix to Chapter I, chapter IB

would organize his kingdom around him and through sacred ordinances, lift that kingdom above its fallen condition. His people would have their own Hall of Osiris where they would wait for the journey to return them to the Father. Without the priesthood, the acts are without effect, but the principles were all in place and we can hope that many of these faithful Egyptians were well prepared to accept the fullness of the Gospel in the Spirit World.

The Holy Hill

Latter-day Saints are taught that the holy hill of the Lord, or mountain of the Lord, is the temple. Therefore, the many verses in Psalms and elsewhere that refers to dwelling in the holy hill, are meant for the living as well as the dead. Psalm 15 begins: "Lord, who shall abide in thy tabernacle? Who shall dwell in thy holy hill?" The answer is then given that this is a place for the righteous. It denotes the idea of standing in holy places, becoming a temple ourselves. Other Psalms use a tree for this same concept[293] and also the idea of wings as a covering as in Psalm 57: 1, "Be merciful unto me, O God, be merciful unto me; for my soul trusteth in thee; yea, in the shadow of thy wings will I make my refuge, until these calamities be overpast."

Therefore, we suggest that a firmament is a set apart sacred space that is for those who have overcome the world through ordinances meant to overcome the effects of the fall. The ship of Zion is such an applicable motif since we are in the process of journeying back to the Father. We can also look at this journey in regards to this earth. We have been taught that this earth will travel back during the Millennium to the presence of Kolob. This is the Atonement earth and has a special and permanent place as the footstool for the center place, Kolob. Enoch wrote: "the earth is his footstool."[294]

When Adam and Eve lived in the Garden of Eden, the Earth was closely orbiting Kolob, like God's home planet. But when Adam and Eve fell, so did the Earth and it was hurled across the cosmos and placed in orbit around our sun in this planetary system. After the Millennium, the Earth will return to its rightful place near God, orbiting Kolob.[295]

---

[293] Psalm 51:8
[294] Moses 6:44
[295] See Church Ensign, March 1997, Page 16 "The Book of Abraham: A Most Remarkable Book," and Journal of Discourses, 7:163 and 17:143

His Dwelling Place

How far is Kolob,
that holy place so near
the majesty of God?

Measure the distance
you imagine in
years of light.
Multiply miles from
Earth to Sun and
number your days
a million times.

Then within these walls
feel His breath
on your cheek as
He says your name
and listen to the Peace
only your contrite
heart can hear.

© Sharon Price Anderson

The hidden pavilion or tabernacle, is a sacred space that is set apart for the righteous to protect them either in death or from the effects of the fall and the dangers of the world. Founded upon the rock of Zion, this is a place of joy where, even with the enemy at the very doors, the righteous sing songs of praise, trusting in God to keep the canopy of protection firm.

5. For in the time of trouble he shall hide me in his pavilion: in the secret of his tabernacle shall he hide me; he shall set me up upon a rock.

6. And now shall mine head be lifted up above mine enemies round about me; therefore will I offer in his tabernacle sacrifices of joy; I will sing, yea, I will sing praises unto the Lord.[296]

Like the seven days of the Feast of the Tabernacles, for seven days in the Lord's time, God's children sojourn away from Heaven. At the end of Millennium, the earth will be brought back to presence of the Father. He and those qualified to assist him, will be the protective covering around the earth as she makes this journey. Christ will be the light of the world at that time. This seems a very good representation of a firmament, a booth of protection. Perhaps the reason the Israelites were not to live in their own home during Sukkot is because we are not home here on earth because we are away from the Father, sojourning in a wilderness experience. To qualify to return, we must become a booth or sukkot (Tree of Life).

To qualify to enter the firmament depends entirely upon our acceptance of Christ and His Atonement, so that we can be covered by the blood of Christ. In addition, the Hebrew word for 'red' also means rush or reed. This Red Sea experience of baptism is the door to the sheepcote, but to move up into higher levels of the firmament, we must go to the temple and keep the covenants made therein. (when baptized we are washed in the blood of the Lamb.)

Again looking at our spiritual journey in light of Moses and his people, after Israel was reborn through the Red Sea, they were attached to their spiritual Father through the umbilical cord and needed sustenance. Travailing in the desert, the candidates for the Promised Land did not know where to go to receive the bread and waters of life. The Lord provided bread from the dews of Heaven. Through the rod of Moses which would soon blossom like a tree bearing witness of a life-saving oasis, the living waters gushed forth.

This ongoing process of development was well portrayed and assisted by the Holy Ark of the Covenant. In Hebrew, 'ark' is translated as 'aaron', meaning box or coffin. The Egyptian god Osiris is the god of death and rebirth and his coffin is also the womb of his rebirth. The lid of the ark is called the Kapparah, meaning 'mercy seat', which is closely related to the word 'womb' in Hebrew, and is from the same

---

[296] Psalms 27:5,6

root as the word for atonement. The ark marked the path Israel was to follow in the wilderness and finally, led the way into the Promised Land. "I will greatly rejoice in the Lord, my soul shall be joyful in my God; for he hath clothed me with the garments of salvation, he hath covered me with the robe of righteousness, as a bridegroom decketh himself with ornaments, and as a bride adorneth herself with her jewels."[297]

In Ephesians, the temple set on the firm foundation is the path to the Father. This takes us back again to that idea of the knot (cross) in the middle that ties the upper world with the lower. It represents the process that applies to our personal progress, that of the church, the earth and the cosmos in general. Circles within circles, the truths we learn can fit together like puzzle pieces to create a beautiful picture of unity.

The foundation rock is laid out in the four cardinal directions, forming a square. The temple (no matter what shape it is) spirals up toward the Father, connecting us together in unity with our fellow saints, with our ancestors and also our posterity, overcoming time and forging eternal links. "For by one Spirit are we all baptized into one body, whether we be Jews or Gentiles, whether we be bond or free; and have been all made to drink into one Spirit. For the body is not one member, but many."[298]

Once released from the yoke of the adversary that is a consequence of this fallen world, the initiate is lifted from the water onto holy ground and given a new yoke. "Come unto me, all ye that labour and are heavy laden, and I will give you rest. Take my yoke upon you, and learn of me; for I am meek and lowly in heart; and ye shall find rest unto your souls. For my yoke is easy, and my burden is light."[299] To exchange the yoke of captivity for the yoke of the Lord, we must be drawn out of the waters of baptism and receive the Holy Ghost, as Nephi tells us in 2 Nephi, chapter 31. He says this gets us into the straight and narrow way. We've passed through the Red Sea, and now is our wilderness journey. Pharaoh no longer holds dominion over the initiate once he/she is beyond the Red Sea, (unless they choose to return to Egypt's 'worldliness').

There are still real dangers from the adversary in that wilderness, as the Israelites learned. "And no unclean thing can enter into his

---

[297] Isa. 61:10
[298] 1 Cor. 12:13–14
[299] Matt. 11:8–30

kingdom; therefore nothing entereth into his rest save it be those who have washed their garments in my blood, because of their faith, and the repentance of all their sins, and their faithfulness unto the end."[300]

The Garden of Eden, in our opinion, was a firmament, a bubble of protection and safety. Paradise would seem to be a good example of a firmament, or in fact more likely a series of firmaments, to separate spirits of various levels of glory through the science of dimensions. The Egyptian *Book of the Dead*, strongly indicates an in-between state between mortality and the place where God resides. The place is a garden of rest on our journey back to the presence of the Father.

---

[300] 3 Ne. 27:19

Chapter Seven: The Garden

"That in the dispensation of the fullness of times he might gather together in one all things in Christ, both which are in heaven, and which are on earth; even in him." (Eph. 1:10) What does the day of gathering mean? Let's take a look at the answer to this through the lens of The Three Pillars of the Gospel.

In the beginning, all things were organized as one. The heavens work on the Zion principle of unity and cooperation. We took part in the creation. This unity was temporarily broken through the important principle of the fall. We were scattered when we were brought into this fallen, telestial world. The beginning of the restoration of the original union is brought about through the temple ordinances empowered by the Atonement. The scriptures are replete with the message that the scattering of Israel is a type for the scattering of the original creators', organizers', prayer circle of creation. Putting it all back together again, the at-one-ment, is what everything is all about. This is done by Christ, the great High Priest and King, and those He commissions to act in His name.

The last days are a time for the restoration of truth but also for the restoration of people and all things to their proper places which are the places they occupied before this life. Ancient Israel was a wonderful type for the return through a wilderness temple experience to the Promised Land that once was their home. But on their return, they were on a higher spiritual level and brought with them their larger families. Likewise, we strive to return to the presence of the Father, reclaiming our place in the council of heaven, only this time it will be reorganized on a higher level as we are progressing to be like our heavenly parents.

Though Israel is found throughout the earth, there is now a remnant that is no longer scattered. The temple grafts the branches back into the original olive tree.[301] In Gethsemane, Christ began the process of bringing us back as one into the Garden of the Lord, grafting us into the Tree of Life. The oil of gladness that comes from the Tree of Life begins the atonement process of reversing first spiritual death, then eventually, physical death.

---

[301] See Jacob 5

The head of a dispensation, a prophet or even a father who has had his salvation sealed upon him, can stand (circles within circles) in that center place of organization. This is an eternal pattern. We are in trouble if we ever see ourselves as the source of power. We must be a conduit, doing all the works we see the Father do. With the opening of the seventh seal, it will be Christ Himself, as the man Aquarius, pouring out the water of knowledge and Spirit. When we plant the seeds of sanctification and are watered by Christ's grace, we will become our own mini Garden of Eden. Once there are enough of those mini-gardens (sanctified members) joined together, then this earth will be prepared to receive the Savior at His Second Coming. In the meantime, it will only be in a garden (temple) state that we find peace and protection as the enemy desperately attempts to retain possession of this earth in the coming decades.

In the beginning we were led by Christ and His general, the archangel Michael. In the final dispensation, what once was will be again. So what did we do in the beginning? We helped plant a garden. What should we be doing now? Helping to plant a terrestrial garden and indeed, for those who have attained certain spiritual promises, they are even beginning their own garden that is rooted into this earth first. Our prophets are doing an amazing job of planting gardens all over the world. Temples are dotting the earth and the plantings from those holy places are being rooted into the righteous homes of spiritual kings and priests.

The Land

Land is often a symbol in the scriptures of a return to a state of unity and also the beginning of individual estates of fruitful increase. A study of the scattering of Israel and the gathering of Israel from the topical guide helps to illuminate the subject. If we become foundations, Adams and Eves for our own creations, then all our creation builds upon us. We can only touch on it here. Ezekiel, chapter 36 gives a partial picture of this concept:

8) But ye, O mountains of Israel, ye shall shoot forth your branches, and yield your fruit to my people of Israel; for they are at hand to come.

9) For, behold, I am for you, and I will turn unto you, and ye shall be tilled and sown:

10)And I will multiply men upon you, all the house of Israel, even all of it: and the cities shall be inhabited, and the wastes shall be builded:

171

11) And I will multiply upon you man and beast; and they shall increase and bring fruit: and I will settle you after your old estates; and will do better unto you than at your beginnings; and ye shall know that I am the Lord.

19) And I scattered them among the heathen, and they were dispersed through the countries: according to their way and according to their doings I judged them.

20) And when they entered unto the heathen, whither they went, they profaned my holy name, when they said to them, These are the people of the Lord, and are gone forth out of his land.

21) But I had pity for mine holy name, which the house of Israel had profaned among the heathen whither they went.

22) Therefore say unto the house of Israel, Thus saith the Lord God; I do not this for your sakes, O house of Israel, but for mine holy name's sake, which ye have profaned among the heathen, whither ye went.

23) And I will sanctify my great name, which was profaned among the heathen, which ye have profaned in the midst of them; and the heathen shall know that I am the Lord, saith the Lord God, when I shall be sanctified in you before their eyes.

24) For I will take you from among the heathen, and gather you out of all countries, and will bring you into your own land.

25) Then will I sprinkle clean water upon you, and ye shall be clean: from all your filthiness, and from all your idols, will I cleanse you.

26) A new heart also will I give you, and a new spirit will I put within you: and I will take away the stony heart out of your flesh, and I will give you an heart of flesh.

27) And I will put my spirit within you, and cause you to walk in my statutes, and ye shall keep my judgments, and do them.

28) And ye shall dwell in the land that I gave to your fathers; and ye shall be my people, and I will be your God.

29) I will also save you from all your uncleannesses; and I will call for the corn, and will increase it, and lay no famine upon you.

30) And I will multiply the fruit of the tree, and the increase of the field, that ye shall receive no more reproach of famine among the heathen.

35) And they shall say, this land that was desolate is become like the garden of Eden; and the waste and desolate and ruined cities are become fenced, and are inhabited.

36) Then the heathen that are left round about you shall know that I the Lord build the ruined places and plant that that was desolate: I the Lord have spoken it, and I will do it.

37) Thus saith the Lord God; I will yet for this be enquired of by the house of Israel , to do it for them; I will increase them with men like a flock.

38) As the holy flock, as the flock of Jerusalem in her solemn feasts; so shall the waste cities be filled with flocks of men; and they shall know that I am the Lord. (Ezek. 36:8–11, 19–30 and 35–38)

Nibley had some very interesting things to say about the creation. In speaking of the Egyptian gods, he writes: "so Geb gave his own entire portion to Horus, the son of his son who was his firstborn. Well, what the theme is here is priesthood and kingship as well as land."[302] Nibley understood far better than we do about the Egyptian connection between priesthood, kingship and the land. Brother Nibley continued this theme, writing about the authority necessary for these sacred offices and the underlying unity behind the transference of those sacred offices as the sealing power comes into effect:

You have a transmission of power, and what is it? Identity? That's what you have in John. The nineteenth chapter of 3 Nephi is the same thing. He goes aside and prays that I may be in you and you, Father, in me; and those that follow me may be in me as you are in me, Father; and that those who follow them (their converts) may also be one as we are one. This idea of being in others and being identified. That's what we have here, and it's one of the keys of Egyptian, this doctrine of identity...[303]

We have discussed the above subject in the past relating to **D&C** 84, the doctrine of the priesthood. Becoming sons of Moses and Aaron, and also Paul telling his converts they are his sons as he is in Christ, is one of the organizational principles that helps bring everything into the body of Christ. The office of apostleship and divine investiture are subjects we would recommend for study. The idea of bringing all things into one and placing them on a foundation beginning with this earth is a concept that will starts to leap out once this subject

---

[302] Hugh Nibley, Teachings of the Pearl of Great Price; Lecture 9, Winter Semester, 1986
[303] Ibid

is studied. Nibley finished his lecture thus: "these things are all related. You'd be surprised how they tie in together."[304]

Orson Pratt wrote about the connection between this earth, an inheritance of land, and eternal inheritance: "And thus, all the different portions of the earth have been and will be disposed of to the lawful heirs; while those who cannot prove their heirship to be legal, or who cannot prove that they have received any portion of the earth by promise, will be cast out into some other kingdom or world, where, if they ever get an inheritance, they will have to earn it by keeping the law of meekness during another probation."[305]

The Garden

In a BYU Devotional, Elder Nelson explained that we were among those intelligences that were organized in the beginning as follows:

> To find answers, let's go back in a mental time tunnel. Before the world was made, "Jesus Christ, the Great I AM, ... looked upon the wide expanse of eternity, and all the seraphic hosts of heaven" (D&C 38:1). The Lord had shown Abraham "the intelligences that were organized before the world was; and among all these there were many of the noble and great ones" (Abr. 3:22). We are no doubt among those he envisioned.[306]

We were among those who assisted Michael under the direction of the Lord, to organize the earth and plant a garden. The Garden of Eden was an outdoor temple. Conversely a temple is a garden, a sacred space made terrestrial. Those gardens, each considered the center place, are being sent out as sparks all over the world to burn away the dross and reclaim that piece of land from the fall. This earth needs to be reclaimed from the Adversary who holds dominion. Place by place, temples, chapels and even homes can become terrestrial. Covenant keeping members can also be redeemed from the fall and stand in holy places. Step by step, this earth can be brought into the millennial reign as the Lord's foundation spreads; the tent stretches outward and the center pole reaches upward.

---

[304] Hugh Nibley, Teachings of the Pearl of Great Price; Lecture 9, Winter Semester, 1986
[305] Journal of Discourses 1, 332–333
[306] Russell M. Nelson, Thanks for the Covenant, BYU Devotional, Nov. 22, 1988

The Garden of Gethsemane gives a crucial clue to being rooted into the foundation garden and watered. Golgotha gives an image of the center post, a dead tree but the middle garden that connects heaven and earth is encompassed in this symbol of life coming from death, the tree becoming enlivened. As mentioned many times, it represents Facsimile 2, fig. 1, the center spot and the beginning of creation.

The direction we want to be heading is to lay the foundation now for our future kingdom. The kingdom of God starts on this earth and will fill the expanse of space starting from these roots. When we grow up hearing that we can become like our Heavenly Father or Mother and create worlds of our own, it is natural to picture ourselves off in our own little corner of the universe, basically working alone with our spouse. Maybe occasionally we would get together with the old family and catch up on things. In actuality, instead of separateness, the scriptures and words of the prophets show there will be eternal unity with those we love and enjoy being with. Those who prove worthy will have their own kingdoms but there will still be a perfect organization, a unity and cooperation with our family and priesthood order.[307]

If each temple is to be looked upon as the omphalos (navel between earth and heaven), then each person who becomes a temple is grafted into the Tree of Life. The original priesthood organization (symbolized by the Original Tree) was unified under Michael and assisted Jehovah with the creation. We become one nation no matter where on earth we are. The pattern is established that was given in the beginning and those who qualify do not have to wait until the final judgment to begin their eternal work as Franklin Richards taught:

In a revelation given to the Prophet Joseph, on Celestial Marriage the Lord, speaking to Abraham, Isaac, and Jacob, says: 'And because they did none other things than that which they were commanded, they have entered into their exaltations, according to the promises, and sit upon thrones; and are not Angels, but are Gods.' All who live on the earth, and faithfully work righteousness, as did those ancient fathers, will receive like blessings of power and dominion, for God is no respecter of persons, but judges all men righteously according to their works. Thus we have a succession of gods from Adam down to Christ and His apostles at least. All men being in the image of their father Adam, even as he is in the image of his father, and possessing a similar knowledge of good and evil, when they receive the keys and powers of the same Priesthood, and by their works attain to its blessings, they will, like Adam, Abraham, Isaac, and Jacob, bear rule and dominion

---

[307] See D&C 84

over their own posterity and have power to redeem, purify, and exalt them, also, to like power and glory.[308]

This pattern was and is put in motion through the Atonement. As Nibley wrote, "Adam in the presence of God is the quintessential atonement."[309] Once again we emphasize that we all have to become as Adam or Eve and make that journey of rebirth. The result, if we claim the highest goal, is to begin our own creation, create our own garden. Thus we see Adam has a crucial role. He begins the job of reorganizing everything into one. The heads of the dispensations work under him to further organize and we would assume that the other prophets in each specific dispensation work under the head of the dispensation and on down to the families as each individual reaches the spiritual point where he/she is authorized to move forward in that office.

Father Adam has the job of bringing his children to their own kingships. The office of kingship belongs to Adam and all who work under him in that office. The Egyptians taught that: "Atum writes the name of the new king on the leaves of the ished-tree; that is, the king is the tree."[310] There is tremendous symbolism in the metaphor of initiates planting the seed, rooting in to the foundation stone and becoming a tree of life. Thus we can become kings/queens/, high priests/priestesses. We can become planters, beginning our garden. Nibley, talking of new kings/queens starting their own creations, explained that the plantings are taken to other places from the Treasure House. The temple is the navel, where all eternal life begins:

"The colonizing process is called 'planting,' and those spirits which bring their treasures to a new world are called 'plants,' more rarely 'seeds,' of their father, or 'planters' in another world. For every planting goes out from a Treasure House, either as the essential material elements or as the colonizers themselves, who come from a sort of mustering-area called the 'Treasure-House of Souls.'

With its 'planting' completed, a new world is in business. A new treasury has been established from which new sparks may go forth in all directions to start the process anew in ever new spaces; God wants every man to 'plant a planting,' nay, he has promised that those who keep his law may also become creators of worlds. Thus you can

---

[308] Franklin D. Richards, Millennial Star 17, 194–196
[309] Nibley, *Temple and Cosmos,* 383
[310] Nibley, *Message,* 289

say there is indeed but one God who fills the immensity of space, yet we are in the act too, as potential creators of worlds."[311]

In the following quote, Brother Nibley identified the treasure house as the temple. It is there that we are brought back and grafted into the Tree of Life and from there take our plantings to begin our own creation:

'It is not too much to say that the dominant theme of the Thanksgiving Hymns of the Dead Sea Scrolls is an ecstatic contemplation of the wonder of man's participation in heavenly affairs going back to the beginning. Man belongs by prior appointment to that community of the Elect. Earthly rites are but the reflection of heavenly events.[the Elect are part of] the family of the sons of Heaven, the council of the Church, and the assembly of the Temple, an establishment, literally, planting, which reaches forever into the future and the past.[312]

When Moses, Elias, and Elijah came to the Kirtland Temple, they brought the keys that restore us to our original state of organization with God. Moses brought the keys of the Gathering of Israel. For a time in the early restoration, this was a physical gathering of Israel to the land of Zion but at length it became a spiritual gathering to Zion. Basically, Moses brought the keys for the temple building which symbolizes the school house. Elias brought the curriculum; the Abrahamic Covenant and the principles given within the school room. Elijah brought the empowerment which is the sealing power that gives the graduate his/her certificate for each level along the way.[313] Here we become part of gathered Israel and we partake of the fruit of the Tree of Life. There will be no cherubim to bar your way because you will know the answers.

Spiritual death is overcome through the substitution of the sacrifice of the Lamb and the initiate can finally return to the presence of the Lord and enter into His rest. Nibley wrote that sacred gardens [firmaments] were a place to rest and gather strength to continue on the journey. The temple has three gardens: the Garden Room, the Celestial Room, (seventh Heaven) and a final garden that is implied and found in the Second Endowment. Washed feet are then ready to be rooted in and then they can begin their own gathering process and begin their own garden. Within these gardens, we are rooted in, watered, enlivened and illuminated, following the pattern of the Feast of the Tabernacles. (John

---

[311] Nibley, *Temple and Cosmos,* 153
[312] Ibid, 187
[313] D&C 110:10–16

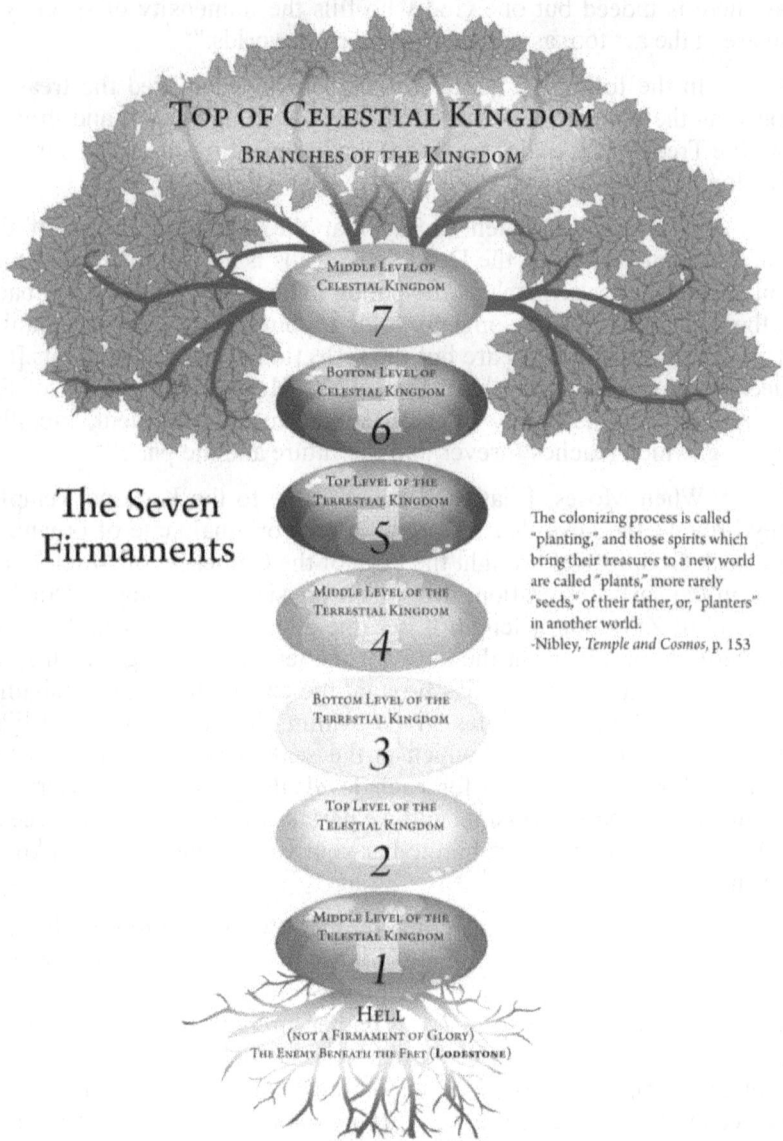

TOP OF CELESTIAL KINGDOM
BRANCHES OF THE KINGDOM

MIDDLE LEVEL OF
CELESTIAL KINGDOM
7

BOTTOM LEVEL OF
CELESTIAL KINGDOM
6

The Seven
Firmaments

TOP LEVEL OF THE
TERRESTIAL KINGDOM
5

MIDDLE LEVEL OF THE
TERRESTIAL KINGDOM
4

BOTTOM LEVEL OF THE
TERRESTIAL KINGDOM
3

TOP LEVEL OF THE
TELESTIAL KINGDOM
2

MIDDLE LEVEL OF THE
TELESTIAL KINGDOM
1

HELL
(NOT A FIRMAMENT OF GLORY)
THE ENEMY BENEATH THE FRET (**LODESTONE**)

The colonizing process is called
"planting," and those spirits which
bring their treasures to a new world
are called "plants," more rarely
"seeds," of their father, or, "planters"
in another world.
-Nibley, *Temple and Cosmos*, p. 153

7:37) This was also called the Festival of Ingathering. Since the name Joseph means 'gatherer' in Hebrew, it is amazing to see how he gathers into the ship of Zion all who will be lifted up and illuminated, watered in and rooted into the terrestrial garden being prepared for the Millennial reign.

A stirring from beneath precedes a stirring from above. In other words, we assist Heavenly Father in helping this desert blossom as a rose, and then He assists us later in transplanting our kingdom (initiated on the rock of our foundation here on earth) to our own place in the universe. Maybe a better word than transplanting would be stretching our kingdom since its roots will always remain in this earth. This is a principle that is subtle but woven throughout the scriptures. Isaiah wrote:

1) Hearken to me, ye that follow after righteousness, ye that seek the Lord: look unto the rock whence ye are hewn, and to the hole of the pit whence ye are digged.

2) Look unto Abraham your father, and unto Sarah that bare you: for I called him alone, and blessed him, and increased him.

3) For the Lord shall comfort Zion : he will comfort all her waste places; and he will make her wilderness like Eden , and her desert like the garden of the Lord; joy and gladness shall be found therein, thanksgiving, and the voice of melody. (Isa. 51:1–3)

This is all part of the Abraham Covenant. Israel will fill the earth but not until she is brought back to the center place (temple) and organized (endowed and sealed) and from there she stretches out the new and higher foundation of the Lord until it fills the earth and brings in the Millennial reign of the Lord. "He shall cause them that come of Jacob to take root: Israel shall blossom and bud, and fill the face of the world with fruit" (Isa. 27:6). Thus will a place be laid for stability and endurance when the wicked are destroyed at His coming. "Therefore thus saith the Lord God, Behold, I lay in Zion for a foundation a stone, a tried stone, a precious corner stone, a sure foundation; he that believeth shall not make haste" (Isa. 28:16). Isaiah talked of the day when the fruit would become a forest, as we become trees of life, rooted into the firm foundation: "Is it not yet a very little while, and Lebanon shall be turned into a fruitful field, and the fruitful field shall be esteemed as a forest? (Isa. 29:17)

Office of Kingship

By studying the role of Adam, we understand that he stands in the office of king, placed there by Christ who is the true center of everything. He is the trunk of the tree, the central pillar, the altar. The Egyptians wrote of his role:

Coffin Text 132: According to Siegfried Schott, this is a drama. The speaker is the man who wants his family 'sealed to him.' 'I am Atum who created the Great Ones.' I am one of the Watchers who danced for joy [prayer circle]. I received my place to rest in accordingly as I went about exploring, taking possession, going the rounds (coming and going). I have assumed dominion of my domains (seats, places). I have toured my domains, my groves, my pastures, my word is that of command of Hw (god) who accompanies me. My two arms are raised to the gods in sacrifice, even the sacrifice of oxen to the Lord of Heliopolis. I am with those who are bound for sacrifice, inasmuch as I am verily with my back to the earth (Geb) (Fac. 2, fig. 1).I have come forth that my family be given to me: my sons and daughters, my brothers and sisters, my father, my mother, and all who come to receive my embrace. O ye who are among their ancestors, whose names are hidden to me, I have the written documents (that say) 'I begot him.'[314]

Adam, Jacob, and Judah are examples of the office of kingship and represent the Egyptian idea of lion, bull, and hawk. The bull gives birth through baptism (Facsimile 2, fig. 5), as shown with the twelve oxen holding the baptismal font. The lion represents many things including the higher sacrifice of the lion couch and the baptism of fire (Facsimile 2, fig. 1). The hawk, which represents the higher aspect of the office of kingship, can fly aloft from the sacrifices to return to heaven. There are many more aspects to these symbols but no room to go into them here.

The Egyptians believed that Horus-hawk represented Pharaoh, the father of his people around which all is organized.[315] They taught that the Apis-bull was a lower form of Horus-hawk.[316] Nibley wrote that the Egyptians believed the office of Atum was given to kings.[317] Through a step by step process, the king added crowns and names. Re-Atum was a name given to the king to represent Re, the sungod and king of heaven, and Atum, the first king on earth. We also believe that we must take upon ourselves the name of Christ and become also as Adam or Eve. Names add upon each other as offices are added and we progress in our ascension. The addition of new offices does not eliminate responsibility for prior offices; for example, holders of the Melchizedek priesthood can also perform the roles of those who hold the Aaronic priesthood.

---

[314] See Isa. 2:3
[315] D&C 86:11
[316] Nibley, *Message,* 289
[317] Nibley, *Abraham in Egypt,* 268

Joseph

We know that Joseph Smith has a unique position among the prophets. Elder Russell M. Nelson, in regards to Joseph Smith said that God the Father and his Son Jesus Christ established once again the Abrahamic covenant, this time through the Prophet Joseph Smith. These are the words of the Lord: ' And as I said unto Abraham concerning the kindreds of the earth, even so I say unto my servant Joseph [Smith]: IN THEE AND IN THY SEED SHALL THE KINDRED OF THE EARTH BE BLESSED.' (D&C 124:58; see also D&C 110:12) The Master conferred upon Joseph Smith priesthood authority and the right to convey blessings of the Abrahamic covenant to others. [Here we can see that role of the dispensation leader to gather and organize all who will come to Christ] Joseph Smith, whose father's name was Joseph, had the same name as Joseph who was sold into Egypt, who millennia before had prophesied of Joseph Smith. This fact is documented in the Book of Mormon (see 2 Ne. 3:6-11). The name JOSEPH carried the connotation both that he was "added" to, and that his mission related to the "gathering" of Israel.

So Israel had ten sons before Rachel finally conceived and bore a son of her very own. She called his name Joseph (see Gen. 30:24). This name had a very special meaning. The word Joseph relates to the Hebrew word YASAPH, meaning "to add." Rachel wanted all to know that this son was added to sons that she already had through her maid Bilhah. Joseph also relates to the Hebrew word ASAPH, which means "to gather" (see Gen. 30:24, footnote 24a in the LDS edition of the King James Version). The name and lineage of Joseph were destined to play an important later role in the gathering of Israel.[318]

Once again, we can see the job of Joseph is to gather in souls and every needful thing beneath the branches of the gospel tree.

Joseph of Egypt watched over the king (pharaoh) and what was his. He fed the people and when times were hardest, he asked them to consecrate their land to the king and in return he sustained their life. When we consecrate to the Lord, He in turn gives the right of usage of land back to us but He is able to bless us abundantly because of our sacrifice and because we and all that is ours has been offered to Him. As Elder Nelson said, "Joseph means added upon; to gather in. This is

---

[318] Thanks for the Covenant, Russell M. Nelson, BYU Devotional, November 22, 1988

the role of the priesthood and the command to gather in . . . an assignment which the children of Joseph hold.

Lehi had two sons, Jacob and Joseph, who were born in the wilderness. The offices of king and high priest may be symbolically represented by those children whom Nephi consecrated to serve the people. Jacob was more vocal and visible as the office of kingship usually is and Joseph was more in the background as usually seems to be the case with the priests. They were both priests but their names and perhaps their roles are a type and shadow, just as the sun is a type for kingship and the moon for the role of high priest (among other things).

Turning the Age

Everything comes back to the Three Pillars of the Gospel; the creation, the fall and the atonement. Hopefully, we can now see that the creation is indeed ongoing. The following quote is about the Egyptian Shabako stone:

In the Shabako stone, the earth is prepared for man's habitation in advance, first by the planting of rushes and papyrus at the gates, and then 'out of Ptah who created Atum came forth all manner of nourishment and food for the creatures who were about to come down and inhabit the earth. 'Praised be the lords of the Fields of Turquoise under the ished-tree in the midst of Heliopolis.' Here the word ished has the determinative not of a tree, but of a green arbor, booth, or bower, suggesting the green bower in which the king, all over the ancient world, sat at the New Year to represent the first man in the garden. Coffin Text 187: 'He made me to sit in the booth at the entrances of the horizon of heaven. I found Khonsu on the way; he came down to Punt' and there organized the subject's family and followers for him. Turquoise and evergreen predominate. There I will cause flowers of all kinds to grow; and the Field of Rushes came into being. We see the subject and his wife together in a pleasant garden where they drink the waters of a stream or pond at the foot of a date palm; at once one thinks of the waters of life and the tree of life the trees, which symbolized natural life eternally renewed,' in the cenotaph of Seti I, 'were meant to go down with their roots' to a canal dug to represent' the waters from which all natural life had sprung.[319]

The Feast of Tabernacles (Feast of Sukkot or Feast of Booths) is believed by many modern Christians and Jews to be the precursor to

---

[319] Nibley, *Message,* 296–7

the establishment of the 1000 year messianic kingdom to be set up at the second coming of Yeshua the Messiah (Christ). It is one of the three pilgrimage festivals God gave the children of Israel in the Bible.[320] It was during these festivals that the Israelites would bring their offerings and firstlings to the Temple in Jerusalem and enjoy a feast!

Following are seven points taught by a religious group called The Ami Israel Torah Study. They are a group of believers in Christ looking for His return and studying the Hebrew roots of the Christian faith. It becomes obvious that more and more truth is being restored to the earth and certain aspects of that truth are spreading to many people:

1) Yeshua has come and will come again, but at this time, He lives and dwells with The Father in Heaven.

2) It should be a believer's goal to want to become part of the "bride of the Messiah".

3) Becoming a part of the Bride is a gift Yahweh (the God of Abraham, Isaac, and Jacob) gives to those who believe He is their God and that His Son (Yeshua) has redeemed them from the penalty of their transgressions against His instructions.

4) We learn how to conduct ourselves as His Bride by learning and living by the instructions He gave us. These instructions are found in the first five books of the Bible (the Torah) and are elaborated on throughout the balance of the scripture (both the old and new testaments).

5) Since the calling of the patriarch Abraham, Yahweh has been working predominately with one group of people - the Israelites and those gentiles who "attach" themselves to Israel (thus becoming Israelites themselves).

6) All Jews are Israelites, but not all Israelites are Jews.

7) Yahweh has commissioned the people of Israel with the responsibility of spreading the good news of that coming Kingdom of God to all the earth.[321]

We can see so many pieces of the truth scattered throughout the world. The idea of a people being prepared as the Bride of Christ is so appropriate for the Feast of Tabernacles. The Church of the Firstborn must be prepared to receive the Savior. Organizing the Saints for that reception and cheering in the Millennium is our goal.

---

[320] See Lev. 23

[321] See http://www.season-of-our-joy.com

Following the example of Joseph the gatherer, may we do as Isaiah prophesied and bring in scattered Israel so that Zion may come forth. The Bible Dictionary refers to Isaiah's prophecies and touches upon the theme of sacred land:

The bulk of Isaiah's prophecies deal with the coming of the Redeemer, both in his first appearance and as the Great King at the last day, as the God of Israel. A major theme is that God requires right-eousness of his people, and until they obey him they will be smitten and scattered by their enemies. But in the end, Israel will be restored; the barren land will be made fruitful and able to support a large popula-tion; and the Lord, the Holy One of Israel will dwell in the midst of his people, who will be called Zion.[322]

This Church is now coming out of the wilderness. With the opening of the Seventh Seal, it is our responsibility to create a beautiful garden of the Lord. This starts with our own temple body as we go through sanctification and grows from there. When the time comes, the great event of Adam-Ondi-Ahman will occur when the heads of the dispensations will return their keys to Adam, the archangel Michael. Then will things be organized as they were in the beginning with the Father placing Christ at the center with no substitutes and Michael as His great general who will lead the followers of Christ. At last, domin-ion will return to the lawful heir and events will move forward to cleanse the earth from the last effects of the Fall and return the earth to her paradisiacal glory. "And to none else will I grant this power, to re-ceive this same testimony among this generation, in this the beginning of the rising up and the coming forth of my church out of the wilder-ness - clear as the moon, and fair as the sun, and terrible as an army with banners." (D&C 5:14)

This is all part of the Abraham Covenant. Israel will fill the earth but not until she is brought back to the center place (temple) and organized (endowed and sealed). From there she stretches out the foun-dation of the Lord until it fills the earth. "He shall cause them that come of Jacob to take root: Israel shall blossom and bud, and fill the face of the world with fruit."[323] Thus will a place be laid for stability and en-durance when the wicked are destroyed at His coming. "Therefore thus saith the Lord God, Behold, I lay in Zion for a foundation a stone, a tried stone, a precious corner stone, a sure foundation; he that believeth

---

[322] Bible Dictionary p. 707
[323] Isa. 27:6

184

shall not make haste."[324] Isaiah talked of the day when the fruit would become a forest, as we become trees of life, rooted into the firm foundation: *"IS IT NOT YET A VERY LITTLE WHILE, AND LEBANON SHALL BE TURNED INTO A FRUITFUL FIELD, AND THE FRUITFUL FIELD SHALL BE ESTEEMED AS A FOREST?"[325]*

Through the unity of Zion, all who are gathered into the ship of the firmament can help increase the power and light so that this earth is redeemed from a telestial to a terrestrial state with the coming of the Lord. Truly, this should be the focus and goal of all members as we move deeper into the challenges of the Last Days.

Overview of Astronomical Events in 2012

After some deliberation, we have decided to share a general overview and further explanation of some of the major astronomical events that happened in 2012. We have hesitated to do this because it could be a distraction to our reader if we laid out the documentation necessary to fully explore some of these rare but significant occurrences. Frankly, it would take a full book to do justice to this astronomy but because 2012 was the year of two important eclipses and the Pleiades crossings, we have decided that we need to again mention them. Some of the following is new and some is a recap but we have been reassured by our readers that repetition helps them assimilate the concepts in this book.

Part of our reluctance to touch on this subject without the luxury of an in-depth study is that these things smack of New Age teachings, or of Hollywood. It almost seems as if the writer of the movie *Thor* took a peek at our research on the Rainbow Bridge, most of which we did not share. These ideas become simple with time and study but we admit that there is quit a lot to bite off in this book and have tried to restrain ourselves from sharing even more.

We never get used to seeing the sacred things we study pop up in movies, TV series and on the Internet. Knowledge has been flooding the earth since the restoration of the gospel and the LDS people are not the only ones who are putting some of the pieces together. In fact, few LDS scholars would touch on these things because they have been exploited to the point where it would be professionally dangerous to wade into these waters so muddied by counterfeits. Yet, we cannot justify leaving alone these concepts that Nibley brought forth that help unveil

---

[324] Isa. 28:16
[325] Isa. 29:17

a far greater understanding of the temple and can help us expand our ability to draw upon the powers of heaven for the protection of our loved ones and assist more fully in preparing the earth for the Second Coming.

So, without going in depth at this time, here is a broad explanation of some of the 2012 astronomical events.

For years, we have wondered why at times, the four cardinal directions were depicted on a straight line instead of in their proper positions. The answer is both simple and stunning. Like cogs in a wheel that rotate until the moment they all line up and click open a valve to release a product, there are times when astronomical bodies line up, opening a conduit of energy that bombards whatever is in their pathway. Think of it as moving from the macrocosm, spread out in the four cardinal directions, to the microcosm, gathering into one great hole. Think of it as joining in unity on the throne that moves upward into the higher state of sanctification.

Ancient Israel rejected the higher priesthood in Sinai. As a result, they had to circumambulate (travel in a circular pattern) their wilderness trial. This motion symbolizes the gathering of enough energy to bring forth their higher spiritual rebirth into the Promised Land, after 40 years of circling around the mobile temple in the sacred and purified space of the wilderness. As we discussed earlier in this book, 40 is the number for growth in the womb and that desert was like a womb. They emerged from the birthing waters of Jordan organized and gathered into a straight line. From there, they spread out into the four cardinal directions (symbolically) and began to restore the land to its promised beauty and fruitfulness.

Modern Israel did not reject the higher priesthood. Instead of circumambulating across the wilderness after miraculously crossing the frozen Mississippi, they traveled in a straight line, gathered in for the journey in an obedient, organized fashion. The energy for their journey was endowed upon them and they did not have to tarry in the wilderness for 40 years. Instead, they moved into their Promised Land, and began to make the desert blossom as the rose. From there, they spread out in the four cardinal directions to stabilize and spread Zion in preparation for the future.

Often, the journey from a lower spiritual state to a higher spiritual place is depicted by a ship. The righteous are gathered in from the four directions. Hopefully by now we can see that this is a term used a great deal in scripture and ancient writings that means, among other things, to bring in people and their possessions from wherever they are, to be gathered as one for a specific purpose. Noah, Lehi, Jared, and other stories that use ships help illustrate the concept we are moving toward. The Tree of Life, that joins heaven and earth, marks the pathway that returns us to the presence of God. It is Jacob's ladder which symbolizes steps of spiritual progression and a series of ordinances as we rise to the Promised Land (the presence of the Father as part of His Heavenly Council). Remembering the Maya teaching that the solar/Galactic crossing is called the Tree of Life, the Cross, and the door, we begin to be enlightened in a new way.

A verse of scripture we often return to is 3 Nephi 27:14, where the Lord said that one of the purposes of His being lifted onto the cross is so that He can lift us up. That symbolic tree can be seen as a ship where the righteous are gathered in for the journey through the dangerous waters until they arrive in the new land where they have to plant seeds and create a beautiful garden-like existence. They spread out a new foundation in the four cardinal directions to create stability and make room for the future. So first there is a gathering in and then there is a journey and finally the initiate becomes established, usually building a temple. There is then an ordered spreading out in all directions to create a beautiful Promised Land. Christ gathers us in, lifts us up, and then sets us by His side as joint-heirs as we are organized around His throne into the 4 directions.

People are the fruits, and when they are rooted into a higher level, they grow into Trees of Life and they become the foundation of the new garden place. This is what must happen before the actual Second Coming. These trees bless and nourish, they wave their branches/handkerchiefs in the air to beckon to weary searchers, and they stand shoulder to shoulder to protect those inside the fort from unauthorized attacks from the enemy.

As an illustration and a reminder, we discussed earlier how the people of Egypt established their Pharaoh, built his pyramid, and sustained him because they believed he would, as a representative of God, be rooted into an eternal place, and then act as a proxy of God to lift up and organize his faithful people on an eternal priesthood order. We will now take this pattern and apply it to 2012.

As we have seen from Chapter Three, a sacred space of time has passed. The year of water, 2008, brought us into the next four years to create 4 symbolic cardinal directions…temple walls of sacred space where we are gathered in for a journey to a higher state. The temple is where all who will come are gathered into the Tree of Life, like Aaron's sacred staff, for the journey upward. In Facsimile 2, figure 4, that sunship depicts this journey. Egyptians used a staff as their symbol for the number one. We believe that this represents God having all life gathered within Himself. We have now the opportunity to become a part of the Body of Christ, wrapped in His robes of righteousness for the journey to a higher place.

The temple represents Christ. Instead of the veil being separated into four directions and times, they are all gathered into one because it is time for the branches of the olive tree to be grafted in for the transition to a higher state. Our moment at the veil represents the New Year, as we have quoted many times from Nibley. That is the moment when all the cogs fall into place. The Maya calendars are like cogs all ending at once. Many other cycles also ended during this time period.

The meaning of the alignment of cycles has been enhanced through our study of astronomy and quantum physics. Each astronomical body gives off an energy frequency. These radio waves not only bring energy but may make communication with our Heavenly Father easier. Radio waves and light are different frequencies of the electromagnetic force given off by matter. When astronomical bodies align, their frequencies align and create a symphony of unity and beauty that pours out upon other astronomical bodies in their path. This endowment of light begins the process of bringing something from a fallen condition, back to a terrestrial state.

On May 20, 2012, an event happened that only happens once every 26 thousand years. In 2012, the year of the Bride bringing forth the new David (the throne of Quetzalcoatl), the righteous members of the Church (most without knowing it) were unified to the point where they were gathered as one. They stood as the catalyst to help the earth begin her transition back to an Edenic condition.

At the veil of the temple, there are 4 distinct events, which could be seen as 4 veils or levels of progression brought together into one. The alignment of the four veils of the temple into one veil would seem to be explained in the May 20th event. There was an alignment of the moon, sun, and the Pleiades at their zenith, and all happened within the house of Taurus.

Adam was upon the earth at the time of Taurus. The bull/cow depicted in Facsimile 2, figure 5, represents the priesthood saving ordinance of baptism (temple oxen) that lifts us above the fallen world. The moon was seen by the ancients as a representative of the Holy Ghost. The sun has been worshipped throughout time as a symbol of God or the Son of God. The Pleiades are the seven sisters, or the mothers of the seven dispensations. All ancient cultures believed Pleiades to be the seed bed, like an ovary where all life originated from. We should not worry about the accuracy or details of that mythology and instead simply look at the type and shadow of the alignment. The starry heavens tell their story.

Joseph has gathered and unified the seven dispensations...the seven sisters of the Pleiades into one unit to hand to the Savior. The Mayas and Aztecs watched for the Pleiades crossing exactly at midnight in November. This was the time of their fire ceremony every 52 years. The old sun would die and a new one would be lit in the heart of the sacrifice. All the fires in the kingdom would be extinguished and then with the sacrificial fire, runners would go to light the fires in everyone's hearth for another cycle. Two cycles of 26 thousand years make 52 thousand years which is simply a larger circle/cycle with the same general pattern and fits the number of weeks in our year. This important larger cycle has now ended and a new sun was symbolically born.

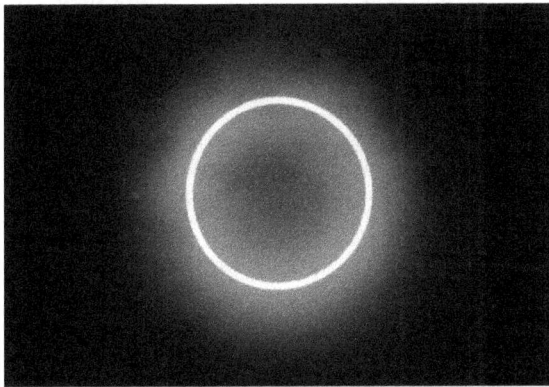

The conception of this new sun was symbolized on May 20th. We have the zodiac time of Taurus representing Adam needing to be reborn. In Hebrew, the word Adam is the root of the word for earth. So earth in its Adamic fallen state will be reborn, endowed with light. The moon (symbol for Holy Spirit) overshadowed the sun (God) as it aligned with the Pleiades at its zenith (directly overhead).

Picture of the recent Lunar eclipse

All the cogs fell into place for a tremendous amount of light to pour down, a gateway opening for a sacred conception. So why does this happen in May and not on December 21st? Nibley often wrote that Eve had to come first. The worship of the Mother-Goddess figure was and is prevalent. The Spirit of God (Creation Council) brooded upon the waters before the light came forth.

For many years we wondered why Nibley insisted that Eve was in the garden first. Studying the concept of Deseret helps explain this

189

idea. The beehive/temple is where the King Bee dies and is protected in that tomb/womb until his rebirth. Nibley wrote that this beehive chapel has the honey that heals and the bee lady is first into the new land to prepare it for settling and rebuilding.[326] Then it would make sense to see the May 20th event as the lifting of the Bride to a higher level for her sacred union and the conception of the new sun.

How easy it is to see the Bridegroom symbolism corrupted through the centuries into worshipping the sun instead of realizing it is a type and shadow of greater things. Remembering that the Father and the Son are both possessors of many offices and titles, we should not be confused when the Lord stands in many roles. Christ, in His role as the Father of Creation, organizes His council around Him. Christ as the King Bee is surrounded by His Bride, the Queen Bee and all she rules over. The bees of Deseret, in their Zion unity, create a circle that draws in and ignites the necessary energy and action to bring forth the light. Eve brought forth Adam in some manner, and then Adam brought forth Eve. The Bride of Christ, the Church of the Firstborn, brings forth the new throne, Christ in His higher role of David, and then afterwards, Christ brings forth His Bride to that higher level.

On June 5th, the rare Venus transit occurred. As Venus is the symbol for the sun, we see the new seed that was conceived on May 20th in its transit across the sun. Think of the new embryo embedding into the womb/Deseret beehive. Merope, the seventh star in the Pleiades, as discussed earlier in the book, is the Bee lady. Nut, the Milky Way, is also sometimes depicted as another aspect of the Queen Bee.[327] The old King Bee is coming to the end of his cycle and is always seen as rebirthing himself. In nature, six months is often seen as the gestational period. So about six months after the Pleiades crossing of May, there is another eclipse. This one would seem to be a type and shadow for the beginning of the journey of the new sun down the birth canal to its birth.

In *The Ascension of Isaiah*, we read that when the Lord came down to take possession of His body, He was veiled from the eyes of all universal creation so they were not aware of His descent into His body. We postulate that the eclipse that was seen from Apocalypse Island (see Chapter 3) on November 13, 2012 was a symbol for the veil-

---

[326] Nibley, Abraham in Egypt, 615
[327] Ibid

ing of the new Venus sun as it symbolically quickens the body and begins labor pains.

Labor ended in birth at dawn of December 21, 2012. Another sacred alignment occurred on that day as the Pleiades appeared low on the horizon, then the new sun, Venus, appeared about 30 minutes before dawn, preceding the old sun as its symbolic replacement. The old year (52 thousand years) died and the new year was born. The New Year Rite was, unknown to most of the world, taking place with the new king establishing his throne. The new king brings his bride with him, symbolically birthing her through the throne.

Notice the seat of the throne in Facsimile 3. This is normally how thrones were drawn with water beneath the seat. A study of ancient temples and palaces shows that most kings had their throne set upon a floor that was made to depict the sea. The Egyptian depiction of water within the seat of the throne brings us back to the Jordan River and Israel being brought forth in a straight line to enter the Promised Land. The movable temple-ship (Ark of the Covenant) goes first, and then Israel is brought forth. Then it is time for Israel to go to work to prepare the new land, planting seeds, spreading out Zion, and defeating the enemy who has usurped the land for himself. All this must be done to prepare for the Second Coming.

This is a lot to take in and we hope our reader will not get bogged down in specifics. Instead, we hope to help illustrate the point that we are living in a very exciting and fulfilling day. With the May alignment, the Bride was finally unified and gathered into the priesthood staff of God to be raised up to blossom on December 21, 2012. Like the olives gathered into the barn in Jacob, chapter five, the new fruit will be planted on a higher level and together we will move toward a beautiful Edenic Millennial existence.

Facsimile 3, Book of Abraham

To a Holy Land

Land of prophets,
scripture, and covenants,
where the buried past
breathes life into our
understanding,
where peace, for some,
is but a place to catch
your breath between fear
and the next war,
for others, a reality that
flows like water springing
from the hopeful ground–

Land of Bethlehem beginnings,
parables, and miracles,
Jerusalem, the Holy City
where Jesus walked
the narrow streets,
Jordan, Nazareth, Galilee,
Golgotha, Cana, Bethany,
and a garden where the
Tree of Life grows–

You call to me
from Earth's other side
to come and be holy, whole,
and my heart, longing
to be complete, listens.
How will I answer?
Will I set aside
uncertainties and concerns,
calendar commitments,
and comfortable convenience?
Will I sacrifice transient
treasure and pay the price
to travel from where I am?

Yes! Even if I never stand
on Israel's sacred land.

© Sharon Price Anderson

Chapter Eight: Bridging Heaven and Earth

The hard work is done. Now it is time to focus on the good news of the Gospel and how it warms our hearts, seeming to glow so much brighter out of frosty winter nights like a shining star on a Christmas tree. For it is now the long Christmas season of that 26,000 Great Year, the birthday of a new throne, which actually spans many of our short mortal years. A new firmament is being prepared for the earth. It is also the New Year celebration of the birthday of the universe when creation first began with the birth of Kolob, the heart of creation, the star of our Savior, Jesus Christ. In the rebirthing process, death and birth are two sides of the coin.

How we weather this historical time depends on our actions. Will we focus on the chilling trials, or will we gather around the hearth which means to stand in holy places and be not moved? To truly accomplish this means we are willing to encircle that hearth in companionship with those who love light. Steadily holding our focus on that pillar of fire, Christ at the center place, is difficult. Brother Nibley's crucial first chapter of *Temple and Cosmos* expounds on the necessity of that constant focus and we want to remind our readers that the information we are sharing in this book will, hopefully, enable us to focus more as we begin to untie the knots of the mysteries hidden within the basics of the gospel.

Our Father has saved many of His most faithful children for this time, who have been foreordained to this work and we must go forward with all determination and courage. Understanding the simple

steps we must take to act our part as the Bride, helps focus our intent and reminds us daily of why we must. In this chapter we will bring all the pieces together and fit them like colored lights onto an evergreen tree of life.

The promise of peace on earth, goodwill toward men gives us the hope we need at this season of the death of the old and rebirth of a new day...a day that will begin to ring in the future bright Millennial Day. Trumpets are spiritually sounding the call periodically in the series of events leading to that day, and we feel certain that one of those trumpet calls coincided with 2012. Step one in internalizing the process is actually a step back. Seeing the bigger picture is so awe inspiring that it helps keep life in perspective with our eye on the ultimate goal. This begins with the structure of the Universe.

Structure of the Universe

According to Nibley, the scientific understanding of the cosmos is what *The Book of Abraham* is all about.[328] This means that we are to learn the science of the universe. God's science is what we must learn to bring order out of chaos. It all begins with the bringing forth of the light through a process of faith and concentration. That first creation and center point of light, Kolob, was the door through which all creation was brought into this sphere of action: "The light which is in all things, which giveth life to all things, which is the law by which all things are governed, even the power of God who sitteth upon his throne, who is in the bosom of eternity, who is in the midst of all things." (*D&C* 88:11–13)

Many years ago, on my mission, I had no idea that the workings of the universe were important or even that it was possible to discover the mechanics of such a thing in this life. However, a few months after beginning my service, I began to have impressions to read here and there in the scriptures and thoughts began to come that opened a whole new idea. The universe was discernible. It has structure and form and this pattern was tied into the hierarchy of the priesthood and the council of heaven. What's more, this same pattern was repeated in smaller and smaller circles and was in fact the structure of all things.

It took many months of study before the picture began to take shape. I called it "the order of the universe" in my own mind and used that as the foundation for my future studies. I had an experience near the end of my mission that convinced me that I needed to take great care and focus almost exclusively on the scriptures for the next few years so I would stay on the straight and narrow. Looking back, I can see that it was necessary for me to learn the pattern of the Three Pillars

---

[328] Nibley, Abraham in Egypt, 179

of the Gospel through the scriptures and temple attendance so I would have a measuring rod with which to judge my future studies.

When the time came, nine years later, that I felt I could begin to branch out, I began with the writings of Hugh Nibley. He had been a hero of mine in my youth. My mother had a hard path to follow with an anti-Mormon husband and on one occasion, she met with Dr. Nibley at his office at BYU. At that time she was still trying to find a way to convert my father and she thought that perhaps some archeological evidence of The Book of Mormon would help. She received an armload of material from Nibley and over an hour of his time. Over the years, he would send her further information and my mother would share this with me.

As I mentioned, my father would often slip anti-Mormon pamphlets into my dresser drawers, and sometimes left books on my nightstand for me to read. I was not yet a teenager when I read his book by Fawn Brodie, *"No Man Knows My History"*. My mother learned of this and gave me another book which I read with a grin on my face. Hugh Nibley's *"No Ma'am That's Not History"* placed that scholar firmly at the top of my list of heroes for some time.

In 1992, when I began to study Nibley's works, I was at first thrilled, then appalled. Quickly, I realized that he was not throwing out random information but was describing the very pattern I had been learning about since my mission; only he was doing it on a much deeper and profound level. My excitement abruptly ended when I came to information that seemed out of line with the Gospel. Always wary of stepping off the straight and narrow line, I set aside his book and did not touch it again for eight months. Then Thomas S. Monson came to town. In a regional conference in Nashville, he asked us if we were studying our Nibley, and assured us that he was.

From that time I began to open my mind and set Nibley's stranger teachings on the shelf, waiting for supportive or negating evidence. I thought I had him a few times but with further research I learned to trust his judgment. Nibley himself recognized that he made errors – they were small and unimportant details, but he had the bigger picture correct. At times I walk away from his books for a few years for my own research and always come back with fresh eyes to see that he understood even more than I had realized. From him, I expanded my understanding about the all-important principle of the law of opposites.

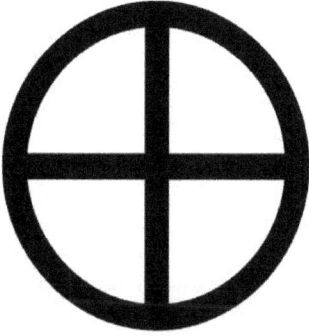

"The sun cross, also known as the wheel cross, Odin's cross, or Woden's cross, a cross inside a circle, is a common symbol in artifacts of the Americas and Prehistoric Europe, particularly during the Neolithic to Bronze Age periods." [329]

The Law of Opposites

Understanding the make-up of the universe brings us back to the cross. For the structure of the universe to have stability, it must have four anchors around a firm center point. The basic structure of the universe is held together by the law of opposites:

Law of Harmony: every positive has a negative, every active a passive; every destroying element is opposed or corrected by a restoring principle. Let the forces of attraction become weak or impaired, will not the repellent forces work destruction? And the converse is no less sure: Let the centrifugal force in any instance fall below the centripetal, or the latter yield to the former, and the consequence will soon be apparent. [330]

Pythagoras held that the Sun is the center of the solar system around which all the planets revolve; that the stars are Suns like ours, each the center of a system; that the earth revolves yearly around the Sun and daily on its axis; that the planets are inhabited, and that they and the earth are ever revolving in regular order, "keeping up a loud and grand celestial concert, inaudible to man, but, as the music of the spheres, audible to God." He was never permitted to declare publicly what he knew and believed but taught his closest pupils all the wonders of his philosophy, under the most binding obligation of secrecy. Pythagoras was forbidden to divulge this knowledge because it would reveal the law of attraction and repulsion, which constituted one of the great secrets of the sanctuary[331]

---

[329] http://www.symbols.com/encyclopedia/29/291.html
[330] http://www.levity.com/alchemy/secret-fire.html
[331] Nibley, *Abraham in Egypt*, 179

Now we begin putting together the puzzle pieces to create a picture of the universe. This is very exciting, yet simple enough for anyone to understand.

Nibley spoke often of the tension between good and evil, and between male and female, one kind being good and the other kind also being good when kept within the bounds the Lord has set. During the era of ancient Israel, the people often went "whoring after other gods". (Judges 2:17) It is now time for us to be a faithful Bride and stay focused on the Bridegroom. That aspect of the law of opposites is the middle crosspiece that lifts others up to safety in the firmament above this fallen earth. We are still rooted into the foundation, and kept in the shadow of our Father's hand above, but we are in a terrestrial place...a temple place. If we stay circled around the altar/throne, we will help maintain that purified, sacred space and we will be standing in holy places. If we break the unity of Zion with those around us, then we metaphorically step away from that circle, out into the cold, where we are in the power of one who hates us.

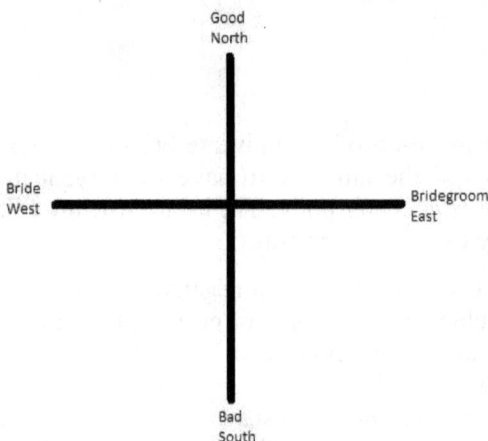

Good
North

Bride
West

Bridegroom
East

Bad
South

We believe that once the council was put in place around the Savior during the creation, time began when words and action put that council in motion, like the ancient round dance Nibley constantly wrote about. Nibley goes on to talk of the temple in regards to the creation of the world, with singing performed in a sacred circle or chorus, so that poetry, music and dance go together in the sacred round dance in the temple. [332] Motion cannot be separated from time. It seems, according to Einstein's theory of relativity, as though time begins when things are put in motion. It appears logical that when creations were put in motion around Kolob, then time began and that was the birthday of the universe. It is likely that this concept was so deeply ingrained in the an-

---

[332] Nibley, *Temple and Cosmos*, 22

cient psyche, that it was natural for the date of Christ's birthday to be established on the day of the birth of the universe and ties in with the ancient celebration of the winter solstice where all the people of the world (symbolically) ritually helped to put the sun in motion for a new year.

"Let's not forget the Shabako Stone there. Let's not forget the Enuma Elish, but especially the Memphite Theology where the oldest record of the human race tells us about this Council in Heaven. And here we have it again. "He thought he saw God sitting upon his throne surrounded with numerous concourses of angels." A concourse is a circle. Of course "numerous concourses" means circles within circles and reminds you of dancing. And what were they doing? Surrounded means "all around." It's the angel chorus "in the attitude of singing and praising their God." It was a choral dance. "And it came to pass that he saw one descending out of the midst of heaven, and he beheld that his luster was above that of the sun at noon-day."[333]

This also brings us back to the ancient New Year Rite, when all the people of the kingdom would come and surround the new king to sustain and support him as he brought his 'new creation' into order. As the people raised their voices as one, the king would be empowered by their faith and honor, for as we know, honor is the source of righteous power.

23 Let the mountains shout for joy, and all ye valleys cry aloud; and all ye seas and dry lands tell the wonders of your Eternal King! And ye rivers, and brooks, and rills, flow down with gladness. Let the woods and all the trees of the field praise the Lord; and ye solid rocks weep for joy! And let the sun, moon, and the morning stars sing together, and let all the sons of God shout for joy! And let the eternal creations declare his name forever and ever! And again I say, how glorious is the voice we hear from heaven, proclaiming in our ears, glory, and salvation, and honor, and immortality, and eternal life; kingdoms, principalities, and powers! (D&C 128:23)

Remember that when Christ came riding into Jerusalem on the last week of His mortal life, the people waved palm branches and raised their voices in honor of Him: "Saying, Blessed be the King that cometh in the name of the Lord: peace in heaven, and glory in the highest. And some of the Pharisees from among the multitude said unto him, Master, rebuke thy disciples. And he answered and said unto them, I tell you

---

[333] Hugh Nibley, Ancient Documents and the Pearl of Great Price, edited by Robert Smith and Robert Smythe, 6

that, if these should hold their peace, the stones would immediately cry out. (Luke 19:38-40)

There is a principle here that shows it is necessary for the king to be sustained even if it is by the lower order of creations. It must happen. Latter-Day Israel is lifting her voice to sustain Messiah who is the new king David, the central throne of the universe.

There are theories that abound suggesting that Kolob is in the center of our galaxy. We will show through scriptures and latter-day prophets that it is in the center of the universe. This does not mean that these theories are worthless. The same pattern plays out on different levels, with others acting in the office of the Father of Creation, Jesus Christ. It is all about the authorized transmission of light. Joseph Smith's explanation of Facsimile 2 helps underscore this cosmic order. The same pattern is laid out on smaller and smaller scales. We believe that there is a similar process for our universe that is laid out similarly for our galaxy and smaller areas of space, on down to our solar system, earth, Church, stakes, wards, and families.

Having a knowledge of the framework of both time and space helps us hold eternal truth in an orderly place. This can help us to remember and also fills us with such reverent awe that it is easier to stay faithful and motivated through trials. Now that we have glimpsed a simple version of the universe, let's fill in a few items to help tie in some of the concepts we have been discussing in this book.

Christ went below all things to establish a foundation, the lodestone to hold the new universe in place. This footstool earth is where this begins. As Quetzalcoatl, the plumed serpent, He shed His skin to be the foundational Atonement. Through the offering of His blood, and His subsequent resurrection, He can endow the worthy with wings to rise above the fall to a firmament of safety and protection until we are ready to return to the presence of the Father. He is staff of life, rooted in southward, and blossoming northward. The wings of His firmament cover those lifted up from the east to the west just as the wings of the Cherubim covered the Ark of the Covenant or the Tree of Life..

Nibley says that the king on the throne would reach up to heaven and also down to the abyss.[334] It is the king who, in the New Year Rite, goes through a ritual suffering in order to save his kingdom. He is then lifted up and is then in a position to lift up his kingdom. It is the high priest and the priesthood of the king working together that encir-

---

[334] Nibley, *Abraham in Egypt*, 414

TOP OF CELESTIAL KINGDOM
BRANCHES OF THE KINGDOM

MIDDLE LEVEL OF
CELESTIAL KINGDOM

7

BOTTOM LEVEL OF
CELESTIAL KINGDOM

6

TOP LEVEL OF THE
TERRESTIAL KINGDOM

5

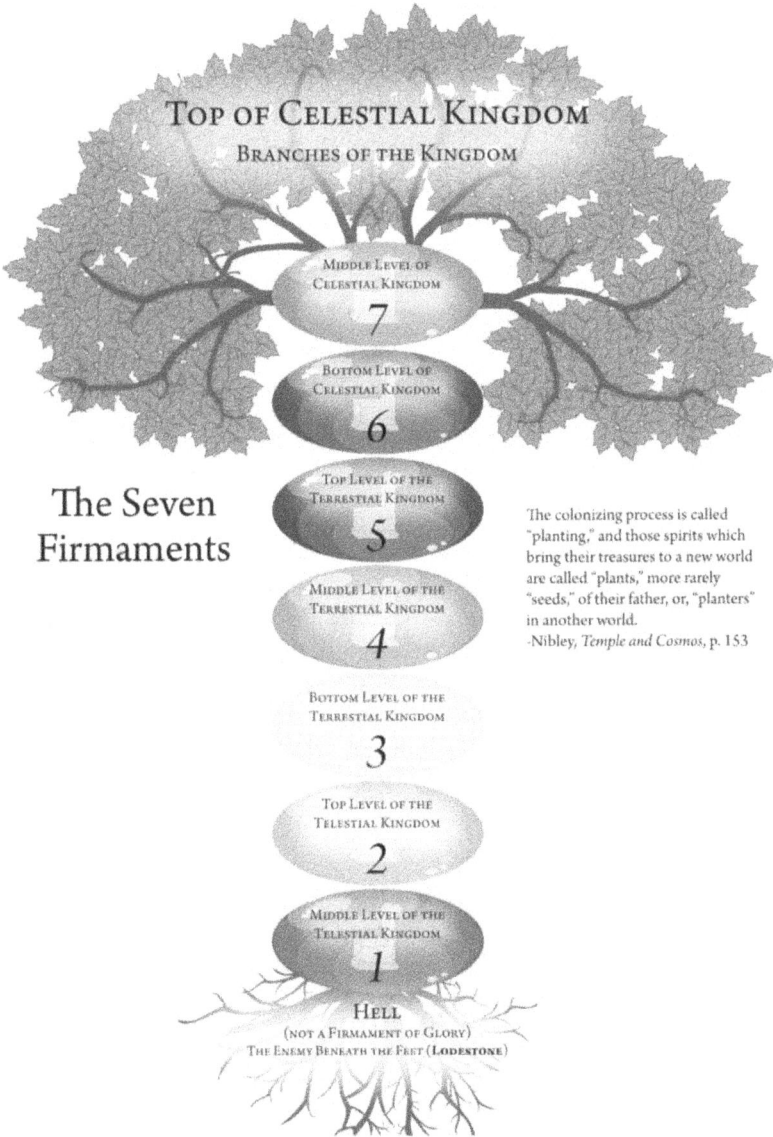

The Seven
Firmaments

The colonizing process is called
"planting," and those spirits which
bring their treasures to a new world
are called "plants," more rarely
"seeds," of their father, or, "planters"
in another world.
-Nibley, *Temple and Cosmos*, p. 153

MIDDLE LEVEL OF THE
TERRESTIAL KINGDOM

4

BOTTOM LEVEL OF THE
TERRESTIAL KINGDOM

3

TOP LEVEL OF THE
TELESTIAL KINGDOM

2

MIDDLE LEVEL OF THE
TELESTIAL KINGDOM

1

HELL
(NOT A FIRMAMENT OF GLORY)
THE ENEMY BENEATH THE FEET (LODESTONE)

cles the righteous citizens in the robes of righteousness, protecting them from the enemy who is waiting to see if they will shed that protection long enough for him to grab his prey.

With the fall, mankind on this earth descended to the base of this structure, into the realm of evil where Satan has dominion. This story is the basis of the wonderful apocryphal work ***The Pistis Sophia***.

Through the Atonement, we are cleansed and gathered up, firmament by firmament, as far as we have the personal spiritual capacity to climb. This process is demonstrated through many types and shadows from Jacob's ladder to the ship of Zion. In Facsimile 2, we find an open boat in figure 3. This boat will journey down to gather in all who will be saved, as did Noah's ark.

A different type is used at the base of the hypocephalus. Figure 5 shows a cow/bull. It is through the waters of baptism that we are gathered in. This is depicted as a lily on the backs of 12 oxen (cow) in the temple basement. We then must obtain certain keys and be tested (figure 7) to see if we qualify to be lifted higher into a firmament of protection that is symbolized by the sunboat in figure 4. This boat is closed, like the Ark of the Covenant, so no corruption can be introduced that would bring future destruction to that firmament or its occupants.

Just as there are seven major firmaments within this universal structure, on the other end of the scale, we establish our own circle within larger circles. Dr. Robert Burton from Brigham Young University wrote a paper in 1980 that was published in BYU Studies. Dr. Burton, an expert in dimensions, postulated that our Heavenly Father lives in a dimension above ours. This would explain eternal progression even though God is perfect and all-knowing. Earth, as the footstool of the Lord, may be the new central point of the next universal round. Although we shared the following illustration earlier, it helps to share it again here when we are discussing the structure of the universe.

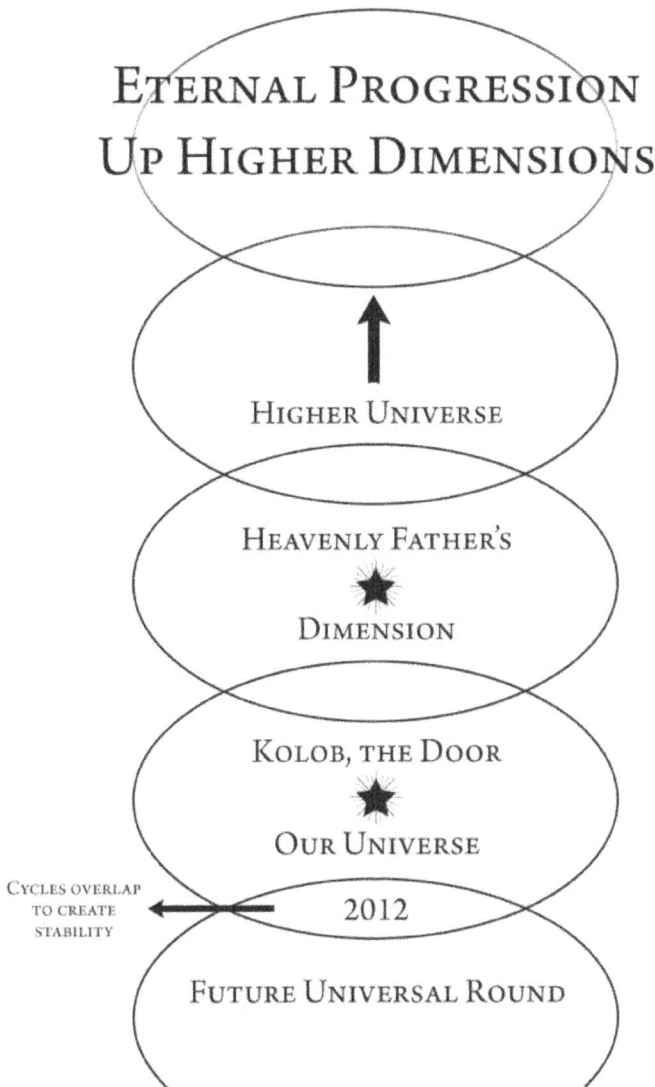

ETERNAL PROGRESSION
UP HIGHER DIMENSIONS

↑

HIGHER UNIVERSE

HEAVENLY FATHER'S
★
DIMENSION

KOLOB, THE DOOR
★
OUR UNIVERSE

CYCLES OVERLAP
TO CREATE   ← ———   2012
STABILITY

FUTURE UNIVERSAL ROUND

2012 marks the moment when the earth pierces the spiritual veil to begin establishing the next firmament. Joseph Smith's hypocephalus, has something that at first glance seems to be a mistake. In figure 2, the headdress of the Maat goddess seems to have been drawn by a sloppy hand. The two tall ostrich feathers that make the headdress reach up beyond that circle (firmament). When one has progressed enough, it is time to move from one rung of the ladder to the next, to a higher firmament. Hidden and protected within this crown, the initiate moves to a higher state, as the earth is now in the process of doing.

(Facsimile 2, figure 2)

The Jaredites

The boat trip in the enclosed Ship of Zion is a perfect illustration of what we need to do in order to fulfill our role as the Bride and protect our families. The type and shadow of the Jaredite journey could not be more fitting. The Jaredites were willing to leave everything behind in the old, corrupted world and take their journey to a higher place in the Land of Promise. Gathering all that was necessary for both physical and spiritual needs, they built enclosed boats. They lived in a day of fierce winds that brought havoc to the world. The seas were filled with monsters that could have crushed them. Even knowing this, they still made that dangerous journey and did those things necessary to ensure a safe voyage. Those things were as follows:

1. Through their priesthood leader, they were able to ascend the mountain and receive Urim and Thummims to light their way. So must we do in the temple as we become endowed with light and power.

2. Then they organized themselves in groups (families, ward, stakes, etc.) that lived in harmony in a very difficult environment.

3. Now this is the hard part, and a crucial key for us to follow: they rejoiced their way across the deep. The terror of the monsters, the unknown destination, the howling winds…none of this tore their focus from worshipping their God with songs of Zion as they journeyed to the Promised Land. Obeying the commandment to be of good cheer will be necessary to propel us forward and will be an inspiration and source of courage for those we love. If we can stand as a firm light when the world shakes with uncertainty, then those in our families who may have wobbly feet will know where to reach out to find stability. If we are rooted in with our enemies beneath our feet and our eye on Heavenly Father; if we are doing our part as the Bride and reaching out to be one with the Bridegroom, then we will have the stability to weather the storm on the Ship of Zion. We will have become a pillar in

the House of our Father to help hold up the new firmament (Facsimile 1, figure 10).

The Jaredite boats were enclosed, like the covered and protected ship of Zion, the sunboat in Facsimile 2, figure 4. We begin to create this higher firmament of protection with the new cycle so that we will survive the final winding up scenes. Only the righteous were in the Jaredite boats. Nephi and his open boat reminds us that the Lord stands still with outstretched arms, beckoning to all to enter in. The Jaredite boats seem more like the ship of 1,000 sunboat where the sanctified have been gathered in. This spiritual separation is necessary in order to create that sacred space we have mentioned many times. We know how important cleanliness is in the birthing place so no infection will bring death. The City of Enoch was physically lifted to a higher state through righteousness and a Zion unity. Similarly but in a spiritual sense, sanctified members are establishing now for the Zion unity that will help to prepare the earth for the Second Coming. Specifically, it is the righteousness of a temple covenant-keeping people that will actually help to bring forth the new cycle at the end of 2012. This is a spiritual ascension process instead of the physical lifting of Enoch's city.

After Enoch's city was taken, there were still people who later qualified for that higher blessing and they were taken up when sufficiently sanctified. Similarly, the process of being spiritually lifted up to be unified with spiritual Israel in the latter-days continues after 2012.

2012 is over, most people have lost interest in the subject but this date is actually a door; one which opens to a series of major events that would be helpful to better understand. We should press forward to understand the process of continuing sanctification learn how to become a Tree of Life. This is how we can become rooted in, bring forth pure fruit, and draw those we love beneath our branches of protection as the prophecies continue to unfold.

Crossing the dangerous time of the beginning of this great cycle, like the Jaredites crossing the ocean, will be much safer if we are in the ship of Zion, that sunboat from Facsimile 2, figure 4. The Milky Way is what births forth the new sun and is compared both to a sacred river and a celestial ocean. A poem by Sharon Price Anderson helps us put that Jaredite crossing in perspective and likens it to our own journey.

The Crossing

Lifted up, arrogant ancients
raised bricks in Babylon,
until foiled and confounded,
they scattered in confusion.

In behalf of family, friends,
Jared's brother sought the Lord.
Gathering food and flocks,
seeds and bees, they followed
a prophet endowed with
knowledge, wisdom, keys.

Prophet-led, we too store food and faith,
prepare for storms and judgments
and the crossing yet to come.
Vessels tight and filled with Light,
we set forth with companies of Saints,
brave fierce winds of tribulation
that drive us toward millennial lands.

Sustained by the Spirit,
secure in God's care,
we pass through terrible tempests,
Encompassed about, we rejoice,
without ceasing sing His praise.

We will safely reach the shore,
shed tears of thanks and joy,
as we receive the promised blessings
and bow before the Lord.

© Sharon Price Anderson

Nephite Forts

As a pillar or a tree of life that has been rooted in, we help create that firmament of safety which is like a fort. Then we help gather in and guard those who need protection. Since fire is a threat to wooden forts, we need earth thrown up over us to keep the enemy from destroying us with a flaming arrow. What is this earth? Through the Atonement, the arrested sacrifice acts as if we did give our blood to the earth. When blood is broken down in the earth, it is separated. The iron becomes a part of the firm foundation, the lodestone to help hold creation in place; but light is also released and clothes upon us. We feel this is why the Egyptians showed the garment of light being stored beneath the throne or footstool.

Being clothed with this light protects us from fire like the earth protected the Nephite forts. Light is the most highly refined aspect of earth.

Dr. Nibley often wrote of the garments of light that are awaiting the righteous to clothe them with an endowment of power. He wrote that crossing the waters at the new birth is when the initiate receives this sacred garment. Nibley identifies two garments, one is a preexistent garment. These garments are metaphorically stored beneath the throne.[335] These garments are kept safe until we are prepared to wear them.

Light from purified earth covers us so we can bear the glory of the presence of the Savior, and keeps us from spiritual danger. We must be gathered to Christ and protected by the wings of protection so the light does not overcome us. Therefore, we should not be surprised by Facsimile 2, figure 4, where the initiate is kept covered by the wings of the hawk in that bright sunboat, so the light can be endured. Whether the symbol is a hawk for protection, a dove for peace, an eagle with the power to lift us to God, those wings come from the power of the priesthood to wrap us in a robe of righteousness and safety.

The Nephite forts are a good type and shadow of that boat/fort. We are in the process of building that fort by becoming trees of life that are endowed with that garment of light and protection. Sanctified members are like trees of life and can become a part of the fort of safety Heavenly Father will build with all who are willing to be a Zion people. If we are in a state of sanctification, we are clothed upon with charity and willing to be one with our families, other Church members,

---

[335] Nibley, *Message*, 489

and all who love God. We can then stand shoulder to shoulder like pillars in the house of the Lord to protect those who come out of the darkness seeking light. At times, some family members or acquaintances become toxic and abusive to the point where we may need to take a step back in order to protect ourselves against too much negativity. In fact, if there is persistent abuse, it may be even more necessary to step back in order to remain loving and forgiving so we do not absorb that destructive toxicity. That is a personal decision for each individual and Heavenly Father but whatever our decision is in those situations, we need to make sure our heart is filled with love and understanding for all mankind.

Although it is true that the Bride will be in danger, perhaps we can remember that when the Nephites were in these forts, even knowing that their enemies were preparing to again come against them, they were happier than they had ever been. (Alma 50:23) How could this be? So many had died, they were removed from their homes and were living with the knowledge of coming danger. We should never be daunted by trials. When measured against the powerful blessing of being kept in the shadow of the Lord's hand, with His Spirit poured out upon us, trials are balanced by the sweetness of communion with fellow Saints. These blessings will outweigh the trials if our priorities are straight and we remain within the sheepfold. Again, being of good cheer is such a key. My father used to tell me, when teaching me to drive, "you will not be swerving all over the place if you lift your vision and look further down the road." Stepping back for a better vision will take the fear out of our last day adventures. The scriptures help with this task.

The great insecurities of life, including major natural upheavals when men can no longer count on the stability of the earth itself, are not without marked psychological effect. A basic teaching of the Talmud is that there is a definite correlation between the behavior of man and the behavior of nature. According to this, the universe is so organized that when man revolts against God's plan of operations, to which all other creatures conform, he finds himself in the position of one going the wrong way on a freeway during rush hour; the very stars in their course fight against him. The blight of nature follows the wickedness of man in every age. Thus, Nibley explained that when Adam fell an angel cut down all the trees of the garden but one. [336] What could that possibly mean? Jesus is the only way back through His Atonement. The lion

---

[336] Nibley, *Abraham in Egypt*, 178

couch of sacrifice in Facsimile 1 becomes the lion throne in Facsimile 3.

Christ provided the only possible means of escaping from the chains of this fallen earth. Those desiring to overcome the effects of the fall and want to return again to the presence of the Father, need to take upon themselves the name of Christ fully and be endowed with enough light to endure the presence of His glory. To do this, we must become a part of the body of Christ, the Tree of Life. In the last days, the scattered branches of the tree are brought together again and grafted back in for the journey to a higher state. Once we have become lifted up and sanctified, we are then made joint heirs with Christ. He lifts us and brings us to his side, Trees of Life surrounding Him in the Garden of Eden, so to speak. Just as the king organizes his kingdom around him once his throne is established each new year, the Lord is ordering His kingdom around Him on the higher level after 2012.

Together we can help to restore an Edenic condition, beginning spiritually before the physical reality takes place. As Nibley's above statement makes clear, only the Lord's tree was left standing representing the only perfect man. As those olive trees surrounded Him when He became rooted in and watered in the Garden of Gethsemane, we will surround Him and sustain His claim to the earth when the throne of David is established and He begins to lay the foundation for His political kingdom upon the earth.

The Rescue

The Bride will be sought by the false husband as Sarah was by Pharaoh. We will need to patiently endure our trials even when destruction seems eminent. Similarly, the Bride of ancient Israel was in bondage, as is mankind to the one who has dominion over this earth. Spiritually we are freed through the ordinances of the Gospel, but we still have residence in Egypt. We all have to start here and be rooted in, eventually crushing our enemy beneath our heel, but first we get a bit bruised. Abraham, Jacob and his children, Moses and the Children of Israel, and even Jesus Christ, had to be rooted into Egypt before making their journey (either in life or death) back through the firmament of the Sinai wilderness to the Promised Land of Israel.

The usurper from the garden, who took temporary control by offering the fruit, will not give up his claim on the Bride easily. Just as Pharaoh needed a lot of persuasion before letting Israel go, Satan will need to be in danger of losing what grip he has left of this earth before letting the Bride return to her rightful husband.

When Pharaoh allowed Sarah to return to Abraham, he sent her laden with gifts of land and treasures. She then gave these gifts to her husband. When the latter-day Bride is released from bondage, there will be a gathering of a representative portion of that Bride to the council of Adam-Ondi-Ahman. There, the Church/Bride will return her keys to Jesus Christ and dominion of the earth will return to the rightful owner. Christ will place Father Adam again as Lord over all the earth and give Him the right to then protect his own.

From that time, the cloud by day and pillar of fire by night will protect the Saints as we build the New Jerusalem and spiritually fortify all the places of refuge as the rest of the world goes through the last of their trials. We should focus on the process that brings about this protection instead of when the specific date of the Second Coming will be.

As we watched the three meltdowns occur at Fukushima, Japan early in 2011, prophecy actually became a comfort to us. We knew the general pattern of how things would play out, so we did not fear when we heard many people claim that the world would soon be coming to an end. We knew it that as serious as the situation was, God's plan would not be thwarted and prophecy would be fulfilled. Our Father in Heaven knows the end from the beginning. Instead of fear, we feel reverent amazement at how He brings about all things to work for our good. He knew that when the world became polluted with radioactive particulates, it would coincide with the time when our solar system would be moving into a place of rescue.

Hugh Nibley discussed the 26,000 year cycle a few times, but our attention was especially grabbed by his article that stated that every 26 million years, our solar system moved into a position in the galactic plane where we would be bombarded with friendly radiation that comes from the Milky Way. [337]

This amazing galaxy is designed to bring earth orbiting into the middle of the galactic plane exactly when we are in such a condition of radioactive pollution that we need extra help. Every 26,000 years, we come into that plane, and every 26,000 million years we are also in the thickest part of the friendly radiation that is like a cloud of protection from dangerous radiation. Like the cloudy nebula of stars around Merope, the seventh star of the Pleiades, this is a type for the unity of

---

[337] http://www.cumorah.org/libros/ingles/Nibley%20-%20Teachings_of_the_
Book_of_Mormon,_vol_3,_Nibley_-_Hugh_Nibley.html#30794

Zion where we stand together in a canopy of protection for earth as she transitions into a higher state.

Science has shown that something strange happened at the beginning of the last Great Year Cycle: "In 26,000 BCE Extraordinary fluorescing X-ray pulses from center of Milky Way."[338] And now again we have moved into the day when both a physical and a spiritual cloud are needed to protect the righteous.

When we see how perfectly timed our journey through the galactic plane has unfolded, we should rejoice at the good news of the Gospel. This beautiful canopy of light, like a shining tree of life, is like protective wings. As we remain encircled by the Lord's robes of righteousness, our love for Him can give us courage when all else fails. Like a prayer circle of palm trees, we can wave our testimonies high for all the world to see, so all can know where they can come to drink of the waters of life in this desert waste. Then we can turn, as saviors on Mt. Zion, and pour out that water to others who thirst.

The Millennium

Does the above concept mean that only those who have attained the highest level of salvation possible in this life can assist in the work of preparing for the Lord? Absolutely not! Anyone who helps bring order out of chaos is assisting in the work. Even if we have just arrived to partake of the fruit, all participate and rejoice at being gathered in. Whether we are the tree, the fruit, or the new initiates gathered beneath sheltering branches of the Tree of Life, as long as we are there on that foundation we are standing in holy places, either because we have become a temple or are sheltering beneath the branches of those who have. And we shall not be moved.

Getting to these spiritual places of safety is becoming more and more important as peace becomes harder to find. According to prophecy, standing in holy places will become even more crucial in the coming days, exactly when, no one knows. If the preparation is not started now, we are in grave danger of being caught in spiritual Sodom as events progress. Christ cannot come until His paths are made straight. Following the example of our prophet and leaders who inspire us through good cheer and rejoicing even when trials are difficult, this example will help ease the bumps in the road that will try us all.

---

[338] http://missionignition.net/bethe/june_solstice.php

The leading brethren of the Church have never been more unified. The example they set is a center place we do well to keep our eye on. The Church leaders have shown the ability to rejoice amidst trials, and to light the world with their hope. As we join them with one heart, we can all help bring in the Millennium, one step at a time. We can be the bright lights on the branches of the Tree of Life that help illuminate a path for those groping in a dark and frightening world; we can help bring in the harvest and, as Joseph's heirs, feed the Lord's sheep. This way we can help the earth to turn smoothly upon the principles of Zion and Christ can come among His people.

The dawn of the new day after the 2012 winter solstice has been the blackest midnight for some and all will feel the heavy hand of the oppressor as the battle for the Bride rages in coming years. Individuals who prepare themselves will be raised to be planted on the Mountain of the Lord. Dawn for the Jews as a group will be when the Lord appears on the Mount of Olives to save them from their Armageddon. Dawn for most of the world will be the Second Coming.

For all those focused on and oriented toward Jesus Christ, the process of sanctification will reverse the effects of the fall and lift them to the Mountain of the Lord. There, Zion as the Congregation of the North will shine brightly, reflecting God's brightness, as that city set on the hill to give light to the dark and weary world. It is our job to gather into that shining ship of Zion symbolized by that newborn sun (Fac 2, fig. 4) and keep our eye firmly on the face of God. Let us follow the example of Moses, Aaron and his sons as they came before the face of God on that holy Mount Sinai in the wilderness of their trials. Similarly today, in a spiritual sense, the priesthood is organizing a circle of faith around the glorious face of God (sunthrone of David) to bless all the earth. The fruit for us, no matter the dire circumstances, is peace.

In order to stand in holy places and come under the most powerful cover of protection, we need to join our canopy of light to the prophet's. Sustaining him will cause a rippling effect like a pebble thrown into a pool. We will be the ones who will benefit the most from the returning ripple. As the arms of Joshua the prophet were held up during the battle for the dominion of the Promised Land, so we now need to jointly raise our prophet's arms as we go forward to reclaim our terrestrial garden, our land of promise. In this way, the Lord can make His arm bare to protect His people.

Doctrine and Covenants 101:21 explains that the curtains that cover the stakes are the strength of Zion. Just as there is a symbolic female aspect of bringing forth, there is a male aspect of action that draws down power and light from heaven. As we make bare our arm to draw down that light, we can help join heaven and earth by empowering and strengthening the cloud or curtain.

The ancient idea of a lightning bolt is a good type and shadow for drawing down that energy of divine power. The cloud is passive, while the lightning is active. Ancient cultures saw the female aspect as passive...to be acted upon and the male aspect as active. "Awake, awake, put on strength, O arm of the Lord; awake, as in the ancient days, in the generations of old. *Art* thou not it that hath cut Rahab, *and* wounded the dragon?" (Isa. 51:9)

The way to battle evil is to focus on love, strange as that may seem. If we love our enemies and they reject that love, it will rebound to us greatly multiplied in that same principle outlined above about a pebble in the water. That love can then envelope us as a protection against hate. We create a canopy of protection through our love of God and our fellowman. The opposition from our enemies and their hatred can actually strengthen our canopy and bless our lives if we effectively draw on the powers of heaven and pour out love instead of giving in to hate. This principle helps explain the importance of the law of opposites, especially between good and evil, love and hate. Love of God and our fellowman is a principle of power. For "on these two laws hang all the law and the prophets." (Matt. 22:40)

An ancient motif has been shown in paintings where Moses is holding his staff in a well of water and that water goes out to each of the twelve tents of the tribes of Israel which encircle him. Behind Moses are the tabernacle and also the seven candles. We are now in the Sabbath of the Earth's seven thousand year period. This Sabbath is like the tabernacle/temple and also, like ancient Israel, we need protection in this dangerous time as we travel to the Promised Land. The water comes from Moses' staff to create a cloud of protection over Israel as we focus on the prophet and his staff of authority. We must surround our living prophet with great faith. He holds the keys, and he is the earthly door to that priesthood power. The living water that is symbolically poured out by Aquarius in the seventh thousand year period will water the Garden of the Lord until the earth is covered during the Millennium.

To conclude and putting our whole book in a nutshell, December 2012 is about the winter solstice, Christmas, the end of the Great Year Cycle, and the beginning of a new cycle. Our job in helping to sustain the bubble of protection during this long New Year challenge and celebration is simple. All three celebrations traditionally focus on 5 things:

1. The emphasis is on the light. We understand the light is Jesus Christ. The following ideas help emphasis the central, life-giving role of the Savior:

a. At Christmas, the evergreen tree of life represents the love of God and reminds us of that sacred babe in the manger.

b. Both anciently and now, at the winter solstice, many burn a yule log to represent the new sun that they help bring forth a new year.[339]

c. The New Year brings forth the new king as the new sun at the center of his kingdom. The king will establish his political kingdom and over time will defeat all enemies and false claimants to his throne. The kingdom sustains the king, and the king protects his people.

2. It is a time for sacrifice. The giving of gifts is a tradition not only for Christians at Christmas but interestingly, it is a tradition as well for those who celebrate the winter solstice. Sacrificing for the happiness of others as an expression of gratitude to the creator is a necessary principle for salvation.

3. Gathering as families and friends brings a warmth found in no other way. This is a tradition at Christmas time and for the winter solstice. Gathering as groups to ring in the New Year is a part of this same idea. It is this Zion principle that unifies the Bride and helps us all be one as a part of the Body of Christ as He gathers us beneath His robes of protection.

4. Being of good cheer and singing songs that lighten the heart is also an integral part of winter solstice celebrations, Christmas and New Year Celebrations.

5. Feasting is an important part of the celebration. As Latter-day Saints, we spiritually feast on the word and the love of God as represented by the fruit of the Tree of Life. That heavenly nourishment seems to distill upon our souls like charity, as the dews of heaven.

All of these five points can be found in the temple and carry actual power. It is no coincidence that we live in the day of temples dotting the earth. These sacred buildings draw down that friendly light that Nibley wrote about which comes from the Milky Way. Righteous saints standing in holy places draw that light which is available in more abundance now, just in time to balance the increase in darkness and

---

[339] http://www.circlesanctuary.org/pholidays/SolsticePlanningGuide.html

chaos on earth. This substance, the light of Christ, is necessary to bring order out of chaos and preserve the earth until the Lord says it is finished. Nibley wrote that combining the office of king and priest is the key to everything. [340]

It all comes down to the interaction between the Bride, who is watched over by the High Priest, and the Bridegroom. The cloud by day represents the Bride with the priesthood of God and the pillar of fire represents the Bridegroom. The unifying of these two offices bridges heaven and earth, opening the door for light to descend and reclaim earth from the fall. As we have learned from Facsimile 2, figure 4, the sunboat is another way to describe this unification. The New Year solar boat that brings the king is the only place of safety when chaos reigns. It is time to get in that boat where only He can calm the storm and bring peace.

To do our part, we have to sacrifice as Abraham did, according to our personal capacity. It is necessary to be willing to let go of the fleshpots of Egypt, gather into the camp of Zion and march toward the Promised Land. Nibley wrote:

> We are in a perfect position to "do the works of Abraham" because we find ourselves in his position. The Book of Abraham was given to us along with a notice of eviction of our present quarters. We have been told by the scriptures in no uncertain terms for the past 150 years what experts in many fields are telling us today: that this present dwelling is rapidly becoming unfit for human habitation, that the place is soon going to be torn down, and that it is high time for us to start looking around "for another place of residence," In the manner of Abraham and to follow his example: get going. [341]

The storms of life will tempt us to lose faith and take our gaze from the Savior but if we do, we will sink. If this happens, we must cry out in faith and then remain firm as a rock, like Peter. Then, we will be raised up by the Lord's miraculous hand to be set up as pillars upon the waters of chaos to stand shoulder to shoulder in the camp of Zion. We will be ordered around the prophet to protect the holy place and bear off the kingdom triumphantly.

---

[340] Nibley, *Abraham in Egypt*, 263
[341] Ibid, 653

Prayer for the Prophet

*Sixty years and more
he served, learning, leading,
staying, graying, preparing
for the heavy, heavenly call.*

*From prophesy's spirit-summit,
he sees invisible perils,
fearsome as Amelek's warriors,
and ominous consequences
dire as defeat.
In mighty supplication,
he pleads our preservation
as the battle rages.*

*Sustain his voice,
unweary his arms,
strengthen his knees,
Wilt Thou steady the staff,
discomfit the enemy.*

*Revealing Thy will,
extend the pavilion
of thy protection.
Encircled in faith,
may Thy people
stand as one
beneath the canopy
of priesthood power.*

© Sharon Price Anderson

Bibliography

Alexander, T. Desmond and Baker, David W., Editors. *Dictionary of the Old Testament Pentateuch*, InterVarsity Press: Downers Grove, Illinois, Leicester, England, 2003

Bitsuie, Roman. "Holy Wind and Natural Law: Natural Law and Navajo Religion/Way of Life," April 21, 1995 <http://www.indians.org/welker/dineway.htm> (February 20, 2012)

Borade, Gaynor. "What does the Lion of Judah Represent?" Buzzle.com 1/17/2012 <http://www.buzzle.com/articles/what-does-the-lion-of-judah-represent.html> (February 20, 2012)

Brayford, Susan. *Septuagint Commentary Series: Genesis,* Boston, Mass: Brill, 2007

Budge, E.A. Wallis. The book of the Dead: The Hieroglyphic Transcript and Translation into English of the Papyrus of Ani, New York: Gramercy Books ; Avenel, N.J. : Distributed by Random House Value Pub., 1995.

Finley, Michael John. "The Dresden Codex: Venus Table", Biblioteca Pleyades 2002 <http://www.bibliotecapleyades.net/ciencia/dresden/dresdencodex04.htm> (February 20, 2012)

Fletcher, Allen J. A Study Guide to the Facsimiles of the Book of Abraham, Springville, UT: Cedar Fort, 2006

Hinckley, Gordon B. "If Ye Are Prepared Ye Shall Not Fear," *Ensign*, Nov 2005, The Church of Jesus Christ of Latter-day Saints, 60.

Hurtak, J. J. *The Book of Knowledge: The Keys of Enoch*, Ava, Missouri: The Academy for Future Science 1987.

Jenkins, John Major. Maya Cosmogenesis 2012: the True Meaning of the Maya Calendar end Date, Rochester VT: Bear and Company, 1998.

Jenkins. "The Watershed: Olmec Antecedents" 1997.
< http://alignment2012.com/waters.htm> (February 20, 2012)

Kaplan, Aryeh. *Sefer Yetzirah: the Book of Creation*, Boston, Red Wheel/Weiser, LLC 1997.

Kimball, Edward L. ed., *Teachings of Spencer W. Kimball*, Salt Lake City: Deseret, 1982.

Spence, Lewis. *Encyclopedia of Occultism and Parapsychology, Part 2*, Kila, Montana, Kessinger Publishing 2003.

Lambdin, Thomas O. *Introduction to Biblical Hebrew*, Harvard University, Darton, Longman, & Todd, 1973, 74

Lethaby, W. R., *Architecture, Mystery and Myth*, London, Percival and Co., 1892.

Littleton, C. Scott., General Editor, *Mythology: The Illustrated Anthology of World Myth and Storytelling*, London: Duncan Baird Publishers, 2002.

Maxwell Neal A. "Brightness of Hope," *Ensign*, Nov. 1994
<http://lds.org/ensign/1994/11/brightness-of-hope?lang=eng> (8 December 2011)

Maxwell. "Meek and Lowly," devotional address given at BYU 21 Oct. 1986.
<http://speeches.byu.edu/reader/reader.php?id=7156>
(5 December 2011)

McConkie, Bruce R., "Christ and the Creation", *Liahona*, Sept. 1983, 22. <http://lds.org/liahona/1983/09/christ-and-the-creation?lang=eng> (8 December 2011)

McConkie. Millenial Messiah: the Second Coming of the Son of Man, Salt Lake City, Deseret Book Company, 1982

Morfill, W. R., Translator, *The Book of the Secrets of Enoch*, Edited by R. H. Charles, Oxford: Clarendon Press, 1896. <http://ia600508.us.archive.org/17/items/bookofsecret sofe00morf/bookofsecretsofe00morf.pdf> (8 December 2011)

Nelson, Russell M., "Thanks for the Covenant," BYU Devotional, Nov. 22, 1988 <http://speeches.byu.edu/reader/reader.php?id=7033> (February 20, 2012)

Nibley, Hugh. *Abraham in Egypt,* The Collected Works of Hugh Nibley, general editor John W. Welch, vol. 14, Edited by Gary P Gillum, Salt Lake City: Deseret Book Co. and Provo Utah: Foundation for Ancient Research and Mormon Studies, The Neal A. Maxwell Institute for Religious Scholarship, Brigham Young University, 1981.

Nibley. *Ancient Documents and the Pearl of Great Price,* edited by Robert Smith and Robert Smythe, Salt Lake City: Deseret Book, 1986.

Nibley. *An Approach to the Book of Abraham,* The Collected Works of Hugh Nibley, general editor John W. Welch, vol. 18, Edited by John Gee, Salt Lake City: Deseret Book Co. and Provo Utah: Foundation for Ancient Research and Mormon Studies, The Neal A. Maxwell Institute for Religious Scholarship, Brigham Young University, 2009.

Nibley and Michael D. Rhodes. *One Eternal Round*, The Collected Works of Hugh Nibley, general editor John W. Welch, vol. 19, Salt Lake City: Deseret Book, and Provo Utah:

Foundation for Ancient Research and Mormon Studies, The Neal A. Maxwell Institute for Religious Scholarship, Brigham Young University, 2010.

Nibley. Teachings of the Pearl of Great Price; Lecture 9 given at Brigham Young University, Winter Semester, 1986 < http://maxwellinstitute.byu.edu/publications/ multimedia.php?id=27>Audio or video file, (6 December 2011).

Nibley. *Temple and Cosmos: Beyond this Ignorant Present*, The Collected Works of Hugh Nibley, general editor John W. Welch, vol. 12, Edited by Don Norton, Salt Lake City: Deseret Book, and Provo Utah: Foundation for Ancient Research and Mormon Studies, The Neal A. Maxwell Institute for Religious Scholarship, Brigham Young University, 1992.

Nibley. *The Message of the Joseph Smith Papyri: An Egyptian Endowment*, The Collected Works of Hugh Nibley, general editor John W. Welch, vol. 16, Edited by John Gee and Michael D. Rhodes, Salt Lake City: Deseret Book, and Provo Utah: Foundation for Ancient Research and Mormon Studies, The Neal A. Maxwell Institute for Religious Scholarship, Brigham Young University, 2005.

Parry, Donald W. "Messiah Becomes the New King: Notes on Isaiah 9:3–7" from "The Disciple as Scholar: Essays on Scripture and the Ancient World in Honor of Richard Lloyd Anderson" The Maxwell Institute for Religious Scholarship 2000. <http://maxwellinstitute.byu.edu/publications/books/? bookid=46&chapid=252> (February 20, 2012)

Plaut, W. Gunther, Editor. *The Torah, a Modern Commentary*, New York: Union of American Hebrew Congregations, 1981.

Porter, Bruce D. "The Book of Isaiah: A New Translation with Interpretive Keys from the Book of Mormon" A review of the book by Avraham Gileadi. FARMS Review: Volume - 4, Issue - 1, Pages: 40-51   Provo,   Utah: Maxwell   Institute,   1992

<http://maxwellinstitute.byu.edu/publications/review/?vol=4&num=1& id=86> (February 20, 2012)

Pratt. Parley P. Key to the Science of Theology: designed as an introduction to the first principles of spiritual philosophy, religion, law and government, as delivered by the ancients, and as restored in this age, Salt Lake City, George Q. Cannon and Sons, 1891.

Rhodes, Michael D. "The Book of Abraham: Divinely Inspired Scripture" *FARMS Review*: Volume-4, Issue – 1, 1992, 120– 26

Richards, Franklin D. Millennial Star Vol.17 <http://contentdm.lib.byu.edu/cdm/compoundobject/collection/MStar/i d/17221/rec/36 > (February 20, 2012)

Sitchin, Zechariah. "Divine Encounters: A Guide to Visions, Angels and other Emissaries, Ch. 8 Encounters in the Gigunu," Biblioteca Pleyades 1995. < http://www.bibliotecapleyades.net/sitchin /divine_encoun/divine_encounters.htm> (February 20, 2012)

Sivan, Dr. Reuven, and Levenston, Dr. Edward A. *The New Bantam-Megiddo Hebrew and English Dictionary,* New York, Bantam books, 1975.

Skinner, Andrew. "The Book of Abraham: A Most Remarkable Book," *Ensign,* vol. 27 no. 3,(March 1997): 16-23.

Steinsaltz, Adin. *The essential Talmud*, translated from the Hebrew by Chaya Galai. New York: Basic Books, 1976.

Talmage, James E. The Articles of Faith: A Series of Lectures on the Principal Doctrines of the Church of Jesus Christ of Latter-Day Saints, Salt Lake City: Deseret News, 1899.

_____. *Doctrine and Covenants Student Manuel: Religion 324 and 325,* The Church of Jesus Christ of Latter-day Saints, Salt Lake City, 1981.

Walker, William R. "Presidencies Part of Gospel's Pattern," *Church News,* Salt Lake City: The Church of Jesus Christ of Latter-Day Saints, April 12, 2008. < http://www.ldschurchnews.com /articles/51878/ Presidencies-part-of-gospels-pattern.html >

Brigham Young Addresses, 1860-1864, A Chronological Compilation of Known Addresses of the Prophet Brigham Young, Vol. 4 [Salt Lake City: Elden J. Watson, 1980]

Willis Roy., General Editor, *World Mythology*, New York: H. Holt, 1993.

Winkel, Richard H. "The Temple is about Families", *Ensign,* November, 2006. < http://lds.org/ensign/2006/11/the-temple-is-about-families?lang=eng>

Young, Brigham., et al, Journal of Discourses of the General Authorities of the LDS Church, vols. 7 and 17

About the Authors

Joy and Roy Bischoff are the parents of six children and have seven grandchildren. Roy served a mission to Caracas, Venezuela and Joy served a mission to Maracaibo, Venezuela. Joy has served in a variety of callings including Relief Society President, gospel doctrine teacher, and institute teacher. Joy is currently involved in developing and running their own entrepreneurial businesses. Joy has a bachelor's degree from BYU in ancient near eastern studies (Hebrew language emphasis). Joy resides in Orem, Utah.

Sharon Price Anderson has received many state and national awards for her poetry and is the *Ensign's* most frequently published poet of recent years. Her poems have also appeared in *BYU Studies*, the *Friend*, the *New Era*, *Utah Sings*, and *Encore* (published by the National Federation of State Poetry Societies). She is the author of *Praising the Prophet: Joseph Smith and the Restoration in History and Verse* and has written and illustrated a series of history time line packets for home schoolers and other educators (www.timelinesetc.com). Her LDS Temple Books, *In Seasons of Joy,* are a beautiful blend of her stunning photographs and insightful poetry (www.inseasonsofjoy.com). Sharon graduated magna cum laude from BYU in 1970 and has held many teaching and leadership positions in wards and stakes in both California and Utah. She and her husband Peter are the parents of nine children. Their posterity includes an ever increasing number of grandchildren and great-grandchildren.